Great Christian Plays

GREAT CHRISTIAN PLAYS

A collection of classical religious plays in acting versions and of selected choral readings suitable for a worship service

EDITED BY

THEODORE MacLEAN SWITZ AND ROBERT A. JOHNSTON

GREENWICH/CONNECTICUT/1956

808.82
S w 6 g

35 461
October, 1957

Foreword

The awakening of our day to the power of drama within the Christian community is a recognition of the emotional appeal of that human drama which is the common concern of each of us from birth until death. For drama is an art which interprets life. Historically, drama has played an important role in the worship life and in the program of religious instruction within the Christian Church. Because of the power of its message, drama continues to be an excellent vehicle in assisting the Church to minister to the needs of men, women, and children. Through drama, the truth as revealed in Jesus Christ may be presented in terms of an action that people can understand and embrace as their own. And what makes drama "religious" is the effect it has on the participants—the audience as well as the actors. Effective Christian drama confronts these participants with situations that are known in their own experience, and leads them through a struggling of the soul to a recognition of God's truth and of man's need to respond to that truth.

The editors of this volume, *Great Christian Plays,* present an anthology which contains some of the outstanding classic Christian drama. In sponsoring this work the Adult Division expresses its gratitude to Dr. Theodore M. Switz, who first sensed the need in the Church for dramatic texts that could be produced effectively by dramatic groups within the Church. He has been of invaluable assistance to this Division both as consultant and editor. Our deep appreciation is extended to Dr. Robert A. Johnston, a professor of drama whose knowledge of the theatre has made possible the presentation of these excellent acting versions of the five great plays. Music appropriate for these plays has been composed by Thomas Matthews.

This volume takes its place alongside the volumes of *The Church's Teaching,* the study courses, and other materials that have been produced by the Adult Division of the Department of Christian Education. Many parishes will use the plays and readings for production in a chancel setting or on a parish house stage. The inclusion of costume sketches, directions, and the musical score will assist in making these presentations as effective as possible.

But this volume has another important use, and one that also contributed to the decision of this Division to sponsor publication. Currently, numerous adult study groups are finding in the reading and discussion of plays and dialogues a satisfaction, as well as a stimulus, to a realistic involvement in, and deeper understanding of, the Christian faith as related to one's daily life. To this end, it is our hope, *Great Christian Plays* will serve the Church.

A. DONALD DAVIES, S.T.M.

Preface

Several years ago a friend invited me to attend a dramatic presentation in a church in Evanston, Illinois. I went reluctantly for I had seen more than enough religious pageants, mostly planned for children. Not many minutes passed before I realized that I was seeing something entirely different in the presentation of *Abraham and Isaac*. Here was reverent, mature drama; it was simple, powerful, poetic; it spoke to both adults and children; it adapted the methods of the theatre to use within the chancel of a church. Once again the resources of the arts—acting, costuming, poetry, and music—were being used to communicate Christian teaching and tradition. Moreover this was not an isolated dramatic presentation: the play was an integral part of a service of corporate worship —Evening Prayer.

It is not an exaggeration to say that everyone who left the church that night was stirred out of his ordinary routine; indeed, the memory of that presentation still remains fresh and vivid for at least one member of that audience. The play was presented by the Drama Department of Northwestern University, which also presented it in various churches of the surrounding community.

The next year, even when a play quite unknown to me, with the strange name *Totentanz,* was offered, I needed no urging to go and see it. Once again, here was drama for adults in the great tradition. All the arts contributed not only to impressing the mind but the heart also.

The question arose at once—must these great medieval plays be offered only by trained actors in a university town, or can they be made available to almost any parish? It is not difficult for a university drama department to do research on text, acting version, costuming, and music; but it is an insuperable task for the average parish. The answer to the problem seemed to be an anthology that would bring together in one volume everything needed, including the music—in other words, an anthology designed for amateur use by church groups.

Why choose the particular five plays that are presented in this anthology? First of all, because even though old, what they have to say and the problems with which they deal seem pertinent to our life today. They arose in the late middle ages at a time when the Church was the Mother of the arts and before the drama had been secularized. They have a vigor, simplicity, and artistic quality that few contemporary plays have, and their message is reinforced, rather than weakened, by the fact that they speak to us across the centuries. Part of our racial heritage, they have been thoroughly tried and tested. One special advantage they have is that they are all suitable for use within the church building itself and, particularly, *as part of a liturgical service.*

These five plays and some of the shorter selections for choral reading in Book II are particularly suitable for special services in Advent and Lent. Most churches have extra services and special programs during these seasons of the Church Year. They are also suitable for Evening Prayer on special occasions, such as the parish anniversary.

The benefit that accrues from the presentation of these dramatic selections is not limited to the congregation that sees and hears them. The cast and all the supporting committees benefit even more from working closely together to serve the Church by giving an artistic and meaningful production. They learn more than they would even in a good study group.

Preparation of one of these plays or choral readings should not be considered a one time affair. If the quality is good, the cast could offer to perform in other parishes in the same or adjacent towns or in churches of other denominations. Or if the work seems too great for a single parish to carry, two parishes might together put on a performance. People outside the parish who are interested in dramatics could also be invited to participate.

Apart from the volume's main use in helping to prepare public performances, it should not be forgotten that it will also be useful to small groups that like to read plays or stories and then discuss their religious implications.

THEODORE MAC LEAN SWITZ

Acknowledgments

We wish to thank:

Professor John Gassner of Columbia University for permission to reprint his version of *Abraham and Isaac* from *A Treasury of the Theatre* (New York: Simon and Schuster, Dryden Press);

Mr. Martin Schloss of Racine, Wisconsin, for permission to publish in English the text and music for his version of *Totentanz,* and to Mrs. Margaret Trinklein for translating it;

Mr. Thomas Matthews of St. Luke's Church, Evanston, Illinois, for his composition of the music for the plays;

Miss Joyce Van Dermark of Park Ridge, Illinois, who made the original costume designs for us;

Mr. Randolph Chitwood of Greenwich, Connecticut, who executed the costume illustrations;

Dr. Lee Mitchell, Director of Theatre, Northwestern University, for his detailed criticism of *The Resurrection* and *The Conversion of St. Paul* before they were put into final form;

Professor Robert Seaver, Director of Religious Drama, Union Theological Seminary, for his reading and evaluation of some of these acting versions;

Mr. William Newey, professional actor of New York City, who read and evaluated some portions of the manuscript;

The staff of the Northwestern University Theatre Department for the generous loan of detailed production notes on *Totentanz* and *Abraham and Isaac;*

The library staffs of the University of Nebraska, Northwestern University, Wright Junior College, the Newberry Library of Chicago, and the Theatre Section of the New York City Public Library for their patient help and advice during the preliminary research for the acting versions of *The Resurrection, The Conversion of St. Paul,* and *Everyman;*

And Mr. Arthur Diamond of Chicago for his patient secretarial work copying music and preparing the manuscript for Book I.

The translation of the *Imitation of Christ* by Henry Parry Liddon is published by A. R. Mowbray and Company, London.

Contents

BOOK I: THE PLAYS

BOOK II: THE SELECTED
CHORAL READINGS

Book I
THE PLAYS

EDITED BY ROBERT A. JOHNSTON

Editor's Note

When Dr. Lee Mitchell, Chairman of the Theatre Department at Northwestern University, called to tell me that he had been asked to recommend someone who might like to work on a book of medieval dramas suitable as parts of religious services, I was extremely interested. Dr. Mitchell recalled that I had done several "acting versions" of ancient Greek drama and that one of these, *The Oresteia* by Aeschylus, was about to be published. He asked whether I would be willing to "move up historically" to the medieval period.

The project excited me. Every student of drama soon learns that there is always a close relationship between man's need for religion and man's need for drama. In no historical period, however, was the art of drama so directly inspired by Christianity as during the thirteenth, fourteenth, and fifteenth centuries. Perhaps, I realized, this relationship could somehow be re-created and strengthened today through more modern productions like the ones Northwestern had done in the Evanston churches.

Now that my part is done, I realize how much there is yet to do before this dream can be realized. Those of us who put this book together are only middlemen, the least important of three groups. More significant are the real writers of this book, the forgotten men who first created these plays in the almost forgotten tongues of Middle English and Middle German. Their work, too, is over. Most important of all now is the third group: you who will be producing these plays. Do them with as much simplicity and sincerity and loving care as you can, for yours is the real task of re-creating them *in your living selves* for the pleasure and instruction of your audiences.

ROBERT A. JOHNSTON

The Brome
ABRAHAM AND ISAAC

AN ACTING VERSION IN MODERN ENGLISH BY JOHN GASSNER

WITH ORIGINAL MUSIC BY THOMAS MATTHEWS

Reprinted from John Gassner, *A Treasury of the Theatre* (New York: Dryden Press, Simon and Schuster, 1951), by permission of John Gassner. The interpolated directions to the actors have been approved by Mr. Gassner. Permission for all productions must be cleared directly through John Gassner, Columbia University, New York 27, New York.

INTRODUCTION

The Brome *Abraham and Isaac,* one of the masterpieces of English medieval drama, was written in the fourteenth century, an age of simple, unquestioning faith. Despite the time that has passed since then, its characters are surprisingly human and recognizable to us today. Abraham and Isaac are not ancient historical figures, remote from our own experiences; they are living representatives of the tender relationship of faith and trust that always exists between good parents and good children and that must grow out of the faith relationship with God.

This play is called the Brome *Abraham and Isaac* to distinguish it from five other surviving early English plays based on this famous Bible story. The original manuscript was found in a house called Brome Manor in Suffolk, England, and critics regard it as the best of the six. The version here is the one done in modern English by John Gassner, critic, author, teacher, and eminent authority on the drama.

How many of us could face Abraham's choice between obeying the unexplained will of God and protecting the life of his best-loved child? It is a dreadful decision to have to make. Yet many of our own decisions seem almost as hard. This play will help us all to become more sharply aware of the need in our lives for faith like Abraham's and trust like Isaac's.*

---

* These three paragraphs may serve as "program notes" for printed programs of performances. Permission to reprint for this purpose is herewith given.

Notes on the Characters

ABRAHAM: This is the familiar Old Testament figure. He is generally thought of as white-haired and with a full white beard. Although old, he is vigorous, strong, and filled with vitality. His faith in God is an unquestioning rock-like faith. He is extremely fond of his son. His suffering is deep and intense; it is caused more by sympathy for his child than by self-pity.

ISAAC: He is an appealing happy-go-lucky boy, probably about twelve years of age (although he may be played by any young actor between eight and sixteen). He is very obedient to his father. This obedience grows out of real affection for Abraham rather than from any rigid sense of duty. Although he agrees to die, there is nothing pompously heroic about him. He must be played as a normal, natural boy.

VOICE OF GOD: God is not seen, but the actor who plays His voice should have a deep, powerful, resonant voice. If a public address system is obtainable (one which conveys the human voice faithfully without distortion and which does not issue forth too many squeaks and squawks of its own), this may be used to give the Voice greater volume. Although there is ferocity and violence in this Old Testament Jehovah, there is also sincere love and tenderness for Abraham based on the knowledge that Abraham will survive the difficult test and be strengthened because of it.

ANGEL: This may be played either by a man or by a woman. The exact age is immaterial. This Angel, like most Angels, is modest and full of sympathy for those who must suffer. At the same time, there is strength, dignity, and a definite sense of divine mission.

DOCTOR: He is a kindly, scholarly man of mature years. If necessary, this character may be eliminated and his lines given to the Angel.

Notes on the Properties

The PROP LIST comprises the following:

> altar (on stage)
> several sticks of firewood (offstage right)
> ram (see below; if used, it is offstage left)
> sword (worn by Abraham)
> flint and small rock (see below; in Abraham's inner pocket)
> enough cord to tie Isaac's hands (in Abraham's inner pocket)
> cloth large enough to tie around Isaac's eyes (in Abraham's inner pocket).

There are two production features in this play which are difficult to stage realistically. One is the building of the fire; the other is the killing of the ram. A real live fire and a real live ram are, of course, out of the question: they would distract the audience and destroy the play by their very reality. Since both are difficult to fake convincingly, it is probably better if they are merely pantomimed. That is, the actor playing Abraham should go through realistic, detailed motions without actually setting fire to the wood or killing a ram. Also, both actors should imagine that they actually *see* the specific actions that are supposedly being performed.

The firewood should probably be real but not the fire. A sense of building a real fire may be given by having Abraham, as he seems to strike the flint against the rock, actually light a cigarette lighter covered from the sight of the audience except for its flame. Thus the idea is planted clearly and the audience is not likely to object to the omission of the big fire itself.

If a toy ram which looks really alive can be obtained, it may be used; but if it looks merely like a lifeless toy, it had better be eliminated. The sword, of course, should be real—or at least real-looking. If Isaac and Abraham will carry the non-existent ram close to them and cover it partially with their arms, cloaks and moving bodies, it is less likely to be missed.

CHARACTERS

ABRAHAM   ANGEL

ISAAC   DOCTOR*

VOICE OF GOD

TIME: *In the days of Abraham*

PLACE: *In the wilderness*

[*At the beginning, music is heard—*
MUSIC CUE 1. ABRAHAM *and his son,*
ISAAC, *enter from the left. They come
to the front left corner of the acting
area.* ABRAHAM *kneels and indicates
that* ISAAC *should also kneel.* ISAAC,
*watching his father intently, does so.
They clasp their hands in an attitude
of prayer. The music continues behind*
ABRAHAM'S *prayer.*]

ABRAHAM: Father of Heaven, omni-
potent
With all my heart to thee I call.
Thou hast given me both land and rent.
And my livelihood thou hast me sent.
I thank thee highly evermore for all.

First of the earth thou madest Adam,
And Eve also to be his wife;
All other creatures from these two
came.
And now thou hast granted to me,
Abraham,
Here in this land to lead my life.

In my age thou has granted me this
That this young child with me shall
dwell.

[*With an affectionate gesture, he indicates* ISAAC.]

I love nothing so much in this,
Except thine own self, dear Father of
Bliss,
As Isaac here, my own sweet son.

[*He reaches out, places a hand on*
ISAAC'S *shoulder without looking at
him.* ISAAC *steals a glance at his father
and then quickly looks down in humbleness again.*]

I who have many children mo'
Love them not as half so well.
This fair sweet child he cheers me so
In every place wherever I do go,
That of no affliction may I tell.

And therefore, Father of Heaven, I
thee pray
For his health and also for his grace.
Now, Lord, keep him both night and
day
That never discomfort nor dismay
Come to my child in any place.

[ABRAHAM *rises. The music stops.*]

Now come on, Isaac, my own sweet
child,
Go we home and take our rest.

[ISAAC *rises.*]

ISAAC: Abraham, mine own father so
mild,
To follow you I am full pleased,
Both early and late.

ABRAHAM: Come on, sweet child. I
love thee best
Of all the children that ever I begot.

[*He puts his arm about* ISAAC'S *shoul-*

---

* May be combined with the role of the
ANGEL.

7

ders, patting him affectionately. They move slowly toward the right. As they reach the other side of the stage, the Angel enters quickly from the left. MUSIC CUE 2. *The* VOICE OF GOD *is heard from offstage, preferably from above or at the back of the audience.* ABRAHAM *and* ISAAC *continue to walk toward the right. When they can go no farther without leaving the stage, they turn and walk directly away from the audience to the far right corner of the acting area. The music continues behind the* VOICE OF GOD.]

VOICE OF GOD: Mine angel, fast hie thee thy way,

And unto middle-earth anon thou
   go—
Abram's heart now will I assay,
   Whether that he be steadfast or no.

Say I commanded him for to take
   Isaac, his young son that he loves so
     well,
And with his blood sacrifice he make,
   If any of my friendship he would
     feel.

Show him the way unto the hill
   Where that his sacrifice shall be.
I shall assay now his good will,
   Whether he loveth better his child
     or me.

ABRAHAM AND ISAAC

All men shall take example by him
My commandments how they shall
keep.

[*When* ABRAHAM *reaches the far right corner, he turns toward the center and comes back toward the center. The music stops, and* ABRAHAM, *as if struck by a sudden thought, kneels quickly.*]

ABRAHAM: Now, Father of Heaven,
that formed everything,
My prayers I make to thee again,
For this day a tender offering
Here must I give to thee certain.

[ISAAC *wanders off toward the right.*]

Ah, Lord God, Almighty King,
What manner of beast would'st thou
fain?
If I had thereof true knowing,
It should be done with all my main
Full soon by me.

[ISAAC *goes off at the right.*]

To do thy pleasure on a hill,
Verily, it is my will,
Dear Father, God in Trinity!

[*The* ANGEL *moves to* ABRAHAM. MU-SIC CUE 3. *As the* ANGEL *begins to speak,* ABRAHAM *looks up with a start.*]

THE ANGEL: Abraham, Abraham, be at
rest!
Our Lord commandeth thee to take
Isaac, thy young son whom thou lovest
best,
And with his blood that sacrifice
thou make.

[ABRAHAM, *in great dismay, starts to rise, then sinks back to his knees.*]

Into the Land of Vision do thou go,
And offer thy child unto thy Lord;
I shall thee lead and show also.

To God's behest, Abraham, accord,

[*The* ANGEL *turns and begins to move toward the left.*]

And follow me upon this green!

[*The music stops.* ABRAHAM *rises, starts to follow the* ANGEL, *then stops with an anguished gesture.*]

ABRAHAM: Welcome to me be my
Lord's command!
And his word I will not withstand.
Yet Isaac, my young son in land,
A full dear child to me has been.

[*The* ANGEL *stops but does not turn around.*]

I had rather, if God had been pleased,
To have forborne all the goods that
I have,
Than Isaac, my son, should be de-
ceased,—
So God in heaven my soul may save!

[*He looks around frantically to the left, searching for* ISAAC. *He apparently sees him a little way off, but this does not comfort him.*]

I have loved never a thing so much on
earth,
And now I must the child go kill!
Ah, Lord God, my conscience lacketh
mirth!
And yet, my dear Lord, I am sore
afeared
To grudge anything against thy will.

[*He lifts his head high.*]

I love my child as my life,
But yet I love my God much more
For though my heart should make any
strife,
Yet will I not spare for child or wife,
But do after my dread Lord's lore.

Though I love my son never so well,
  Yet smite off his head soon I shall.

[*He kneels, lowering his head humbly.*]

Ah, Father of Heaven! to thee I
  kneel—
A hard death my son shall feel,
  For to honor thee, Lord, withal!

[*The* ANGEL *turns and faces* ABRAHAM.
He lifts one arm over ABRAHAM *in
blessing.*]

THE ANGEL: Abraham, Abraham, this
  is well said,
And all these commandments look that
  thou keep,—

ANGEL

But in thy heart be nothing dismayed.

ABRAHAM: Nay, nay, forsooth, I hold
  me well repaid
  To please my God to the best that I
    may.

For though my heart be heavily set
  To see the blood of my own son,
Yet for all that I will not let,
But Isaac, my son, I will go get,
  And come as fast as ever we can.

[MUSIC CUE 4. *The* ANGEL *goes out at
the left.* ABRAHAM *rises. He is trembling slightly and has some difficulty in
getting to his feet. He turns toward the
right. As he starts to speak, the music
stops.*]

ABRAHAM: Now, Isaac, my own son,
  dear.
Where art thou, child? Speak to me.

[ISAAC *enters, skipping, from the right.
He drops to his knees.*]

ISAAC: My father, sweet father, I am
  here,
And make my prayers to the Trinity.

[*He clasps his hands in an attitude of
prayer and closes his eyes.*]

ABRAHAM: Rise up, my child, and fast
  come hither,
  My gentle bairn that art so wise,
For we, too, child, must go together,
  And unto my Lord make sacrifice.

[ISAAC *rises and comes to* ABRAHAM.]

ISAAC: I am full ready, my father, lo!
  Given to your hands, I stand right
    here;
And whatsoever ye bid me do, even so
  It shall be done with glad cheer,
    Full well and fine.

[ABRAHAM *looks steadily into the eyes*

of his son and speaks with great sincerity.]

ABRAHAM: Ah, Isaac, my own son
    so dear,
God's blessing I give thee, and mine.

[*He crosses to the right, moving in front of* ISAAC *to do so. He exits momentarily to pick up a piece of firewood, then enters with it.*]

Hold this faggot upon thy back,
    And I myself fire shall bring.

[*He gives the faggot to* ISAAC. ISAAC *takes it, runs in front of* ABRAHAM *to the right, exits momentarily and comes on with several stacks of firewood. He places this heavy load on his little back.*]

ISAAC: Father, all this here will I pack;
I am full fain to do your bidding.

[*At this,* ABRAHAM, *in great pain, turns away abruptly.*]

ABRAHAM: Ah, Lord of Heaven!

[*He looks up to heaven. He wrings his hands.*]

This child's words all do wound my
    heart!

[*He controls himself and turns to* ISAAC.]

Now, Isaac, son, go we on our way
    Unto yon mount with all our main.

[*He indicates a position in the center of the acting area.*]

ISAAC: Go we, my dear father, as fast
    as I may;
To follow you I am full fain,
    Although I be slender.

[*They move toward the center.* MUSIC CUE 5.]

ABRAHAM: Ah, Lord, my heart break-
    eth in twain
This child's words, they be so tender!

[*The music stops.* ABRAHAM *again controls himself. He turns toward* ISAAC.]

Ah, Isaac son, anon lay it down,
    No longer upon thy back it hold,
For I must make ready prayer soon
    To honor my Lord God as I was
    told.

[ISAAC *drops the faggots.*]

ISAAC: Lo, my dear father, here it is.

[*He moves close to him tenderly.*]

To cheer you always I draw me near.

[*He looks at his father anxiously, seeming to notice his great worry for the first time.*]

But, father, I marvel sore at this,
    Why ye make this heavy cheer,

[ABRAHAM *moves quickly to the wood, strikes flint and lights the fire.*]

And also, father, even more dread I—
    Where is your quick beast that ye
    should kill?
Both fire and wood we have ready
    nigh,
    But quick beast have we none on
    this hill.

[*He becomes more anxious.* ABRAHAM *turns away and cannot answer.*]

A quick beast, I wot well, must be
    slain,
    Your sacrifice to make.

[ABRAHAM *draws his sword and turns around slowly to face* ISAAC.]

ABRAHAM: Dread thee nought, my child, I would fain;
Our Lord will send me unto this place
Some manner of beast for to take
Through his command.

ISAAC: Yea, father, but my heart beginneth to quake
To see that sharp sword in your hand.

Why bear ye your sword drawn so?
Of your countenance I have much wonder.

[ABRAHAM *turns suddenly and moves a step toward the left.*]

ABRAHAM: Ah, Father of Heaven! Such is my woe,
This child here breaks my heart in sunder.

[ISAAC *moves to* ABRAHAM *and touches his arm tentatively.*]

ISAAC: Tell me, my dear father, ere that ye cease—
Bear ye your sword drawn for me?

[ABRAHAM *moves away from* ISAAC'S *touch, another step toward the left.*]

ABRAHAM: Ah, Isaac! sweet son, peace, peace!
For in truth thou break'st my heart in three!

ISAAC: Now truly, on something, father, ye think,
That ye mourn thus more and more.

[*He shakes his head wonderingly.*]

ABRAHAM: Ah, Lord of Heaven, let thy grace sink,
For my heart was never half so sore!

ISAAC: I pray ye, father, that ye me know will let
Whether I shall have any harm or no.

ABRAHAM: Alas, sweet son, I may not tell thee yet,
My heart is now so full of woe.

ISAAC: Dear father, I pray you, hide it not from me,
But some of your thought, I pray tell me.

[ABRAHAM *turns suddenly and faces* ISAAC.]

ABRAHAM: Ah, Isaac, Isaac, I must kill thee!

ISAAC: Kill me, father? Alas, what have I done?

If I have trespassed against you aught,
With a rod ye may make me full mild;
And with your sharp sword kill me naught,
For in truth, father, I am but a child.

ABRAHAM: I am full sorry, son, thy blood for to spill,
But truly, child, I may not as I please.

ISAAC: Now I would to God my mother were here on this hill.
She would kneel for me on both her knees
To save my life.
And since that my mother is not here,
I pray you, father, change your cheer,
And kill me not with your knife.

[*He drops to his knees before* ABRAHAM *and seizes his cloak.*]

ABRAHAM: Forsooth, my son, save I
thee kill,
I should grieve God right sore, I
dread;
It is his commandment and also his
will
That I should do this same deed.

He commanded me, son, for certain,
To make my sacrifice with thy blood.

ISAAC: And is it God's will that I
should be slain?

[ABRAHAM *wrings his hands*.]

ABRAHAM: Yea, truly, Isaac, my son so
good;
And therefore my hands I wring!

ISAAC: Now father, against my Lord's
will,
I will never grouch, loud or still.
He might a-sent me a better destiny,
If it had been his pleasure.

ABRAHAM: Forsooth, son, if not this
deed I did,
Grievously displeased our Lord would
be.

ISAAC: Nay, nay, father, God forbid
That ever ye should grieve him for
me!

Ye have other children, one or two,
Which ye should love well in natural
kind.
I pray you, father, make you no woe;
For, be I once dead and from you go,
I shall be soon out of your mind.

[ABRAHAM *slowly shakes his head to
deny this*.]

Therefore do our Lord's bidding,
And when I am dead, then pray for
me.

[ISAAC *rises*.]

But, good father, tell ye my mother
nothing,
Say that I am in another country dwell-
ing.

ABRAHAM: Ah, Isaac, Isaac, blessed
mayest thou be!

My heart beginneth wildly to rise
To see the blood of thy blessed
body!

ISAAC: Father, since it may be no
other wise,
Let it pass over as well as I.
But, father, ere I go unto my death,
I pray you bless me with your hand.

[ISAAC *kneels;* ABRAHAM *places his
hand on the lad's head*.]

ABRAHAM: Now Isaac, with all my
breath
My blessing I give thee upon this land,
And God also thereto add his.
Isaac, Isaac, son, up thou stand,
Thy fair sweet mouth that I may
kiss.

[ISAAC *rises. They kiss briefly*.]

ISAAC: Now farewell, my own father so
fine,
And greet well my mother on earth.
But I pray you, father, to hide my eyne
That I see not the stroke of your
sharp sword
That my flesh shall defile.

[ABRAHAM *begins to sob.*]

ABRAHAM: Son, thy words make me to
weep full sore;
Now, my dear son Isaac, speak no
more.

ISAAC: Ah, my own dear father! wherefore?
We shall speak together here but a
while.

And since that I must needs be dead,
Yet, my dear father, to you I pray,
Smite then but few strokes at my head
And make an end as soon as ye may,
And tarry not too long.

ABRAHAM: Thy meek words, child, do
me dismay;
So "wellaway" must be my song,

Except alone for God's good will.
Ah! Isaac, my own sweet child,
Kiss me yet again upon this hill;
In all the world is none so mild!

[*They kiss again.*]

ISAAC: Now, truly, father, all this tarry-
ing,
It doth my heart but harm—
I pray you, father, make an ending.

ABRAHAM: Come up, sweet son, unto
my arm.

[ABRAHAM *takes cord from an inside
pocket of his cloak and binds* ISAAC'S
hands together behind him.]

I must bind thy hands too
Although thou be never so mild.

[ISAAC *cries out in anguish.*]

ISAAC: Ah, mercy, father! Why should
ye do so?

ABRAHAM: That thou should'st not
stay me, my child.

ISAAC: Indeed nay, father, I will not
stay you.
Do on, for me, your will;
And on the purpose that ye have set
you,
For God's love, keep it steadfast
still.

I am full sorry this day to die,
But yet I will not cause my God to
grieve.
Do your desire for me hardily;
My fair sweet father, I do give you
leave.

But, father, I pray evermore,
Nothing to my mother tell,
If she wist it, she would weep full sore;
Indeed she loves me, father, well,
God's good blessing may she have!

[*He speaks slowly and quietly.*]

Now farewell, my mother so sweet,
We two are like no more to meet.

ABRAHAM: Ah! Isaac, Isaac, son, thou
makest me grieve,
And with thy words thou so distemper-
est me.

ISAAC: Indeed, sweet father, I am sorry
to grieve you;
I cry you mercy for what I have
done,
And for all trespass ever I did do.
Now, dear father, forgive all I have
done—
God of Heaven be with me!

[*He sighs audibly.*]

ABRAHAM: Ah! dear child, leave off thy
     moans!
In all thy life thou grieved me never
     once.
Now blessed be thou, body and bones,
     That ever thou were bred and born;
Thou hast been to me child full good.
     But in truth, child, though I mourn
          never so fast,
     Yet must I needs here at the last
In this place shed all thy blood;

Therefore, my dear son, here shalt
     thou lie,—

[*He places* ISAAC *upon the altar.*]

     Unto my work I must proceed.
In truth, I had as lief myself to die
     If God were pleased with the deed
     That I my own body should offer.

[*He breaks down into uncontrollable
sobbing.*]

ISAAC: Ah, mercy, father, mourn ye no
     more;
Your weeping maketh my heart sore
     That mine own death I am to suffer.

Your kerchief, father, about my eyes
     wind.

ABRAHAM: So I shall, my sweetest child
     on earth.

ISAAC: Now yet, good father, have this
     in mind,
And smite me not often with your
     sharp sword,
     But hastily that it be sped.

[ABRAHAM *takes a cloth from the inside
pocket of his cloak and binds it loosely
around* ISAAC'S *eyes.*]

ABRAHAM: Now farewell, my child so
     full of grace.

[ISAAC *begins to wince, not being able
to see when the sword will fall.*]

ISAAC: Ah, father, father, turn down-
     ward my face,
For of your sharp sword I am ever
     adread!

[ABRAHAM *looks up to Heaven re-
signedly.*]

ABRAHAM: To do this deed I am full
     sorry,
But, Lord, thine behest I will not with-
     stand.

ISAAC: Ah! Father of Heaven, to thee I
     cry;
Lord, receive me thou into thy hand!

[ABRAHAM *falters and pleads again.*]

ABRAHAM: Lo, now is the time come
     for certain,
     That my sword in his neck shall bite.
Ah, Lord! my heart riseth there again,
     I may not find it in my heart to
          smite.
     My heart will not now thereto!
Ah, fain I would work my Lord's will,
But this young innocent lies so still,
I may not find it in my heart him to
     kill.
     Oh, Father of Heaven! what shall I
          do?

[*He moves a few steps to the left. He
sheathes his sword.*]

ISAAC: Ah, mercy, father, why tarry ye
     so,
     And let me lie there so long on this
          heath?

Now I would God the stroke were done
    also;
Father, heartily I pray you, shorten my
    woe,
    And let me not wait thus for my
      death.

ABRAHAM: Now, heart, why would'st
    thou not break in three?
    Yet shalt thou not make me to my
      God unmild.
I will no longer stay for thee,
For that my God aggrieved would be.
    Now have thy stroke, my own dear
      child.

[ABRAHAM *draws his sword again, lifts
it high and is about to strike.* MUSIC
CUE 6. *The* ANGEL *enters suddenly and
seizes the sword as it is lifted high just
before it can descend.* ABRAHAM *is
frozen with surprise. The music continues behind the* ANGEL'S *speech.*]

THE ANGEL: I am an angel, thou
    mayest see blithe,
    That from heaven to thee is sent.
Our Lord thanketh thee a hundred time
    For the keeping of his command-
      ment.

He knoweth thy will, and also thy
    heart,
    That thou dreadst him above all
      thing;
And some of thy heaviness for to de-
    part
    A fair ram yonder I did bring;

[*He indicates with a gesture the ram
offstage at the left.*]

He standeth, lo, among the briars tied.
Now, Abraham, amend thy mood,
For Isaac, thy young son, here by thy
    side
    This day shall not shed his blood.

[*The sword drops to the ground.* ABRA-
HAM *looks up with great rejoicing.*]

Go, make thy sacrifice with yon ram.
Now farewell, blessed Abraham,
For unto Heaven I go now home,—
    The way is full straight. . . .
      Take up thy son now free!

[*The* ANGEL *goes off at the left. The
music stops.* ABRAHAM *drops to his
knees.*]

ABRAHAM: Ah, Lord! I thank thee for
    thy great grace,
Now am I eased in diverse wise.

[*He rises, goes to* ISAAC *and begins to
loosen the cord that binds his hands.*]

    Arise up, Isaac, my dear son, arise,
Arise up, sweet child, and come to me!

[ISAAC *cries out, not understanding.*]

ISAAC: Ah, mercy, father, why smite ye
    naught?
Ah, smite on, father, once with your
    knife.

[ABRAHAM *removes the cord, then removes the cloth from his face.*]

ABRAHAM: Peace, my sweet son, and
    take no thought,
    For our Lord of Heaven hath
      granted life
    By his angel now,
That thou shalt not die this day, son,
    truly.

ISAAC: Ah, father, full glad then were
    I;
In truth, father—I say, I—wis,
    That this tale were true!

ABRAHAM: A hundred times, my son
    fair of hue,
For joy thy mouth now will I kiss.

[*He kisses him lightly, but* ISAAC *is
troubled.*]

ISAAC: Ah, my dear father Abraham,
Will not God be wroth that we do thus?

ABRAHAM: No, no! hardly, my sweet
    son!
For yon same ram he hath now sent
Hither down to us.

[*He points offstage left.*]

Yon beast shall die here in thy stead,
    In the worship of our Lord, alone.
Go fetch him hither, my child, indeed.

ISAAC: Father I will go seize him by
    the head,
And bring yon beast with me anon.

[*He runs off to the left and brings back
the ram.*]

Ah, sheep, sheep, blessed may thou be,
    That ever thou were sent down
        hither!
Thou shalt this day die for me,
In worship of the Holy Trinity.

Now come fast and go we together,
    To my father of Heaven.
Though thou be never so gentle and
    good,
Yet I had liefer thou shed thy blood
    In truth, sheep, than I!

[*He takes it to his father.*]

Lo, father, I have brought here, full
    smart,
    This gentle sheep, and him to you I
        give.

[*He breathes a sigh of relief.*]

But, Lord God, I thank thee with all
    my heart!
    For I am glad that I shall live,
        And kiss once more my dear
            mother!

[ABRAHAM *takes the ram.*]

ABRAHAM: Now be right merry, my
    sweet child,
For this quick beast, that is so mild,
    Here I shall offer before all other.

[ISAAC *begins to lean down to blow
upon the fire.*]

ISAAC: And I will fast begin to blow;
This fire shall burn a full good speed.

[*He hesitates, however.*]

But, father, if I stoop down low,
Ye will not kill me with your sword,
    I trow?

ABRAHAM: No, hardly, sweet son; have
    no dread.
My mourning is past!

ISAAC: Yea, but would that sword were
    sped—
For, father, it doth make me yet full
    ill aghast.

[ABRAHAM *kneels before the altar.*]

ABRAHAM: Now, Lord God of Heaven
    in Trinity,
    Almighty God omnipotent,
My offering I make in the worship of
    thee,
    And with this quick beast I thee pre-
        sent.
Lord, receive thou mine intent,
As thou art God and ground of our
    grace.

[*He kills the ram.* MUSIC CUE 7. ISAAC
kneels but averts his face so that he

does not see the killing. The VOICE OF
GOD *comes out of the darkness. The
music continues.*]

VOICE OF GOD: Abraham, Abraham,
          well mayest thou speed,
    And Isaac, thy young son, thee by!
Truly, Abraham, for this deed,
    I shall multiply both your seed
        As thick as stars be in the sky,
          Both of bigger and less.
And as thick as gravel in the sea,
So thick multiplied your seed shall be;
    This grant I you for your goodness.

Of you shall come fruit unknown,
    And ever be in bliss without end,
For ye dread me as God alone
And keep my commandments, every
          one.
    My blessing I give wheresoever ye
          wend!

[*The music stops.* ABRAHAM *rises. He
and* ISAAC *move toward the left.*]

ABRAHAM: Lo, Isaac my son, how
          think ye
Of this work that we have wrought?
Full glad and blithe may we be
    That 'gainst the will of God we
          muttered naught
        On this fair heath.

ISAAC: Ah, father, I thank our Lord
          every deal
That my wit served me so weel
    For God to fear more than my death.

[ABRAHAM *places his hand on his son's
shoulder tenderly.*]

ABRAHAM: Why, dear-worthy son, wert
          thou afraid?
Boldly, child, tell me thy lore.

ISAAC: Yea! by my faith, father, be it
          said,

I was never so afraid before,
As I have been on yon hill!

[*He points to the spot at which the
sacrifice was made.*]

Ah, by my faith, father, I swear
I will nevermore come there,
    Except it be against my will!

ABRAHAM: Yea, come on with me, my
          own sweet son,
And homeward fast let us be gone.

ISAAC: By my faith, father, thereto I
          agree!
I had never such good will to go home,
And to speak with my dear mother!

ABRAHAM: Ah, Lord of Heaven, I
          thank thee,
    For now I may lead home with me
          Isaac, my young son so free,
The gentlest child above all other,—
    This may avowed be.
Now, go we forth, my blessed son.

ISAAC: I grant, father, let us be gone,
For my troth, were I home then,
I would never go out as thus again.
I pray God give us grace evermore
          true,
And all those that we be beholden to!

[ABRAHAM *leads him off at the left.*
MUSIC CUE 8. *The* DOCTOR *enters
from the right and crosses to the right
corner of the stage near the audience.
He speaks directly to the audience.
The music continues.*]

DOCTOR: Lo, now sovereigns and sirs,
          thus did we show
    This solemn story to great and small.
It is a good lesson for both learned and
          low,
    And even for the wisest of us all,
          Without any barring.

For this story showeth you deep
How to our best power we should keep
   God's commandments without
      doubting.

[*He moves to the center.*]

Think ye, sirs, if God sent an angel,
   And commanded you your child to
      slay,
By your truth, is there any of you
   That would balk or gainsay?
How think ye now, sirs, thereby?

[*He pauses, then continues.*]

There be three or four more, I trow,
And those women that weep so sor-
      rowfully
   When that their children from them
      die
      As nature takes of our kind.
It is folly, as I may well avow,
Against God to grudge or to grieve so
      low;
For ye shall never see them mis-
      chiefed, well I know,
   By land or water,—have this in
      mind!

And grudge not against our Lord God,
   In wealth or woe whatever he you
      send,
Though ye be never so hard bestead;
   For when he willeth, he may it
      amend,
His commandments truly if ye keep
     with good soul,
   As this story hath now showed you
      before,
And faithfully serve him, while ye be
     whole,
   That ye may please God both even
      and morn.

[*He lifts his arms high.*]

Now Jesu, that wore the crown of
     thorn,
   Bring us all to heaven's bliss!

[*He brings his arms down and goes
off slowly to the right. The music dies
away.*]

DOCTOR

ABRAHAM AND ISAAC
MUSIC CUE 1

MUSIC CUE 2

MUSIC CUE 3

MUSIC CUE 4

MUSIC CUE 5

MUSIC CUE 6

Continue and repeat III commencing at •

MUSIC CUE 7: *Repeat Music Cue 2.*

MUSIC CUE 8

The York
RESURRECTION

AN ACTING VERSION IN MODERN ENGLISH BY ROBERT A. JOHNSTON

WITH ORIGINAL MUSIC BY THOMAS MATTHEWS

INTRODUCTION

At York, in the thirteenth, fourteenth and fifteenth centuries, a great cycle of plays, presenting all the biblical themes from Creation to the Judgment of the Last Day, were given annually on the feast called Corpus Christi. All day long, from early dawn until late night, the people crowded the streets to watch this cycle performed. Each guild presented a separate scene on a rolling platform that moved from corner to corner, repeating its performance at each stop. Some of the guilds participating were the Fishers and Mariners, who presented Noah and the flood; the Goldsmiths, who re-enacted the visit of the three Kings at the Nativity; and the Butchers, who reproduced the Crucifixion with a realism that would shock and revolt modern audiences. Even though he could not read, a person came to know intimately and directly, through these presentations, the themes of the whole Bible.

The great climax of the cycle was the *Resurrection,* a play assigned to those who followed Christ's own craft, the Carpenters. Immediately following, the Winedrawers pulled up in the next wagon to present the most touching and most beautiful of the scenes, the visit of the three Marys at the tomb and Christ's appearance to Mary Magdalene. The play that follows here is a version that combines these two playlets.

No one knows who wrote these plays originally, but it is certain that they affected powerfully the lives of the people who saw them. And it is hoped that they will mean as much to you today as they did long ago to the people of York.*

Notes on the Characters

PILATE: He is a mature, dignified man of great position and authority. Although he is pompous and overbearing, he has more intelligence than Caiaphas and Annas. Also, underlying his confident outer nature is an inner suspicion that Jesus may really be the Christ. This makes him uneasy at times. He is basically an affectionate man. There is a kind of weakness about him that makes him rely too much on others even when his own superior intelligence prompts him to a different course. He is finally revealed as utterly unscrupulous when it is politically expedient to be so.

CAIAPHAS: Caiaphas and Annas, heads of the Temple, are crafty, calculating, and opportunistic. Caiaphas is middle-aged. He is more forceful than Annas, and he usually speaks up first. He imagines himself to be the leader of the two. He also believes himself the superior of both Pilate and Annas in intelligence, although he is, of course, too polite to say so. He is positive and dogmatic. He definitely believes Jesus to be a fraud.

ANNAS: Annas is colder and quieter than Caiaphas but equally malicious. He is inclined to wear a sneer on his

---

* These paragraphs may be used as program notes in printed programs of productions.

face, thus revealing that he is not at all sure that Pilate or Caiaphas or anybody else has any sense at all. He is, of course, too wise to allow Pilate or Caiaphas to see this superior air. He is sharp-eyed and seems to notice more that goes on than Caiaphas does. He is middle-aged but probably a little younger than Caiaphas.

THE CENTURION: He is wise, old, grizzled, and thoroughly reliable. There is a blunt honesty about him which gains him the sympathy of the audience. He is devoted to duty but even more devoted to truth. He is an outdoor man, rugged and strong. It is evident that he has been soldiering all his life. (His costume is the same as that of Saul in the next play.)

FIRST SOLDIER: The four Soldiers may be of various ages but are probably all young men. The First Soldier is more fearless than the others and a leader among them. He is also more honest than they are.

SECOND SOLDIER: He is more inclined to self-pity and complaining than the others. There is an air of preciseness about him. He has an imaginative alertness which enables him to think quickly, but he sometimes seems to be more accurate than he really is.

THIRD SOLDIER: He is rather surly and phlegmatic. He is less inclined to get excited than the others. He considers himself to be very hard-headed and practical.

FOURTH SOLDIER: He is somewhat nervous and excitable. He is also an incurable pessimist. He is very much afraid of dying. He is not very happy with the profession of soldiering, but it is the only thing he knows how to do.

FIRST MARY: She is young and more than usually beautiful. Her suffering and sense of loss are deep and passionate. Until Jesus strengthens her faith, she finds it difficult to grasp the ideals of faith in the abstract, believing only those things which can be perceived by the senses. She moves gracefully, and her voice is lovely, clear, and full of tenderness.

SECOND MARY: She is more matronly than the others. There is a strong maternal quality in her, and she has a deep sense of responsibility and practicality. Her grief is as deep as the others, but she is perhaps more serene, more dignified, more resigned.

THIRD MARY: She is small, gentle, sensitive. There is a delicacy about her that makes her seem almost unreal. Her grief is bitter, but her faith is strong and free from doubts.

AN ANGEL: Although described as a child in the text, the role may be played either by a child, or by an adult, of either sex. In any case, the Angel should be attractive, solemn, quiet, kind, and compassionate. There should always be a quality of modesty in the voice and movements, and we should feel that this is the Guardian Angel who protects us all.

JESUS (The GARDENER): Even when He is the Gardener, He is regal and divine. He should be played by an actor who is strong and masculine but, at the same time, gentle and affectionate. His dominant emotion in this play is a combination of sorrow and pity for the suffering Mary. His comments on His own qualities are made for the purpose of alleviating her pain by helping her to understand better what has happened; they are not made from any conceit or didacticism.

Notes on the Properties

The PROP LIST comprises the following:

sceptre (carried by Pilate)

four spears (carried by Soldiers)

four shields (carried by Soldiers; may be omitted if necessary)

large white cloth (carried by Angel)

vial of yellow oil (carried by First Mary)

vial of blue oil (carried by Second Mary)

vial of red oil (carried by Third Mary)

coins (in money bag worn by Pilate).

The sceptre can easily be made out of an old table leg or any available piece of rounded lumber. Carving grooves all the way around and alternating these with wood or metal strips forming an interesting design will make the sceptre look more elaborate. It should be painted with gold or silver paint if possible.

The large white cloth should be of heavy material to make it look as much like a shroud as possible. If heavy material is not available, an ordinary bed sheet will do. It should look large enough to wrap a body in, and it should be loose and wrinkled, not neatly folded up. It should, how-ever, be clean except for dark blood stains which can be created effectively with brownish-red tempera or water paint. Be sure to put the stains where they would naturally be. Be very careful also not to overdo this; the primary effect must be one of whiteness and purity, not one of bloodiness and garishness.

The vials should be large enough to be seen easily by the audience but small enough to be concealed from view at first by the hands of the women. Vinegar bottles or other interestingly shaped bottles from the grocery store with labels removed may be used. The liquids inside should be vividly bright. Easter egg dye, clothing dye, or water color paint from a child's paint set, can be mixed with water to form this "oil." The bottles should be nearly full but not completely full so that the water will move in the vials as the Marys move, thus showing the audience that they really do contain liquid.

The money bag can be any piece of felt, burlap, or other heavy material caught up and tied to form a bag. Real coins need not be used since Pilate does not take them out. Nuts and bolts or other heavy metal objects should be put inside, however, to give weight and to clink realistically when Pilate slaps his money bag.

CHARACTERS

PILATE	FOUR SOLDIERS
CAIAPHAS	THE THREE MARYS
ANNAS	AN ANGEL
THE CENTURION	JESUS

Scene 1

PLACE: *Pilate's Council Hall*
TIME: *Late on Good Friday*

[MUSIC CUE 1. PILATE *enters from the right and marches in a dignified but somewhat pompous manner to the center of the acting area. He carries a sceptre and wears an ornate crown. Following him are* CAIAPHAS *and* ANNAS *dressed as bishops.* CAIAPHAS *takes a position left of* PILATE, *crossing in back of him to do so. When he gets there, he stops, then turns solemnly and formally to face* PILATE. ANNAS *takes a similar position to the right of* PILATE. PILATE *faces the audience and lifts his hands toward* CAIAPHAS *and* ANNAS. *The music stops as he begins to speak in a loud, commanding voice.*]

PILATE: My lords, please listen now to me.

[CAIAPHAS *and* ANNAS *bow formally.* PILATE *now indicates the whole audience with his hands and speaks directly to them.*]

I speak to all of each degree,
all ranking chiefs of royalty
    assembled here.
As I command, so shall you be.
    Is that quite clear?

[CAIAPHAS *and* ANNAS *nod their heads*

solemnly. PILATE *turns to* CAIAPHAS.]

First, Sir Caiaphas, chief of state.
We took advice from you of late
to put to death this Man you hate:
    Jesus His name.
Do you declare His death this date
    was not a shame?

CAIAPHAS: Yes, sir, that deed we shall
    defend.
Every move was legal. Sir, attend,
consider that you saw the trend
    as well as we.
His words have vanished with His end,
    no more to be.

[PILATE *turns to face* ANNAS.]

ANNAS: The people, sir, have made
    their choice,
and you have spoken with their voice,
and you have stopped this traitor's
    noise,
    just as you swore,
and now the people should rejoice.
    Need we say more?

PILATE: Indeed we must speak of this
    thing,
for since the time of burying
we have not learned of anything
    the people say.

30

CAIAPHAS: The Centurion will surely
        bring
    us news today.

[PILATE *turns toward* CAIAPHAS.]

We sent a Centurion, who is wise,
to see if any rebels rise
or if the public should despise
    us or be offended.
If any do, at the next assize,
    they, too, will be ended.

[*Enter the* CENTURION *from the left.
He is shaking his head and talking in
awed tones to himself.*]

PILATE

CENTURION: Ah, blessed Lord, my
        Master, aye!
What may these marvels signify
that there were shown so openly
    unto our sight?
This day when Jesus had to die
    gave me a fright.

It is so strange a thing to tell,
this wonder that to us befell,
that only prince or priest know well
    what it may mean.
I must describe the dark which fell
    and what I've seen.

[*He crosses over to* PILATE, *walking in
front of* CAIAPHAS *to do so. As he begins to speak, he indicates both* CAIA-
PHAS *and* ANNAS *with his hands, bow-
ing his head slightly to each as he does
so. Then he bows more deeply to*
PILATE.]

God save you, sirs, on every side.
May worship, wealth and joy abide
with you in this great world and wide
    both day and night.

[PILATE *reaches out a hand to the* CEN-
TURION *and clasps his warmly.*]

PILATE: Centurion, welcome to our
        side,
    our handsome knight!

We wondered where you were so long.

CENTURION: Pray God that He will
        keep you strong.

PILATE: Centurion, praised in every
        song,
    what is your will?

CENTURION: I fear that you have done
        most wrong.
    It makes me ill.

[*At this, the others are disconcerted.*

They look at one another in amazement.]

CAIAPHAS: It makes you ill? I pray
    you, why?
Declare your reason for this cry.

CENTURION: I will, sirs, tell you all,
    for I
  am diligent.
The Man Whom you did crucify
  is innocent!

[*The other three gasp audibly. Then*
PILATE *controls himself and speaks deliberately and calmly.*]

PILATE: Centurion, hold us in more
    awe.
You are a man who knows the law.
If any witness we should draw,
  our will to excuse,
you'd testify there was no flaw,
  and not refuse.

[*The* CENTURION *speaks defiantly.*]

CENTURION: No, nothing but the truth
    I'd say.
When I saw Jesus die today,
I knew that God's Son we did slay,
  His flesh we tore.

CAIAPHAS

ANNAS

This I now say; this will I say
forevermore.

[CAIAPHAS *speaks angrily*.]

CAIAPHAS: Shame, sir. Talk like this
you'll rue.
Such counsel should not come from
you;
your job should be to tell us true
what things befell.

CENTURION: Such wondrous things I
never knew
I have to tell.

[ANNAS *speaks coldly*.]

ANNAS: Tell us these things. Be quick,
we pray.

CENTURION: Nature itself, both night
and day,
began to mourn in every way
in every place
as if they knew it was God Who lay
there in disgrace.

[CAIAPHAS *shakes his head at this. He
glances significantly at* ANNAS.]

The sun grew pale and white for woe;
the stars and moon stopped shining so;
the earth began to shake below;
the dead men woke;
the stones that never stir did grow
and then they broke.

[ANNAS, *with a look of disgust, turns
his back on the* CENTURION.]

The dead men rose, both great and
small.

[PILATE *tries to speak calmly, but he
is obviously disturbed*.]

PILATE: Centurion, beware of all
this folly; you know wise men call
sights like this one

eclipses when dark shadows fall
on moon or sun.

CAIAPHAS: Yes, and if the dead rose
bodily,
that might be done through sorcery.
Therefore we say most comfortably:
this means no ill.

CENTURION: All that I tell, I tell truth-
fully
and always will.

From all this work that you did do,
not just the sun was touched with blue.
The veil in the temple ripped in two!
This caused alarm.

PILATE: Such rumors, if they're spread
anew
will do us harm.

[ANNAS *turns and crosses over to the*
CENTURION, *speaking while he walks*.]

ANNAS: Centurion, go off a way;
such words we did not hear you say.

CENTURION: Then, sirs, I bid you all
good day
since you won't hear.
God grant you grace. For you I pray.
You will know fear.

ANNAS: Withdraw at once or fear our
wrath,
for we cannot retrace our path.

[*The* CENTURION *goes out at the left
quietly and with great dignity and humility.* PILATE *looks after him thought-
fully*.]

PILATE: Such wonders as he told we
hath
not heard before.

[CAIAPHAS *crosses over to* PILATE *in
front of* ANNAS, *speaking as he goes*.]

CAIAPHAS: To words like these, try but
    to laugh.
Worry no more.

On matters like this do not dwell,
for all this may end very well.
But let us keep good watch to quell
    the people's fear.
We pray you, sir, to listen well
    to our words here.

And to this story patiently
attend, for Jesus openly
said something that was heresy
    and bold display:
that He would rise up bodily
    on the third day.

If that be true, as He has said,
His second death is more to dread
than is the first time He is dead.
    Let us beware.
Perhaps we should consider ways
    to take more care.

ANNAS: Why sir, if Jesus did say so,
He has no life to rise and go,
but if His men should hide below
    and His corpse steal,
that would to us and others show
    His words were real.

For then they'd say with mighty moan
that He rose by Himself alone.
Let's guard Him better than the throne
    with rugged men
until three days have come and gone.
    We're finished then.

[PILATE *has listened carefully to both*
CAIAPHAS *and* ANNAS.]

PILATE: In truth, good sirs, you are
    both wise.
We shall do just what you advise.
We shall by force prevent His rise
    and spoil their plan,

and none will steal this Man who dies,
    for no one can.

[*With a gesture,* PILATE *summons the*
FOUR SOLDIERS. *They enter from the*
left. They halt just inside. They carry
spears and shields. PILATE *crosses over*
to them, going in front of both CAIA-
PHAS *and* ANNAS *as he does so.*]

Sir knights, it is no flattery
to praise you for your chivalry
and count upon your bravery
    both nights and days.
I charge you: guard most carefully
    the corpse always.

Especially to you I say,
guard Him well on the third day,
and let no man take Him away
    out of His bed,
for if you fail in this, I say,
    you shall be dead.

[*The* FIRST SOLDIER *takes one step for-*
ward. He is obviously the leader.]

FIRST SOLDIER: My lords, you need
    have no despair.
No one will take him from our care.
Both day and night we'll be aware
    of what goes on.
Sir knights, this burden we will share,
    so let's be gone.

[*All four* SOLDIERS *go out at the left.*
PILATE *crosses in front of* ANNAS *and*
CAIAPHAS *and goes out at the right.*
ANNAS *and* CAIAPHAS *shake their heads*
at one another. Then they go out at
the right, whispering to one another as
they go. MUSIC CUE 2 *swells up, indi-*
cating a change of scene. Somewhere
in the musical bridge, the music stops
and three separate, distinct chimes are
heard, indicating the passage of three
days.]

Scene 2

PLACE: *Beside the Tomb of Jesus*

TIME: *Easter Day*

[*When the music stops, the* FOUR SOLDIERS *enter from the left. They are laughing and jostling one another. They wear cloaks over their tunics, and their heads are covered with hoods over which the helmets are placed. As the* FIRST SOLDIER *starts to speak, the others quiet down and listen to him. During his speech, he points to a place where each man should stand guard. As he does so, each man moves into place and sits down, laying his shield and spear beside him. The* SECOND *and* FOURTH SOLDIERS *remove their helmets and place them at their side, but the* THIRD SOLDIER *keeps his on. As he finishes speaking, the* FIRST SOLDIER *sits down also.*]

FIRST SOLDIER: Now, certainly, we all
    are bound
to keep this Man down in the ground.
On every side let us sit down.
    Here, you sit there.
If a robber comes, we'll crack his
    crown.
    Let's watch with care.

[MUSIC CUE 3 *is heard. It is resurrection music accompanied by bursts of thunder—or its musical equivalent. The* FIRST *and* SECOND SOLDIERS *half rise in amazement, then fall to the ground in a deep sleep. The* THIRD *and* FOURTH SOLDIERS *try to crawl away, but they too fall into sleep. The music continues for a little while in great exultation and then gradually shifts to quieter music. The* ANGEL *enters from the right as quietly and unobtrusively as possible. He holds behind him a large white cloth which the audience does not yet notice. He takes a position near the altar. The* THREE MARYS *enter from the left. They stand in a group. They have their hands clasped in attitudes of prayer. Inside their clasped hands are vials of brightly colored oil which are concealed from the audience. They all speak with deep grief, simply and sincerely. The music stops as the* FIRST MARY *begins to speak.*]

FIRST MARY: Alas! To death let me be
    taken,
so deep in sorrow I am shaken.
My tears of pain cannot awaken
    the blessed He.

SOLDIER

THE FIRST MARY   THE SECOND MARY

My Christ, my Lord, in death is taken
   away from me.

Ah, I saw what He could endure
before He lost His life so pure.
For every ill, He was the cure
   and health for all.
To all His servants, help was sure
   if Him they'd call.

SECOND MARY: Alas, who shall my sor-
            rows hide
when I think of His bleeding side?
Jesus, always loving others, tried
   to harm no one.
For no good reason, He has died,
   God's only Son.

THIRD MARY: For no good reason they
            have killed
the loveliest Lord that ever filled
the heart with joy. His blood is spilled;
   His soul has fled.
To soothe my anguish, who is skilled
   since He is dead?

[*As she begins the next speech, the*
FIRST MARY *unclasps her hands, re-*
vealing to the audience the vial of
bright yellow oil.]

FIRST MARY: Since He is dead, my sis-
            ters dear,
let us continue without fear
with our anointments fair and clear

[The SECOND MARY unclasps her hands, revealing the vial of bright blue oil.]

which we have brought
to wash the gash in His side from the
    spear
        that the soldier wrought.

[The THIRD MARY unclasps her hands, revealing the vial of bright red oil. Then the SECOND MARY takes the arm of the FIRST MARY. The THIRD MARY takes the arm of the SECOND MARY, and the three begin to move very slowly toward the altar.]

SECOND MARY: Let us go, then, sisters
    free.
His sacred corpse, I yearn to see.
Yet I don't know how that may be.
    We are alone.
Without some help, how can we three
    remove the stone?

THIRD MARY: That we can surely never
    do,
for it is large and heavy, too.

[The FIRST MARY suddenly sees the ANGEL. She seizes the SECOND MARY. They all stop.]

FIRST MARY: Sisters, look! Can it be
    true?
    A solemn sight!
A child is there where we go to,
    dressed all in white.

SECOND MARY: Surely, sisters, we need
    not hide—
the heavy stone is put aside!

THIRD MARY: Why, yes! To see what
    is inside,
    near let us wend
to see Him and with Him abide
    Who was our Friend.

[They move toward the ANGEL. He speaks to them simply and with great sympathy.]

ANGEL: Ye women, mourning in your
    thought,
here in this place Whom have ye
    sought?

FIRST MARY: Jesus, that unto death
    was brought,
    our Lord so free.

ANGEL: Women, here you will find
    Him not.
Come near and see.

[They come closer and stare in consternation at the altar. The SECOND

THE THIRD MARY

MARY *gives a little cry. The* ANGEL
continues to speak in soothing tones.]

He is not here, to you I say.
The place is empty where He lay.
They wrapped Him in this shroud the
  day
  when He grew cold.

[*He holds up the white sheet for them
to see.*]

Now He is risen, has gone away
  as he foretold.

As He foretold, so has He done.
With power mightier than the sun,
He is risen, flesh and blood. If one
  would find Him, go
to His disciples, every one,
  and tell them so.

SECOND MARY: This angel's voice has
  cleared my woe.

FIRST MARY: My sisters dear, since
  now we know
that out of death He is risen so—
  our Lord is free!—
away from here I will not go
  till Him I see.

[*The* SECOND MARY *takes her arm.*]

SECOND MARY: Marie, we must not
  longer stay;
to Galilee let's make our way.

[*The* FIRST MARY *shakes her head.*]

FIRST MARY: Here I must wait; here I
  must pray.
  My sisters, go.
While I stay here, to the others say
what now we know.

THIRD MARY: As we have heard, so
  shall we say.
Dear sister Mary, then, good day!

[*They all clasp hands with one another.*]

FIRST MARY: May very God, as He
  well may
  with His great might,
be ever with you on your way
  and lead you right.

[*The* SECOND *and* THIRD MARYS *go off
at the right. The* FIRST MARY *goes to
the altar and kneels before it.*]

Alas, what will become of me!
My lowly heart will break in three
when I think on that body free,
  how it was spilt!
Both hands and feet nailed to a tree,
  and without guilt!

And without guilt my Lord was slain
Who never sinned nor fought for gain.
He suffered wounds in cruelest pain
  for all my sins.
For me He let Himself be slain—
  and death begins.

[*The* ANGEL *hands her the white sheet
which she reverently takes.*]

How might I worship Jesus sweet
Who suffered nails in hands and feet
and Who, for love of me, in this cold
  sheet
  was laid away.
Nothing again until we meet
  shall make me gay.

[MUSIC CUE 4. MARY *rises and goes
sorrowfully out at the right. The* AN-
GEL, *as if to protect and watch over
her, follows her out. When they are
out, the* FIRST SOLDIER *begins to stir
in his sleep. Finally he wakes up suddenly and jumps to his feet. The music
stops.*]

FIRST SOLDIER: What! Gone, alas!
     What shall I say?
Where is the corpse that right here lay?

[*He runs to the* SECOND SOLDIER *and shakes him. The* SECOND SOLDIER *wakes up and speaks sleepily.*]

SECOND SOLDIER: What ails you, man?
     Is He away,
  the one we guard?

FIRST SOLDIER: Rise up and see.

[*The* SECOND SOLDIER *grabs his spear and gets up and looks. Then he speaks excitedly.*]

SECOND SOLDIER: Help! Gone away!
  Oh, this is hard.

[*He throws himself down on the ground and begins to wail. The* THIRD SOLDIER *wakes up and speaks crossly.*]

THIRD SOLDIER: What devil tempts the
     two of you
to make such noise? And crying, too!

[*The* FIRST SOLDIER *goes to the* FOURTH SOLDIER *and tries to wake him, but he does not succeed at first. He speaks with great excitement.*]

FIRST SOLDIER: Where did He go?

[*The* THIRD SOLDIER *gets up.*]

THIRD SOLDIER: Alas! Gone! Who?

SECOND SOLDIER: He that here lay.

THIRD SOLDIER: What, how—How
     could He do
  it, get away?

[*On this last phrase, the* FOURTH SOLDIER *finally wakes up. He jumps to his feet, seizes his shield and spear. He picks up his helmet and puts it hurriedly on his head.*]

FOURTH SOLDIER: What? Has He escaped the grave
while we watched here, so good and
     brave?
Has He walked off, the crooked knave?
  He got away?
Now we are ruined sure. God save
  us all this day.

[*The* FOURTH SOLDIER *falls onto his knees and begins to pray silently.*]

FIRST SOLDIER: Alas, what shall we do
     this day?
The Jewish traitor's gone away!
And do you know, I think He may
  have risen alone?

SECOND SOLDIER: If Pilate hears of this
     affray,
  he'll make us groan.

[*The* SECOND SOLDIER *begins to wail again.*]

THIRD SOLDIER: Say, can't we find a
     better plan?

[*The* FOURTH SOLDIER *is still kneeling.*]

FOURTH SOLDIER: We'll die if we have
     lost this man.

[*The* SECOND SOLDIER *rises to his feet, gains control of himself and begins to speak more deliberately.*]

SECOND SOLDIER: The exact time He
     left, none of us can
determine now.

FIRST SOLDIER: Alas, how bad my luck
     has ran.
  I'm cursed, I vow.

[*The* FOURTH SOLDIER *rises to his feet.*]

FOURTH SOLDIER: Sir Pilate, learning
     that instead
of guarding, we slept while He fled

will order us to join the dead—
  unless mercy wins.

SECOND SOLDIER: Let's us make up
      some lies instead
to save our skins.

THIRD SOLDIER: Yes, I agree that is
      our quest.

FOURTH SOLDIER: And I agree that
      plan is best.

[*The* SECOND SOLDIER *suddenly gets an
idea and begins to speak enthusiasti-
cally.*]

SECOND SOLDIER: I'll say some men
      removed our guest,
  and they were armed;
a hundred men upon us pressed,
  and we were harmed.

[*He begins to pantomime a limp, and
he holds his head as if it were bruised.*]

FIRST SOLDIER: No, I do not agree we
      should.

[*The other three look at one another
in dismay.*]

There is no lying quite so good
as truth. Let's say, "Alone He stood,
  then went His way."
Sir Pilate may tear off my hood;
  this I dare say.

SECOND SOLDIER: What, dare you to
      Sir Pilate's face
give him the truth in this strange case?

[*The* FIRST SOLDIER *now speaks simply, without a trace of smugness or
conceit.*]

FIRST SOLDIER: Yes, and if death I
      must embrace,
  we die once only.

THIRD SOLDIER: Let's pray the Body
      from this place
finds His death lonely.

FOURTH SOLDIER: Then, good sir
      knights, let us proceed
to great Sir Pilate.

[*He addresses the* FIRST SOLDIER.]

                    You may lead.
I fear that we shall have great need
  of mercy there.

FIRST SOLDIER: I'll tell him just how
      Christ was freed.
This will I dare.

[MUSIC CUE 5. *The* SOLDIERS *go out
at the left.*]

Scene 3

PLACE: *Pilate's Council Hall*
TIME: *An hour later*

[PILATE *enters from the right, followed
by* CAIAPHAS *and* ANNAS. *The* SOLDIERS
*re-enter from the left. When they have
all halted, the* FIRST SOLDIER *crosses
over to* PILATE *and reports to him formally. The music stops.*]

FIRST SOLDIER: Sir Pilate, prince with-
      out a peer,
Sir Caiaphas and Sir Annas here,
and all you others who are near,

[*He indicates the audience and speaks
to them as well as to* PILATE, CAIA-
PHAS, *and* ANNAS.]

  this I proclaim:
God save you all from cold, from fear,
  from sin, from shame.

[PILATE *puts a hand on the* FIRST SOL-

DIER'S *shoulder and speaks to him with friendly condescension.*]

PILATE: You are most welcome, pleasant knight.
Have you some stories for tonight
that may provide us some delight?
  We hope you do.

FIRST SOLDIER: Our watchfulness did not go right.
  We have failed you.

[PILATE *drops his hand from the* SOLDIER'S *shoulder. He tries to speak, but he is astounded; he cannot get the words out.* CAIAPHAS *speaks up angrily.*]

CAIAPHAS: Failed? Alas! Do not say so.

[*The* SECOND SOLDIER *crosses over to stand beside the* FIRST SOLDIER *before* PILATE.]

SECOND SOLDIER: The prophet Jesus Whom you know
is risen and gone. We're filled with woe,
  for we did fail.

[PILATE, *in great anger, crosses in front of the* FIRST *and* SECOND SOLDIERS *and speaks to the* THIRD *and* FOURTH SOLDIERS.]

PILATE: The devil must have struck this blow.
  I'll make you wail.

Clumsy cowards, I'll make you crawl.
Have you let Him go from you? All?

[*The* FOUR SOLDIERS *drop to their knees.*]

THIRD SOLDIER: Sir, we did feel mighty small
  when we found out.

FOURTH SOLDIER: We were so scared.
  We tried to call
but could not shout.

[ANNAS *steps forward and speaks to the* FIRST *and* SECOND SOLDIERS.]

ANNAS: Had you no strength to bind Him first?
You traitors, you. You should be cursed.
Both Him and the men who on you burst
  you might have tied.

FIRST SOLDIER: No mortal man could do the worst,
  or we'd have tried.

SECOND SOLDIER: We were so frightened there alone.
When Jesus thrust aside the stone,
we turned to stone from cause unknown
  and could not stir.

PILATE: What?

[*He turns toward the* FIRST SOLDIER *but does not cross over to him.*]
  He rose by Himself alone?

FIRST SOLDIER: That He did, sir.

FOURTH SOLDIER: We never heard since we were born,
nor did our ancestors forewarn
us of such music, noon nor morn,
  as we heard there.

[CAIAPHAS *speaks philosophically.*]

CAIAPHAS: Alas, then we must grow forlorn
  and sad with care.

SECOND SOLDIER: Good note of time I carefully took.
He rose when the earth beneath us shook.

All courage then my heart forsook
  till He ascended.

FOURTH SOLDIER: I was so scared, I
      dared not look.
  My strength was ended.

THIRD SOLDIER: I could not stand, I
  felt such pain.

[PILATE *crosses in front of the* FIRST
and SECOND SOLDIERS *and* ANNAS. *He
speaks to* CAIAPHAS. *His voice is tinged
with sarcasm.*]

PILATE: Sir Caiaphas, you have a
      brain.
If we have loss instead of gain,
  we'll pay a price.
Therefore what actions now remain?
  Give your advice.

[CAIAPHAS *first pantomimes that* PI-
LATE *should dismiss the* SOLDIERS.
PILATE *motions for the* FIRST *and* SEC-
OND SOLDIERS *to go over to the extreme left with the other two. All* FOUR
SOLDIERS *rise and form a tight little
group at the extreme left of the acting
area.* ANNAS *moves closer to* PILATE
and CAIAPHAS. *Before* CAIAPHAS
speaks, he looks first to make sure the
SOLDIERS *are out of hearing distance.*]

CAIAPHAS: I always try to counsel
      wisely,
so if we now proceed discreetly,
these men may try to hide completely
  what they have done.
We ought to order them right calmly
  to tell no one.

[ANNAS *steps forward, not to be out-
done in advising.*]

ANNAS: Sir Pilate, let me now implore
you strongly, as I've done before,

to take strong action to explore
  this case, but now
say twenty thousand men or more
  began this row.

Pay off your knights with golden cash
to tell the story of that clash.

PILATE: Although such lies seem some-
      what rash,
  I'll take the chance.

[PILATE *crosses over to the center of
the area and speaks to the* SOLDIERS.]

Sir knights, do not stand there
      abashed.
  You may advance.

[*In great fear, they come toward him,
halting a few paces before they reach
him.*]

Listen well to what I say.
Tell every man along your way
ten thousand men in full array
  came up to you.

[*The* SECOND, THIRD *and* FOURTH
SOLDIERS *all look quickly at the* FIRST
SOLDIER. *He looks down shame-
facedly.*]

With force of arms they took away
  this Jesus, too.

This shall you say throughout the land,
and for obeying my command,
a thousand pounds, please understand,
  shall come to you.

[PILATE *pats the money bag which he
wears at his side.*]

This gold I'll place in each man's hand.
  This I will do.

[CAIAPHAS *crosses over toward the*
SOLDIERS *but stops just before crossing
in front of* PILATE.]

CAIAPHAS: You each will get a good
  promotion
if you describe this false commotion.

FIRST SOLDIER: Wherever we go, as
  fits your notion
  by night or day,
in every land, on every ocean,
  so shall we say.

PILATE: Yes, good. Remember always
  then
wherever you travel among men
that no man hears the truth again
  as you've told us.
Forget what you have seen and heard.
  Pretend
  it happened thus.

You men were overcome by force.
The people will believe this source,
and we'll condemn, with words like
  yours,
  His followers.
And we will back you up, of course.
  Goodbye, good sirs.

[PILATE *turns to* CAIAPHAS *and*
ANNAS.]

Thus shall the truth be bought and
  sold,
and falsehood shall for fact be told.

[*He turns to the* SOLDIERS *again.*]

So in your hearts forever hold
  this secret hid.
Now, fare you well, both young and
  old.

[*The* SOLDIERS *go out at the left. As
he leaves, the* FIRST SOLDIER *buries his
face in his hands.* PILATE *speaks to*
ANNAS *and* CAIAPHAS *triumphantly and
with great finality in his voice.*]

  Of Christ we're rid!

[PILATE, CAIAPHAS *and* ANNAS *go out
at the right. They are still pompous
and dignified, but they are also vaguely
troubled.* MUSIC CUE 6.]

Scene 4

PLACE: *In a Garden*
TIME: *A Few Days Later*

[*The* FIRST MARY *enters from the
right, the white sheet still in her hand.
She crosses to the altar and lays it at
the foot of the altar. She speaks sorrowfully. The music stops.*]

FIRST MARY: Alas, I am filled with ill
  dismay,
torn with more anguish than I can
  stand.
The dark dread deed they did that day
has crushed the happiness in this land.
Jesus of Nazareth has gone away,
has disappeared with the wind like
  sand.
Now all my light is locked in clay;
my head I uncover with this hand.

[*With her hand, she removes her head
covering.*]

My wits are lost: I totter, I fall.

[*She falls to the ground.*]

The pain in my heart has vanquished
  me.
I cannot move from here at all.
The Jews nailed Jesus to a tree.
My love is gone, and I cannot call
Him near to soothe or comfort me.
My heart is drenched with bitter gall.
Please help me, God in persons three.

[*She gets up into a kneeling position,
facing left, and begins to pray.*]

Most holy God of every country
Who watches over day and night
making both sun and moon shine
brightly,
grant me the grace to have one sight
of my sweet Lord—or a messenger
saintly.

[MUSIC CUE 7 *begins.* JESUS, *disguised as a gardener and carrying a hoe, enters from the right and crosses over to her. He stands behind her and places one hand gently on her shoulder. In fright, she pulls away from Him and falls forward to the ground, crying. He crosses to her left and speaks to her with infinite kindness. The music stops as he starts to speak.*]

JESUS

JESUS: Thou woman of sorrow avoiding the light,
why weepest thou so? Why cry?

[*Her crying subsides a little.*]

Even faintly?
Whom seekest thou? Do not take
fright.

[*She cries out again in anguish.*]

Ah, weep no more; lift up your head.
Rise from the ground there where you
lie.
Tell Me your troubles now instead.

[*He kneels beside her and lifts her head. She looks at Him but does not recognize Him.*]

FIRST MARY: My Christ has gone
away, and I
am lonely. For my sins He bled.

JESUS: Thou faithful friend, try not to
cry,
for He will soon to you be led.
You will know comfort; He is nearby.
He is alive. He is not dead.
Jesus Christ shall never die!

[*She rises.*]

FIRST MARY: Sir, I have looked both
far and near
to find my Lord but found Him not.

[*He also rises from the kneeling position.*]

JESUS: Woman, weep not. Be of good
cheer.
I know the place where He was
brought.

FIRST MARY: Sir, if you took Him far
away,

for the sake of the prophets let me
know
where now He is without delay,
and there with great haste I will go.
Good gardener, to you I pray
that you'll have pity on my woe.
In the name of Jesus, if I may,
I beg you. Where did Jesus go?

[*He shakes his head slowly and speaks
with gentle reproof.*]

JESUS: Why do you seek His body
only?
The soul, more than the body, is dear.
You could not save Him from His
destiny.
His wounds would hurt you if He were
here.
But His spirit shall help make mankind holy,
and what is cloudy He shall make
clear,
and all who are lonely shall be happy,
and all shall be brave who are touched
with fear.

FIRST MARY: Ah, yes. But if I could
only see
Him once, my blessed Lord of light!
Dry and not wet my eyes would be.
I sorrow only for the worldly sight.

[MUSIC CUE 8. JESUS *drops his head
covering back so that she may see
Him more plainly. She recognizes Him
and sinks to her knees.*]

JESUS: Maria, mourn no more, but
look
upon this wound within My side.

[*He parts His garment at the side,
revealing the ghastly wound.*]

For all the sins of man I forsook
My life. Look at these nail holes wide.

[*He holds up His hands, revealing the
bleeding nail holes.*]

I am He Whom soldiers took.
Upon the cross I hung and died.
Know this, sweet Mary: good shall
hook
to more good when the flesh in earth
shall hide.

[MARY *rises and goes toward Him, her
arms outstretched to embrace Him.
The music stops.*]

FIRST MARY: Ah, master! I have waited
long.
Let me embrace You if I may.

[JESUS *moves a step backward and
raises a restraining hand to her. She
stops.*]

JESUS: No, Mary. Touch Me not. Be
strong
and listen well to what I say.
I am He Who does no wrong,
the God Who is with you today.
With bitter death and sorrow's song,
I bought God's mercy for man's way.

Therefore, good Mary, speak with Me
and let your happiness be great.

[MARY *picks up the white sheet from
the foot of the altar and moves toward
JESUS.*]

FIRST MARY: My Lord, I know that
Thou art He.
Let me with this Thy blood abate.

[JESUS *moves another step backward.
He shakes His head sadly.*]

JESUS: Touch me not! It may not be,
my love. You must for touching wait.
First to My Father, fair Marie,
I must ascend. It is My fate.

[MARY *kneels before Him again.*]

FIRST MARY: Have mercy on my
    mortal soul.
Sweeter than honey is Thy love.
To be worth Thy mercy is my goal.
Saviour mine, from God above
plead mercy for my mortal soul.
I once was sinful. Thy sweet love
and mercy into my heart stole.
Welcome, Lord, my gentle dove.

[*With great humility, she puts her head
covering back upon her head.*]

JESUS: Maria, write this in your heart.
Christ's armor, rich and strong and
    bright,
is a leather jacket, torn apart.

[*He indicates with a gesture His
garment and the tear in it at the side.*]

This symbolizes all the white
and sacred flesh of men who start
with faith in God. The crown of light
is a crown of thorns.

[*He indicates with a gesture His crown
of thorns.*]

                        God's chart
shows this means dignity and right.

FIRST MARY: Ah, blessed body,
    crowned and clad
in shining light and meaning this.
For our sins, not Thy fault, Thou had
to suffer pain for mankind's bliss.

JESUS: To God, Who is My Father,
    soon
I shall ascend, for I have done
what was assigned for mankind's boon,
and now He calls His on!y Son.
Tell to all people, morn and noon,
My story of the victory won
by life over death. Tell those who
    swoon

with suffering: love heals everyone.

[MUSIC CUE 9 *starts quietly in the
background.* MARY *speaks in great
ecstasy.*]

FIRST MARY: For joy my soul begins to
    sing.
My breast is filled with ecstasy,
for Jesus lives, and everything
seems beautiful and wise to me.
Love, sweet Love, is now crowned
    king.
My Jesus died upon a tree,
but rose again with angel's wing,
and has come back to comfort me.

[*The music stops.*]

JESUS: Go, tell My friends in Galilee
to preach My teachings as they ought.
In Galilee they think of Me
and live in fear lest they be caught.
Tell them that I appeared to thee
and said to take courageous thought.
Blessings on those who serve with Me,
who try to live as I have taught!

[MARY *bows her head in reverence.*]

FIRST MARY: Thy love surpasses every-
    thing.
Praised be Thy everlasting love.

[JESUS *moves toward her and holds
His hand over her head in benediction.*
MUSIC CUE 10.]

JESUS: Bless you, my sister. Of mercy
    sing
to everyone. I go above.

[JESUS *goes out slowly at the left.
When He has gone,* MARY *rises, stands
looking after Him for a moment, then
slowly turns and goes out right. She is
still holding the white sheet close to her
with loving tenderness.*]

MUSIC CUE 1

MUSIC CUE 2

RESURRECTION

MUSIC CUE 3

MUSIC CUE 4

MUSIC CUE 5: *Repeat Music Cue 1.*

MUSIC CUE 6

MUSIC CUE 7

MUSIC CUE 8

RESURRECTION

MUSIC CUE 9

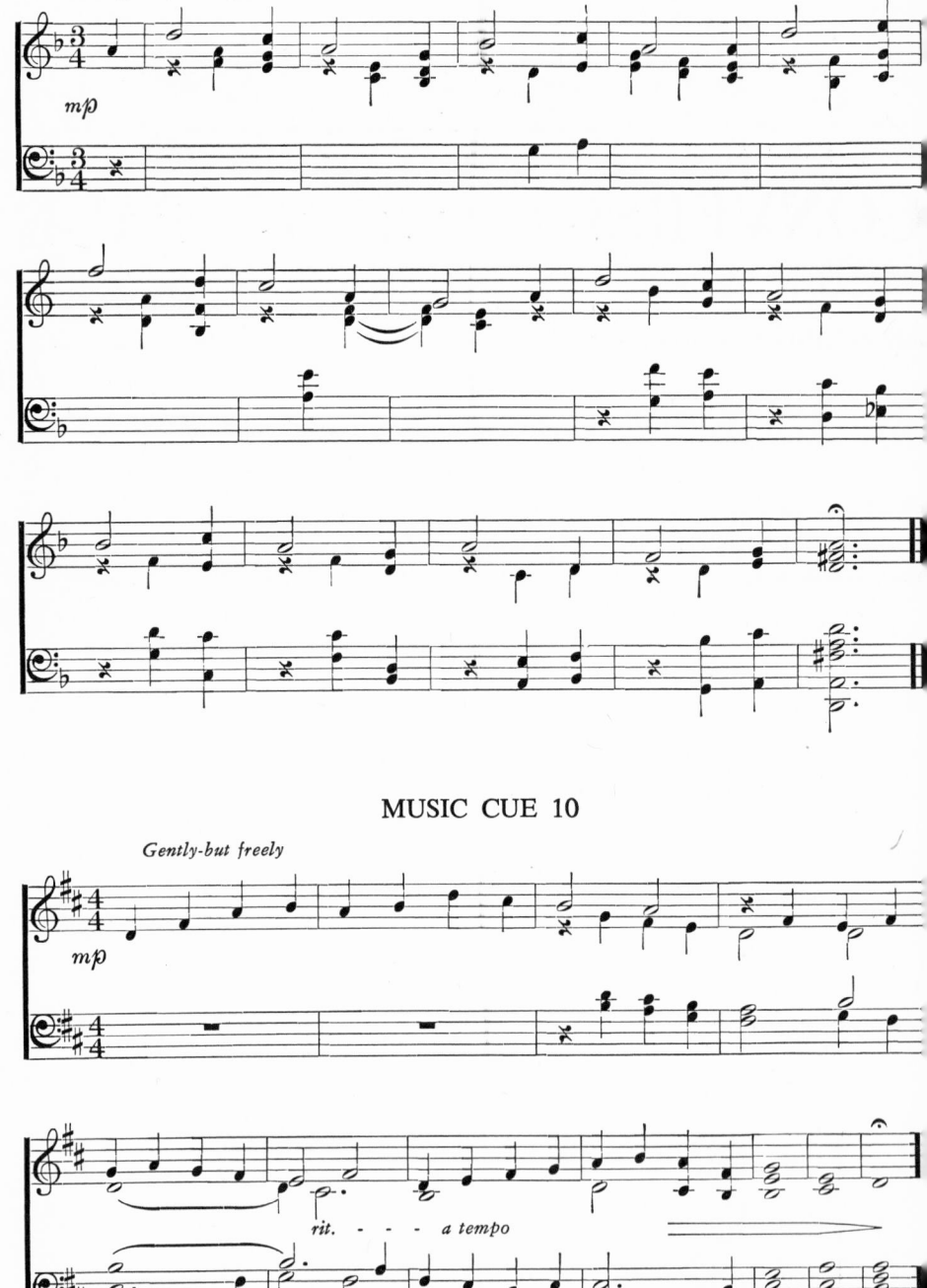

MUSIC CUE 10

The Digby

CONVERSION OF ST. PAUL

AN ACTING VERSION IN MODERN ENGLISH BY ROBERT A. JOHNSTON

WITH ORIGINAL MUSIC BY THOMAS MATTHEWS

Permission is hereby granted to church and educational groups to perform, without payment of royalty, this version of The Digby CONVERSION OF ST. PAUL. Dr. Johnston will appreciate it, however, if any group presenting the play will so notify him at Wright Junior College, 3400 North Austin, Chicago 34, Illinois.

INTRODUCTION

It is said that God moves in mysterious ways. Certainly His selection of the great persecutor of Christianity to become one of its saints seems almost incomprehensible to our limited human intelligence. And yet He did.

This play is one of the old miracle plays of medieval times. It was originally presented not as mere entertainment but to teach the people that God was capable of changing anybody from bad to good, no matter how evil or how proud he might be to begin with. Many things have changed since then, but God's abilities to strike the mighty low or to raise the humble to holiness have not.

That this play still has high literary merit and exciting theatrical effectiveness today is perhaps surprising. Part of the reason may be the deep sincerity of its author and his clear desire to communicate his own firm faith to others. The *Conversion of St. Paul* was anonymously written, as all medieval plays were, and so the unknown author received no public recognition for his work. His only glory was in being able to serve God in an artistic way. It is his faith which endures and speaks to us today.*

Notes on the Characters

POET: The poet is a kind of commentator, and he represents the unknown author. He is a thoughtful,

dignified, wise person. The role may be played either by a man or by a woman. It would certainly be appropriate and effective to have the rector or vicar himself play this role. It would probably be better to have the lines memorized, but it is entirely possible to present the play with the Poet reading his lines from the book. If the lines are to be read from the book, the Poet should practice so that he can frequently look up at the audience while reading, without losing his place.

SAUL (ST. PAUL): This is a difficult role because the actor must present convincingly two different characterizations and yet, at the same time, make it seem consistent that such a reversal of character should occur. It should be remembered that certain characteristics unify Saul before and after his conversion: his great physical strength, his superior mind, his qualities of leadership, his fearlessness in the world of men, and his intense devotion to duty as he sees it at the time. Before his conversion, of course, he is proud, egotistical, overbearing. The audience should not sympathize with him. After his conversion, he is humble, unselfish, and modest. The audience must change its mind about him and decide to like him. He must convince us during the conversion scene that an actual miracle takes place, and that by God's entering into his heart, he is a completely changed man. The actor's voice should be strong and forceful, and he should be the most talented of the available men.

---

* These three paragraphs may serve as "program notes" for printed programs of performances. Permission to reprint for this purpose is herewith given.

53

CAIAPHAS: Whether it is because they are older now than they were in the York *Resurrection,* or whether it is because the plays were written by different authors, Caiaphas and Annas, high priests, are somewhat different in characterization from what they were in the *Resurrection.* Basically they are still the same: crafty, calculating, opportunistic. Caiaphas, however, is more of an old fuddy-duddy in this play. He is not dogmatic and positive; in fact, he often seems dubious and insecure in trying to make up his mind. He is still, of course, vicious and unscrupulous.

ANNAS: Annas is less of a sneerer in this play, but he is still shrewd and observant. He makes decisions quickly, and he has become the real leader of the two. The two priests are completely friendly to each other in this play and do not seem to feel the necessity of trying to outdo one another. Annas has a touch of laziness in him, too, as seen in his willingness to let Saul take over the arduous duties so long as Annas can have the credit if they are successfully performed.

TWO SOLDIERS: The Soldiers are not distinguished from one another by individual characterizations as the soldiers in the *Resurrection* were. They are simply two young men, loyal and naive, who try to be faithful to Saul as long as possible but who decide ultimately that he must be crazy. The supernatural events confuse them a great deal, and they are completely incapable of comprehending exactly what has occurred.

FIRST SERVANT: The First Servant may be of any age, but he is probably younger than the Second Servant. He is wittily comic. He is also vulgar. He has no sense of dignity nor respect for others. He is physically quick and agile. If played properly, he should be a very humorous character.

SECOND SERVANT: He is the foil for the First Servant and the recipient of his wit. He should be a kind of comic caricature of Saul in his pride and conceit (as Belial is in a different sense later on). He can be exaggeratedly pompous because dignity is not natural with him but only put on. He is very disconcerted at the teasing by the First Servant. His change to complete servility at the end of the scene is a comic parallel foreshadowing the serious conversion of Saul himself. If properly played, he can be even funnier than the First Servant.

VOICE OF GOD: See the description of the Voice of God, p. 5. Remember, however, that in this play we have the New Testament conception of a God of mercy and compassion, who has recently tested mankind with the death of His own Son. There is firmness and strength, however, as well as gentleness and love.

ANANIAS: Ananias describes himself in the text as "meek and weak but pious." This is an accurate description of him. He should seem smaller than Saul and much less powerful physically. He is probably middle-aged or old. He has been a priest for many years, and his relationship with God has been close and intimate. He is a very holy man, but at the same time, he is very human, too.

BELIAL: Belial is one of the most evil, most intelligent, and most hard-working of the devils. He is fiery, animalistic, and full of explosive vitality. He has greater self-control than Mercury and is definitely superior to him in rank. While watching Belial, one senses that Saul's earlier egotism must have been an unconscious imitation caused by the influence of Belial. In fact, all excessive pride seems to be his special province, and it is on this point that the specific conflict between him and St. Paul arises in this play.

MERCURY: Derived from the respected god of messengers of classical antiquity, Mercury has here become messenger of the devils. He is flighty, excitable, violent, uncontrolled, and not too bright. Probably originally both devils were rather comic, and it is quite in order for Mercury to be so still. The comedy should not be allowed to obscure the fact, however, that he is evil and revolting.

PRIESTS' SERVANT: He is surly, sly, and downright mean. He is a bully and a coward. He is meek and obsequious with Caiaphas and Annas, but he is afraid of them and of the possibility that they will ask him to kill the powerful Saul. He may be of any age.

AN ANGEL: In marked contrast to Mercury, this other messenger is serene, happy, poised, and dignified. The Angel may be either a man or a woman. There is a quality of firmness in this Angel, but it is tempered with pity and goodwill.

Notes on the Properties

The PROP LIST comprises the following:

> two letters with official seals (in Annas' inner pocket)
> two staffs (carried by the Soldiers)
> two devil's forks (carried by Belial and Mercury; these are optional and may be omitted if desired)
> a cross (in Saul's inner pocket).

This is a simple play as far as properties are concerned. The letters should be the rolled-up scroll kind, and the seals can easily be made by painting them on and perhaps gluing bits of ribbon to the paper. The staffs should obviously be strong enough to support the weight of Saul when one of them is offered to him. The devil's forks are not necessary but may add an interesting touch to complete the traditional appearance of devils. The cross is the most significant of the properties. It should be rather large. Care should be taken to make it bright enough to be seen easily but yet not flashy or gaudy. It is probably most appropriate to have it made of wood although cardboard painted to resemble wood will do.

CHARACTERS

POET	VOICE OF GOD
SAUL (later ST. PAUL)	ANANIAS
CAIAPHAS	BELIAL*
ANNAS	MERCURY*
TWO SOLDIERS	PRIESTS' SERVANT †
TWO SERVANTS*	AN ANGEL†

Scene 1

PLACE: *Jerusalem*

TIME: *Shortly after the death and resurrection of Christ*

[MUSIC CUE 1. *The* POET *enters from the right side of the acting area. He crosses to the center of the stage and kneels. As he begins to pray, the music grows softer.*]

POET: Glory to God, the omnipotent
King Who
by divine power refreshes the earth;
to Mary, the purest of queens, let us
sing true
glory, for She gave our Jesus His birth;
all glory to Jesus, Whose goodness and
worth
are limitless! From Him I now request
influence
to bless and to govern this worshipping
audience.

[*The music stops. The* POET *rises and speaks directly to the audience.*]

Now, honorable friends, with your
kindest permission,
we plan to present, if you'll listen and
look,

the *Conversion of St. Paul.* The Bible's
expression
of this strange, true story which took
place long years ago is best. Read that
great Book
for yourselves. And now, if we may,
we'll act out
the story of how such a miracle once
came about.

[MUSIC CUE 2. *The* POET *goes out at the right as* SAUL *enters from the left.* SAUL *strides to the front left corner of the acting area and addresses the audience. His manner is haughty and aristocratic. As he begins to speak, the music stops.*]

SAUL: Look at me. Firmly I stand on
the ground,
wealthy with many a rich royal garment.
No one superior to me can be found
throughout this whole world from orient to occident.
My fame is the widest known under
the firmament.
All people everywhere fear and respect me.

---

* Characters omitted in shortened version.
† Additional characters omitted in the very
shortened version that ends with Scene 4.

No one dares ruffle or injure my dignity.

Saul is my name, I do hereby announce to you.

I am the one man who threatens and menaces

the wicked disciples of Jesus. Before I'm through,

they will be brought for their illegal trespasses

up for cruel punishment in the priests' palaces.

They must be suppressed, for they really have no business

preaching and giving examples of lawlessness.

[*The high priests* CAIAPHAS *and* ANNAS *enter from the right and go to the front right corner of the acting area.*]

In the name of the devil-god Belial, I will

go forth to the princes Caiaphas and Annas

to form an alliance for friendly support until

I can pursue through Libya and Damascus

these criminal Christians and bring them to justice.

For trial we'll transport them into Jerusalem,

all children as well as adults that we find of them.

[SAUL *crosses to* CAIAPHAS *and* ANNAS. *He bows slightly to them and they return his bow. He speaks to them in a dignified manner but with less condescension than he showed toward the audience.*]

Most noble prelates and princes of regality,

I hereby petition of your friendly worthiness

some letters or epistles from your most official sovereignty

to grant permission to subdue rebellions caused by stubbornness

which Christian groups are fostering with clever, sly finesse

among the common people. Now I need your support.

If we join forces, we can bring each one of them to court.

[CAIAPHAS *and* ANNAS *exchange satisfied glances.*]

CAIAPHAS: With your righteous attitude, great Saul, we perfectly agree

POET

and grant the petition which you hereby ask.

We know your reputation for strength and dignity

and are content that you will be successful in your task.

[*He raises his hand solemnly and speaks in an official tone, almost a chant.*]

We now proclaim a law outlawing Christians.

[*He resumes his natural voice and speaks directly to* SAUL.]

Now we ask

that you proceed to persecute them. Stop this Christian cause.

We must take sterner measures against those who break our laws.

[ANNAS *reaches into an inner pocket in his garment and produces two letters with large official seals upon them. He shows them to* SAUL.]

SAUL

SAINT PAUL

ANNAS: Here, then, are two letters
which give you authority
to strike where the danger is, no matter where.
Whether they're paupers or people of
property,
bring them to us, and we will prepare
harsh judgments against them. See that
you bear
these documents with you wherever
you go.
We trust you to spare neither friend,
sir, nor foe.

[*He gives the letters to* SAUL.]

SAUL: These letters I accept. I understand
what I must do.

[*He raises his hand solemnly and
speaks in the more formal tone used
by* CAIAPHAS *in proclaiming the law
above.*]
         I make my oath
to spare no man nor woman in this
land.

[*He resumes his normal voice.*]

I trust that this will satisfy you both.
To do this kind of work, I am not
loathe,
for I can do it well.

[CAIAPHAS *and* ANNAS *go out at the
left.* SAUL *crosses to the center and
gestures to his* SOLDIERS *offstage at the
right.*]
         Good soldiers, ho!

[TWO SOLDIERS *enter from the right
and come over to* SAUL. *They kneel
before him. He speaks to them in an
authoritative tone.*]

We'll now go to Damascus as soon as
we can go.

FIRST SOLDIER: Whatever you command, I'll always do.
I'll never hesitate, complain nor fret.
Throughout Damascus I will go with
you,
and we will stop these foul rebellions
yet.

SECOND SOLDIER: Me too. As long as
you will let
me serve you, I'll obey your will.
These Christians we will either catch
or kill.

SAUL: To me it is a happy consolation
to hear your earnest vows of loyalty.
Your intelligence deserves my com-
mendation.
You are both men of special quality,
for you can recognize my royalty.
But now, since time is moving, bring
to me
my swiftest horse. We'll start immediately.

FOR SHORTENED VERSION,

CUT THE FOLLOWING SCENE

[SAUL *crosses in front of the* SOLDIERS
*and goes off at the right. They rise and
go off at the left.* MUSIC CUE 3. *The*
FIRST SERVANT *enters from the left,
walking backward and calling offstage.
The music stops as he begins to speak.*]

FIRST SERVANT: Say, stable boy, one
peck of oats and some hay!
Hurry it up, or we'll get rid of you.
Hey! Hey there, you doing it? Be on
your way.
You could move just a bit speedier,
too.

[*The* SECOND SERVANT *enters from the
left. He is very pompous and affected.*]

SECOND SERVANT: How dare you address me as stable boy, you!

Why, I am a gentleman's gentleman, son.

One word more from you and I must whack you one.

[*The* FIRST SERVANT *bows low in mock humility.*]

FIRST SERVANT: Your pardon, sir, please. I see now very well

you are either a gentleman or a big fool.

One look at those sweet ugly features would tell

that you were a gentleman straight out of school.

But I saw you fall flat in that slippery pool

of slithery mud which then spattered your face,

so I thought you a stable boy, lowly and base.

[*The* SECOND SERVANT *starts toward the* FIRST SERVANT. *The* FIRST SERVANT *runs to the right side of the stage. The* SECOND SERVANT *stops in the center.*]

SECOND SERVANT: You are making this up. Why, this is not true.

I never fall down, and most certainly not

in the mud. I stand upright and elegant, too.

My master's so pleased with the way I can trot

that he trusts me with everything that he has got.

FIRST SERVANT: Oh, isn't that mud, then, on your pretty face?

[*The* SECOND SERVANT *automatically feels his face. The* FIRST SERVANT *laughs gleefully.*]

I'll never get over my fearful disgrace.

I see you're a higher type, truly you are.

One can see you're a gentleman's servant, old bean.

That's not mud on your face. It is probably tar.

[*The* SECOND SERVANT *again feels his face and begins to look uncomfortable. The* FIRST SERVANT *laughs again.*]

SECOND SERVANT: It is not tar. My features are perfectly clean.

[*He runs toward the* FIRST SERVANT, *hand upraised. He tries to hit him, but the* FIRST SERVANT *dodges and runs to the front left corner of the acting area. The* SECOND SERVANT *stops at the center.*]

FIRST SERVANT: If you are a gentleman, where is your hood?

SECOND SERVANT: I once had a hood that was perfectly good.

FIRST SERVANT: Oh yes, I am sure of it. Was it a double?

The man who made your hood was too good to live.

Did he harness and yoke you to keep you from trouble?

[*The* SECOND SERVANT *runs to the* FIRST SERVANT *again. Again he tries to hit him, but the* FIRST SERVANT *dodges and runs to the front right corner of the acting area. The* SECOND SERVANT *runs all the way after him this time and catches hold of him. He is just about to hit him when the* SOLDIERS *enter from the left. As soon as the* FIRST SOLDIER *starts to speak, the*

SECOND SERVANT *lets go and the* FIRST SERVANT *runs off at the right.*]

FIRST SOLDIER: Hey, stable boy, will you go quickly outside
and saddle the horse so your master can ride?

[*The* SECOND SERVANT *loses all his pomposity and becomes meek and servile. He crosses to the* SOLDIERS.]

SECOND SERVANT: Yes, sir, he is ready. You may tell our great Saul
that I have him all saddled and ready to go.

[SAUL *enters from the right. The* FIRST SOLDIER *crosses in front of the* SERVANT *and goes to* SAUL *as he speaks.*]

FIRST SOLDIER: Sir Saul, this good stable boy tells me that all
is ready for you. Shall we now go below?
We all shall our faithfulest loyalty show
and follow wherever our master shall lead
by night or by day and whatever your creed.

SHORTENED VERSION

RESUMES HERE

SAUL: Let us quickly proceed to Damascus to chase
all obstinate beings, rebellious and proud,
who transgress our laws. I lift up my face
and declare that with diligence I shall erase
all Christians from off of the crust of this earth.

Such a mission accomplished will prove my great worth.

[SAUL *and the others go off at the right.* CAIAPHAS *and* ANNAS *enter from the left and watch them leave.* MUSIC CUE 4. *This continues as background music behind the next two speeches.*]

CAIAPHAS: Now Saul has begun his wonderful voyage
to persecute rebels of every degree.
He will not permit any to have clear passage
in this, our whole region, unless they agree
to give up their notion of Christianity.
Whenever this Saul takes our problems in hand,
he proves he'll be able to govern this land.

ANNAS: When Saul is in charge, we others may rest.
He'll do our defending, and we will be bound
to love him as one of our great country's best.
The champion in everything noble, we've found
him to be. There is none alive over the ground
who is anything like him. None is his peer:
we've looked both east and west, both far and near.

[*They go out at the left. The* POET *enters from the right and crosses to the center. As he begins to speak, the music stops.*]

POET: We must now conclude this episode
and beg the audience to move with us
to another place on a lonely road

where Saul is going to far Damascus.

For best understanding, it is a good practice

to read the Bible with its famed intelligence.

And now we commend you to God's magnificence.

[*He goes out at the left.* MUSIC CUE 5.]

Scene 2

PLACE: *The Road to Damascus*
TIME: *Two days later*

[SAUL *enters from the right followed by the* TWO SOLDIERS *and the* TWO SERVANTS* *in a procession. The* TWO SOLDIERS *carry staffs. All but* SAUL *stop just inside the entrance.* SAUL *crosses to the front right corner and speaks directly to the audience. As he begins to speak, the music stops.*]

SAUL: This is my journey to Damascus. There I do intend

to give pursuit to these disciples. Vigor I'll apply

in breaking down their churches. I will not condescend

to save one soul who worships Jesus just to gratify

some silly notion. Our strict laws we must apply,

and all the ones who into Christian ways have been perverted

must, by our force, to pagan ways be once again converted.

[*He crosses to the back and center as he speaks the next lines.*]

No, we cannot allow these evil Christians to exist.

---

* In shortened version, the TWO SERVANTS may be omitted.

The princes of our land have fully guaranteed that they

will join with me in punishing the ones who still persist

in violating laws made by our government today.

To Caesar, Caiaphas and Annas they must kneel and pray.

Thus we'll subdue the wretches of that pointless nomad life.

We shall spare none among them, neither man nor child nor wife.

[*He begins to move straight forward toward the audience. The* TWO SOLDIERS *move center and then turn forward and follow him. The* TWO SERVANTS *likewise move center following the* SOLDIERS *and then move forward. In other words, the whole procession moves left to the center and then turns and comes straight toward the audience. As soon as all are facing forward, there is a tremendous crash of music* [MUSIC CUE 6]. *If stage lighting is available, lightning flashes. The music continues with crashes of thunder.* SAUL *falls to his knees, looking upward in great fear. The* TWO SERVANTS *run off, one to the right and one to the left. The* TWO SOLDIERS *move to either side of* SAUL, *looking frantically all about them. Then they, too, drop to their knees at either side of* SAUL. *The* VOICE OF GOD *speaks from some hidden place, preferably from above or in back of the audience. The music continues throughout God's speech.*]

GOD: Saul, Saul, Saul, why dost thou Me pursue?

It is not good to pit your strength against what I defend.

I am thy holy Saviour, omnipotent and
    true.
The earth I made, and every living
    creature is My friend.
Against God's chosen followers, O
    Saul, do not offend.

[*The music stops.*]

SAUL: O Lord, I am afraid. I pray
    Thee, tell me while we're here
what Thou wouldst have me do, my
    God. I'm trembling with fear.

[MUSIC CUE 7. *The music is still commanding but gentler in mood.*]

GOD: Arise and go with happy cheer
to the little city just ahead,
and I shall take away your fear.
Nothing there is that you need dread.
I shall provide your daily bread
and shall soon tell you what to do.
Arise and go, I now bid you.

[*The music stops.* SAUL *tries to rise to
his feet, but he gets halfway up and
then falls back to the ground.*]

SAUL: O merciful God, what's wrong
    with me?
I am lame. I am lame! My legs grow
    weak.

[*He suddenly seizes his forehead in
great pain.*]

My eyes! I am blind! I cannot see.

[*He looks frantically with staring eyes
all about him. Then he places his
hand across his eyes.*]

What is this pain that crosses my
    cheek?
Soldiers and servants around me,
    speak.

[*He pauses. There is no answer. The
TWO SOLDIERS look at one another in
terror.*]

All gone from me? Then God give me
    grace.
What shall become of me in this place?

[*He falls forward and lies prostrate on
the ground. The SOLDIERS rise quickly
and move toward him. They touch him
reassuringly on the shoulders.*]

FIRST SOLDIER: Two of us stay to help
    in your need.
We will not leave you while you are
    sick.

[SAUL *looks up at them, but since he
cannot see them, he looks in a slightly
wrong direction.*]

SAUL: Then to the nearby city, lead
me soon. In God's name, please be
    quick.

[*The* SECOND SOLDIER *offers* SAUL *his
staff.*]

SECOND SOLDIER: Hold up your hands
    to grasp this stick.

[*He helps* SAUL *to do so.* SAUL *rises
painfully during the next lines, leaning
heavily on the staff and held up by the
SOLDIERS.*]

Now, gently rise. We'll take you there
and we will give you all our care.

[*They lead him off at the left. As they
leave,* SAUL *gives a low moan of pain.*
MUSIC CUE 8.]

Scene 3

PLACE: *The hut of Ananias in the
nearby city*
TIME: *Three days later*

[ANANIAS *enters from the right and*

*starts toward the left. As he reaches
center, the* VOICE OF GOD *speaks.* ANA-
NIAS *drops to his knees, facing forward. The music continues.*]

GOD: Ananias, Ananias, where art
thou, my Ananias?

ANANIAS: Here, my Lord. Here is Thy
priest, so meek and weak but
pious.

GOD: A task for Me I bid thee pursue:
go out into the busy street
and there I shall tell you what to do
to get to a certain house to meet

ANANIAS

a man named Saul whom you will
greet
and comfort.

[ANANIAS *looks shocked. He shakes his
head, makes a negative gesture and
begins to speak. The* VOICE OF GOD,
however, continues and ANANIAS *does
not actually get any words out.*]

Do not be ashamed.
He's humble. "Wolf" he once was
named,
but through My punishment the wolf is
tamed.

[ANANIAS *lifts his hands in supplica-
tion.*]

ANANIAS: Lord, I am afraid, for always
in my mind
I think of all I've heard of his cruel
angry fury.
If I but call his name, to death he'll
surely put me.

GOD: No, Ananias, no.

[ANANIAS *lowers his hands and bows
his head.*]

I can in truth assure thee
he will be glad to know thee. He now
awaits thy coming.

[ANANIAS *looks upward again.*]

ANANIAS: Ah, Lord, but I'm afraid. I
know for certain fact
that saints of Thine upon this earth to
pieces he has hacked.
These evil things about him I have for
long been learning.
Behind the hand of Saul, the arm of
highborn priests will give
him power of death or life over me, to
kill or let me live.

GOD: Do not be frightened of this. He
    is My chosen vessel
appointed, like thee, Ananias, by My
    holy election.
He will be My promised priest to the
    weeping children of Israel.
By many pangs of sharpest pain, he
    soon will learn correction.
He'll then become a learned doctor
    with a kind complexion.
He will in time, I promise thee, a holy
    minister be,
a very pinnacle of faith and high divin-
    ity.

[ANANIAS *bows his head and clasps his
hands together in resignation.*]

ANANIAS: Lord, Thy commandment I
    shall fulfill.
To Saul at once I'll make my way.

GOD: Be not afraid for good nor ill.
Farewell, My priest, tell Saul what I
    say.

[*The music stops.*]

ANANIAS: My Lord, defend me as
    Thou may.

[*He rises and starts toward the right.*]

Greatly I fear the cruelty of Saul,
but when God bids, I shall do all.

[*He exits right.* MUSIC CUE 9.]

Scene 4

PLACE: *The house where Saul is
fasting*
TIME: *A few minutes later*

[*The* TWO SOLDIERS *enter from the left
and cross to slightly right of center. As
the* FIRST SOLDIER *starts to speak, the
music stops.*]

FIRST SOLDIER: I marvel greatly what
    it may mean.
We found our master in this strange
    state.
And that wonderful light all gold and
    green
that struck him down and changed his
    fate!
It seemed to me that beside the gate
I heard the sound of a voice delectable
which caused this sudden and marvel-
    ous miracle.

SECOND SOLDIER: Certainly the light
    was fearful to see,
the live sparks of flame that fluttered
    about
setting on fire the grass and that tree.
But that it was good, I most strongly
    doubt.
To find out what this may all be about,
let's go to Caiaphas and Annas to tell
them about this strange miracle thing
    that befell.

[*They go out at the right as* SAUL *enters from the left. He is still blind and
much humbled. His hands are clasped
in prayer. He walks slowly as if in
great pain. He moves toward the right,
turns, and then walks slowly back to
the left during the following prayer.*]

SAUL: Lord, of Thy comfort much I
    do desire.
Mighty King of goodness and of pity,
    too, I think,
Thou hast rewarded me with legs and
    eyes of flaming fire,
and for three days I've taken neither
    food, my Lord, nor drink.
But happiness is high in me, O gra-
    cious God, I think
that I shall be Thy servant as long as
    I have breath

and that I shall be Christian and, like
Jesus, suffer death.

[ANANIAS *enters at the right.* SAUL *stops
walking as soon as* ANANIAS *speaks.*]

ANANIAS: Peace be in this place. Peace
be on this roof.
Who is within? Speak at once in Jesus'
name!

[SAUL *turns to face him.*]

SAUL: I am here—Saul, good sir. Of
God's will I have proof,
but what is your will, stranger? Please
tell me without blame.

ANANIAS: From mighty God above I
am sent.

SAUL: Tell me what's your name.

ANANIAS: Ananias men have always
called me where I dwell.

SAUL: What will you do with this blind
man? I pray you, sir, to tell.

[*They walk toward each other, meeting
at center stage.* SAUL *kneels before*
ANANIAS.]

ANANIAS: Give me your hand, once
mighty Saul.

[*He does so.*]

By God's most gracious will
I'm sent to give instructions that you
live a holy life.
He asks that you be steadfast and that
you try to fill
with humbleness your useless bowls of
pride and angry strife.
Remember when the thunder crashed
and pain, like a blunted knife,
came sweeping down across your eyes,
leaving you struck blind.
Remember Ananias by these signs
within your mind.

[SAUL *nods his head in humbleness.*
ANANIAS *lets go of* SAUL'S *hand. He addresses both the audience and* SAUL *in
the following stanza.*]

Know that God's celestial power
can hurl to the ground the proudest
king.
Nothing can stop Him at any hour,
and He can accomplish anything.
We stand, we sit, we shout, we sing
only because God wills it so.
This is His power, above and below.
Whoever lacks godliness lacks a
friend:
this is the message that God doth send.

SAUL: His mercy to me is welcome at
last.
I'm glad that it has happened thus.

[MUSIC CUE 10. *The* HOLY GHOST *descends upon* SAUL *and* ANANIAS. SAUL
rises in great fear. ANANIAS *indicates
with his hands and follows with his
eyes the descent of the invisible* GHOST.]

ANANIAS: Be of good cheer. Stand not
aghast.
The Holy Ghost descends upon us.
With grace It inspires both of us.

[*He reaches for* SAUL'S *hand.*]

Put forth your hand and go with me.

[SAUL *does so.* ANANIAS *leads him a
few steps to the left.*]

As Saul, you were blind. As Paul, you
can see.

[*They stop. In great joy,* SAUL *lifts his
hands to his eyes and begins to look
about him as if he were seeing for the
first time in his life. He then raises his
arms high above his head, throws his
head back, and speaks in exultation.*]

SAUL: O Lord, my God, my humble prayers to you shall never
cease. The darkness falls from my two eyes.
Once I was blind and lame. O God, forever
I shall praise Thee. Please hear my grateful cries.

[*The music stops. He sinks to his knees and bows his head.*]

From this time forward, Saul of Corinth tries
to serve Thee, God. My heart is filled with sorrow,
for once I gave offense. But I shall serve tomorrow.

Where once I used such sharp intensity
to persecute Thy followers throughout the land,
I now will use the broad immensity
of the power Thou givest me to understand
Thy simple teachings and to spread on every hand
Thy message.

[*He looks up at* ANANIAS *who is watching him with kindness and tenderness.*]

Therefore, Ananias, please baptize me. I am humbly on my knees.

ANANIAS: Rise, O Paul, for first we must go to the well
which has the purifying water blessed with special grace.

[SAUL *rises.*]

SAUL: Go before me, Ananias. Ananias, tell
me how to praise the Lord and how I should abase
myself and cleanse myself before I reach His holy place.

ANANIAS: First you will kneel upon the ground
and receive baptism with good intent.
The noxious poison which seeps around
your heart will be drained away and sent,
with your sins, into nothingness. This Christ meant
when he taught forgiveness. The fiends from below
have no hold over those whom Christ has changed
into Christians, whose lives are so arranged.

[*They go off at the left.* MUSIC CUE 11. *The music continues as the voice of* ANANIAS *comes solemnly from offstage left.*]

I christen you, Paul, as one chosen by God.
With this touch, I receive you into our religion.
You must always be sturdy and straight as a rod
and constant forever without variation.
Let the Christians rejoice for this great demonstration
of God's mighty will. Rejoice, heavenly host!
In the name of the Father, Son and Holy Ghost.

Amen.

[*The music swells into a great Amen, then stops.* SAUL *enters from the left followed by* ANANIAS.]

SAUL: Like an eagle floating over the clouds,
I feel happy and free at this sacred moment.

ANANIAS: Come with me, Paul, past these silent crowds.

[*He indicates the audience. They begin to cross the stage to the right, walking slowly. When they are almost out, they stop.*]

You have just received the blessed sacrament.
Take some food now for your body's nourishment.
In long days to come, much work lies ahead,
but now be comforted, warmed, cheered and fed.

SAUL: God wills that great Saul should be guided by you.
I humbly will follow your every request.
Ananias, as you command, so will I do.
God grant that I pass this most rigorous test.
Through your teachings of wisdom, I'll learn what I need.
Go ahead, Ananias. I'll follow; you lead.

[ANANIAS *crosses in front of* SAUL *and goes out at the right.* SAUL *bows his head, clasps his hands and follows him out.* MUSIC CUE 12. *The* POET *enters from the left and crosses to the front left corner of the acting area. As he addresses the audience directly, the music stops.*]

POET: Thus, friends, as you see, the cruel tyrant named Saul
is changed through a miracle by Jesus' will
to the humble and Christlike person named Paul.
His noble behavior and teachings still

serve as examples to all those who will remember to read the Bible. Paul tried
to follow our Lord Who was crucified.*

[*He crosses to the center.*]

Let us now move our scene to another location
to see what occurred after St. Paul had fled.
The soldiers reported at one distant station
to Annas and Caiaphas. What they might have said
will shortly be shown to you. If you have read
the Scriptures, you'll recognize all of the action
and our play will give you much more satisfaction.

[*He goes out at the right.* MUSIC CUE 13.]

Scene 5

PLACE: *The palace of Caiaphas and Annas*
TIME: *A day later*

[CAIAPHAS *enters quickly from the left and crosses to the center.* ANNAS *follows him. Both are obviously nervous and irritated. The* SOLDIERS *follow them in, but they stop just inside the entrance. As* CAIAPHAS *begins to speak, the music stops.*]

CAIAPHAS: I am sure this wild story can never be true.

---

* For a very shortened version, the play could be ended at this point and it would still have a kind of dramatic unity. In this event, Music Cue 18 would come in here and the Poet would go out at the right.

What! Saul is converted from our supreme laws?
He purposely went to Damascus to
  pursue
the rebellious disciples of that foolish
  cause
with stubborn persistence. Saul never
  withdraws
from a struggle until he has won it by
  force.
What do you think, Sir Annas? It's
  nonsense, of course?

ANNAS: I agree, Sir Caiaphas, for I
  know Saul well.
This story is fraudulent. Saul will not
  turn

from our side until he can kill or expel
every miscreant Christian. Mark me,
  he'll earn
high praise when no Christian is left
  to be burned.

[*He crosses over to the* SOLDIERS *and
speaks angrily to them.*]

You soldiers, tell truth now. Give us
  your reason
for this false report, or we'll try you
  for treason.

[*He seizes the* FIRST SOLDIER *by the
collar. Both* SOLDIERS *drop to their
knees in fear.*]

CAIAPHAS

ANNAS

FIRST SOLDIER: You may put, sirs, our bodies to the torture test,
but nothing that we said was stated in jest.
With our eyes we saw lightning and all of the rest.

[ANNAS *lets go abruptly, turns and crosses to the center.* CAIAPHAS *crosses to the* SOLDIERS, *walking in front of* ANNAS *and speaking as he moves.*]

CAIAPHAS: By the greatest gods, I truly marvel greatly.
If this is so, as you have related,
then Saul shall repent of his foul treachery,
and all shall learn how he is fated
to suffer for this. O, Saul shall be hated
as a traitor to his country and to his priests.
This is evil beyond the worst actions of beasts.

[*With a gesture, he dismisses the* SOLDIERS. *They run off at the left.* CAIAPHAS *watches them out.*]

ANNAS: It is up to us, I think, Caiaphas, to guard well the law.

[CAIAPHAS *nods his head but he does not turn.*]

The law must never be allowed to fall into decay.
The people must be taught by force to hold in dreaded awe
the rule of rigid government today and every day.

[CAIAPHAS *turns to face* ANNAS.]

It never must be said of us that any favorite may
defy great Caesar, Emperor of all the world around.

[ANNAS *crosses to* CAIAPHAS.]

Let's summon up those supernatural forces that we've found.

IN SHORTENED VERSION,
FOLLOWING SCENE IS CUT AND
ANNAS AND CAIAPHAS MERELY
GO OUT LEFT AT THIS POINT AS
SAUL ENTERS FROM THE RIGHT

[*The two of them nod their heads solemnly and lift their hands slowly straight up into the air as if pulling spirits up from the ground. Weird supernatural music is heard—*MUSIC CUE 14. *They drop their hands and turn so that they face right. Then they go through the pulling up motions again, walking backwards out at the left as they do so. The music becomes more violent as* BELIAL, *a devil, enters from the right. With a bearing reminiscent of* SAUL'S *first entrance in the play,* BELIAL *crosses to the center and addresses the audience with great haughtiness. The music continues.*]

BELIAL: Ho, ho, behold me, audience, prince of the parts infernal.
Next to Lucifer himself, I'm best in excellency.
Belial is my name, and I am doomed to life eternal
in hell where I assist with all my might and majesty
to make the principles of hell supreme. My mighty sovereignty
extends over souls condemned by sin. I crush them, then devour
them, but first woo them through false priests till I have them in my power.

[*He crosses to the left.*]

BELIAL

My prelates, Caiaphas and Annas, I
    have moved for years,
and in the latest battle, I have asked
    them to pursue
and quell the Christian rebels. Every
    one shall sink in tears
throughout Damascus, Libya, and
    every country, too,
where those who serve Jehovah try to
    see what they can do
to break the power Lucifer almost gets
    over all.
Our greatest human helper is the
    mighty soldier, Saul.

[MERCURY, *another devil, enters from
the right.*]

MERCURY: Ho, I suffer! O, my pain!
    Alas, this sudden chance.
We will bewail this horrid day with its
    dreadful cursed adventure.

[*He stamps on the ground.* BELIAL
crosses to the center.]

BELIAL: Mercury, what ails you? Stop
    this silly dance
and tell me what has caused this dis-
    play of displeasure.

[MERCURY *crosses to him. He looks
extremely depressed.*]

MERCURY: Displeasure, yes! Of that
    you may be very, very sure.
I fear some day these struggling efforts
    we've so often made
will only decay to nothingness. God
    will win, I'm afraid.

MERCURY

[BELIAL *draws himself up arrogantly.*]

BELIAL: How can that be? Why, Mercury, it surely is not possible.
Consider, fool, the centuries we've spent in the continuance
of war with God. Decay, you say! It surely is not credible.
Of perjury, false news and lies you're famous for the utterance.
Behold how people stand and serve in fatuous attendance
my every whim; to please the devil is their sole desire.
With pride's corruption, I have set all human hearts on fire.

Sometimes, it's true, some sinners do for a moment or two repent
and we lose them a while, but soon you will smile for you can plainly see
the sinners come back to follow the track of temptations we have sent,
and they bring along a mighty throng, enlarging our company.
The people, I tell you, prefer by far our flashing majesty
to the drabness of God's prosaic way. Now, why are you amazed?
What fury has hit you, Mercury? You seem completely dazed.

MERCURY: Ho, he that I trusted of all my allies,
the one whom I hoped would be my special aid,
has turned good and noble and holy and wise.
Our former friend, Saul, whose big soul was just made
for our purposes has become good, I'm afraid.

[BELIAL *moves one step backward, shocked.*]

Now he serves only God with a great intense love.
Like lightning, holiness struck from above.

He was baptized, anointed, confirmed and ordained
as a specially appointed servant. He made
strong promises. Why, such grace he has obtained
it is doubtful if Saul's faith ever will fade.
So I suffer. Of Saul much we could have made.

[BELIAL *pounds his hands together.*]

BELIAL: Ho! What have we lost? Of what can we boast?
Saul was our chosen whom we loved the most.

[*He moves closer to* MERCURY *and studies his face closely.*]

Are you certain of this? This is not some new lie?

MERCURY: It is so, master Belial. Why should I feign?
I'm so distressed I can do nothing but cry.

[BELIAL *turns and walks away to the left as he speaks.*]

BELIAL: This grieves me much worse than hell's violent pain,
the conversion of favorite subjects once vain
and sinful like us. This sharp persecution
is worse than the furies of our hellish dungeon.

[BELIAL *stops.* MERCURY *crosses to him, speaking as he goes.*]

MERCURY: It does not help us to continue to lament.

Let us seek out a remedy as soon as we can.

Let us both go at once, if you will assent,

to the priests Caiaphas and Annas. The man

who betrayed us must die. These hirelings can

find some way to cure this incredible grievance

and keep Saul from making a dreadful disturbance.

[BELIAL *turns and claps him on the shoulder.*]

BELIAL: Well said, my friend Mercury. You are most wise.

[*He crosses in front of* MERCURY *and moves to the front right corner of the acting area.*]

O Saul, we shall make you regret this rash act.

You will find that the harsh law of treason applies

to your hasty defection. We'll order you tracked;

your too human body with pain will be wracked.

We may have lost one man, but millions remain.

For the one that we've lost, twenty subjects we'll gain.

Some people we'll tempt with pride and conceit,

and others with greediness, gossip or spite.

Among Christians — so-called — you never will meet

less charity than at this hour. Both night

and day with anger and sloth we will fight

Christianity. Gluttony, envy, and lust will rise. We will win the whole world. Yes, we must!

[*He crosses to* MERCURY.]

Come, Mercury. Long ago at another time we vowed

we'd never rest nor shirk till we had won.

Let's delay no longer. The earth's great crowd

waits for our bidding. Let our will be done!

Sin is the one thing men do not shun.

First we must conquer the disciple St. Paul.

MERCURY: Yes, for if we've lost him, we may lose it all.

[*They go out at the left.*]

SHORTENED VERSION
RESUMES HERE

[*The music shifts suddenly to quiet, holy music—*MUSIC CUE 15. SAUL *goes to the center of the stage, kneels and prays.*]

SAUL: That Lord Who is shaper of sea and of sand,

Who hath wrought with His Word all things at His will,

bless all this assembly who sit here or stand.

Grant us Thy mercy may be with us still.

Grant me, O Lord, Thy own will to fulfill

and send me the speech to be able to say

the truth and to move this audience if I may.

[*He rises, moves straight forward to the audience and addresses them directly.*]

My well beloved friends, there are seven mortal sins

and these are the very princes of poisons.

First there is pride where all evil begins.

Withholding all faith, pride feeds and fattens,

PRIEST'S SERVANT

sucking the good from the best of intentions.

Pride is the root of all vices, my friends.

Humility saves when excessive pride ends.

[*The* PRIESTS' SERVANT *enters from the left and stands just inside the entrance, watching* SAUL *through narrowed eyes.*]

Dread nothing but sin, for sin is but folly.

Besides pride, sloth and gluttony also are sins.

There are also wrath, covetousness, lechery and envy.

I plead with you to give these up. A holy life begins

when these depart from you. I beg you, give up sins.

Jesus said to those about him, "I wish to be meek."

Meekness makes our faith grow strong and sins grow weak.

The greater you are, the lower try to be.

This will save you from falling into wrong.

Never bear yourself as better because of your degree.

The humbler the singer, the more perfect is his song.

With all the teachings of our Saviour, try to go along

and say but little, learn of many, boast of little, think much,

and you will find within yourself heaven and all the rewards of such.

[*The* PRIESTS' SERVANT *crosses to* SAUL *and seizes his arm roughly. The music stops.*]

PRIESTS' SERVANT: What, are you the same Saul who formerly did rage against the Christian followers? Did you not once oppress
all Christ's disciples? I thought that on the bloody page
of history you wrote a promise to kill and to suppress
all those who went astray. Did you not one time stress
the point that churches of the Christians should be laid to waste,
your journey to Damascus for that purpose made in greatest haste?

[*With some dignity,* SAUL *shakes the* SERVANT'S *hand loose from his arm.*]

SAUL: Yes, certainly, Saul is my proper name.
I held in my power a great dominion.
To hide my identity would be a shame and a mortal sin, in my opinion.
Once I served Caesar and priests of the religion
of the war god Ares who is very hideous.
Now I serve only my King, Christ so precious.

PRIESTS' SERVANT: Before Annas and Caiaphas, then, I must bring you. Come along now and make no delay.

[*He makes a threatening gesture which* SAUL *ignores.*]

SAUL: Without fear I shall follow you off to
the princes of priests to hear what they say.

[*The* SERVANT *crosses to the left entrance.* SAUL *follows him.* ANNAS *and* CAIAPHAS *enter suddenly at the left. The* SERVANT *drops on his knees before them.*]

PRIESTS' SERVANT: Holy priests of high power who rule night and day,
here is Saul. Behold him. Look at him closely.
He is another man than he was formerly.

[*They cross in front of the* SERVANT *and study* SAUL *closely.* SAUL *takes a cross from an inside pocket of his garment and holds it up. They react with violent antagonism toward it.*]

SAUL: I am the servant of Jesus Almighty,
Creator and Maker of earth and of sea,
Who lives in the kingdom of blue heaven's glory,
Who comforts and soothes both imprisoned and free.
Against Him, no power can stand, as you'll see.
He is the true Ruler of heaven and hell.
Above all things, His goodness and grace will excel.

[*He turns suddenly, crosses the stage and goes out at the right.* ANNAS *and* CAIAPHAS *look at one another. The* SERVANT *rises slowly to his feet.*]

CAIAPHAS: My heart is greatly troubled at this sight.
I cannot understand why Saul is transformed so
into a different man. I wonder if he might
have been bewitched by devils. Shall we go?

[*He takes* ANNAS' *arm and they begin to walk slowly toward the center.*]

Alas, my heart is struck with bitter woe,
for he is taken from us by perversion.

What do you think, Annas, of this
    strange conversion?

ANNAS: Like you, Caiaphas, I am
    much depressed.
I cannot understand this sudden shift.
To see so great a change puts to the
    test
all my customary poise and sanity. No
    gift
is great enough to cause my spirits to
    lift.
Whether he is traitorous or insane,
    however,
we must kill him, or he'll ruin us for-
    ever.

SERVANT

CAIAPHAS: You are right. With Caesar,
    we'll get into trouble.
Let's kill Saul very soon. Let's think
    of whom to hire.

[*He glances around briefly at the* SERV-
ANT. *The* SERVANT *looks away.*]

If Saul continues thus, our problems
    first will double,
then will triple, then quadruple.
    Caesar's ire
will—

ANNAS: Yes, I'd rather he were burnt
    in fire
than let great Caesar find this out,
    either now or later.
Saul was subtly false to us, the worst
    kind of sly traitor.

[*The* SERVANT *looks back at* CAIAPHAS.
CAIAPHAS *gestures authoritatively to the*
SERVANT.]

CAIAPHAS: We will command that all
    gates to the city
be shut. All walls will be guarded se-
    curely.
If he should escape now, it would be a
    pity.
He must die before sunrise.

[*Again he gestures to the* SERVANT, *indicating that he should go out and pass
these commands to those who will
carry them out. The* SERVANT *runs off
at the left.*]

ANNAS: That he must surely.
This crime constitutes the worst act of
    disloyalty
I've ever known. We must silence this
    new Saul.

[ANNAS *crosses to the left and calls
loudly offstage.*]

Now every soldier guard with diligence
    his wall!

[*The* SERVANT *enters, out of breath,
and drops on his knees before* ANNAS.]

PRIESTS' SERVANT: The gates, sir, are
    shut. He cannot escape.
Every wall of the city is guarded by
    men
who are loyal and in good strong
    physical shape.
Right now it's impossible, by any
  . means, then,
to get out of the city or back in again
without being seen. And when we find
    Saul,
we'll bring him to you.

ANNAS: No, just kill him, that's all.

[ANNAS *and* CAIAPHAS *go out at the
left, walking in front of the kneeling*
SERVANT. *The* SERVANT *rises, shakes
his head worriedly and follows them
off at the left.* MUSIC CUE 16. SAUL
*enters slowly from the right. He crosses
a few steps toward the center. The*
ANGEL *enters from the right and stands
behind him. The music continues as
the* ANGEL *speaks.*]

ANGEL: Holy St. Paul, I bring you a
    warning.

[SAUL *turns to look at the* ANGEL.]

The princes of evil are planning to kill
    you,
but God is on your side. Before a new
    morning
dawns over the city, you will escape.
    But still you
must always obey and serve God. St.
    Paul, will you?

SAUL *drops to his knees and crosses
himself.*]

SAUL: I will.

ANGEL: Then God will promise you
    this.
After death, you will live in perpetual
    bliss.

[*The* ANGEL *turns and goes slowly out
at the right. The music dies away.* SAUL
rises and moves toward the audience.]

SAUL: God's will is the only will that
    always must be done
in heaven or earth, by the young or by
    the old.
God's plan is that I run away before
    the rising sun
hidden in a basket or in a blanket
    rolled
and carried out by Christ's disciples in
    a daring, bold
manner.

[*He goes to the right and looks anxiously offstage.*]

Every wall is guarded; every gate is
    closed;
but I trust in my God.

[*He crosses to the left.*]

            I will not be exposed.

[*He exits left.* MUSIC CUE 17. *The*
POET *enters from the right and crosses
to the center. As he begins to speak,
the music stops.*]

POET: Thus we leave St. Paul inside
    the closely guarded city,
but as the Bible tells us, in the darkest
    hour of night
Christ's disciples smuggled Paul out of
    the guarded city,
and Paul lived on for many years to
    use his holy might
to teach the word of God and to dis-
    tinguish wrong from right.

His truth remains. I beg of you to read
    his great advice.
You will find it in the Bible in words
    clear and precise.

[*He crosses to the right front corner
of the stage.*]

And now our play is ended. We do
    sincerely pray
that you'll excuse our clumsiness and
    crude inadequacy.
We hope that you will understand the
    purpose of our play
which was to show St. Paul's conver-
    sion with as much accuracy

as possible. It is impossible for inner
    ecstasy
to be portrayed in drama's outer ac-
    tions.

[MUSIC CUE 18.]

        And now, if I may,
I commend you all to Jesus' mercy.
    Let's bow our heads and pray.

[*He bows his head. The minister leads
the audience in prayer. At the end of
the prayer, the* POET *goes off at the
right. The music stops.*]

MUSIC CUE 1

MUSIC CUE 2

CONVERSION OF ST. PAUL

MUSIC CUE 3

MUSIC CUE 4

MUSIC CUE 5

MUSIC CUE 6

CONVERSION OF ST. PAUL

MUSIC CUE 7

MUSIC CUE 8

MUSIC CUE 9

MUSIC CUE 10

MUSIC CUE 11

MUSIC CUE 12

MUSIC CUE 13

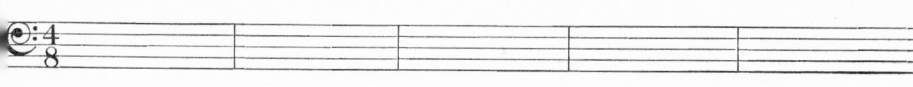

CONVERSION OF ST. PAUL
MUSIC CUE 14

MUSIC CUE 15

MUSIC CUE 16: *Repeat very slowly and softly Music Cue 2.*

MUSIC CUE 17: *Repeat Music Cue 12.*

MUSIC CUE 18

TOTENTANZ

A Medieval Morality Play

IN A MODERN VERSION BY MARTIN F. SCHLOSS

TRANSLATED FROM THE GERMAN BY MARGARET TRINKLEIN

INTRODUCTION

Totentanz (*The Dance of Death*), like so many other morality plays of the Middle Ages, rejects confinement by time or space. The stage is only the symbol of man's existence. On one side is the Door of Life from which the characters enter, and on the other side is the Door of Eternity through which all mortal beings must ultimately pass. In the fourteenth century, many versions of this play were performed in Germany, in Holland, in Belgium, in Spain, in France, and in England. They were given special meaning because of the widespread fear of the Black Death, that dreaded pestilence that sometimes wiped out whole cities without warning. The fear, in our own day, of hydrogen bombs and biological warfare gives us a rough parallel.

Our version has been translated by Margaret Trinklein from the German text of Martin F. Schloss, a biochemist who believes the power of literature to be as great as that of science. He recovered and made public this text in 1922, and since then it has been acted in many German cities by the dramatic group of the University of Heidelberg. Its American premiere was given at Northwestern University in 1953.

Which of the characters in this play will you most resemble when your time comes to dance to Death's violin? It is our prayer that the music in that hour will, to all of us, be pleasant and welcome. It is our further hope that, in thinking about how the people in this play die, you may discover the most important secret of all about how to live.*

Notes on the Characters

The characters in this play represent abstractions. The purpose of each actor, therefore, is to represent a *typical* specimen of whatever his name indicates. In other words, each actor is primarily representing a type of individual rather than a specific person.

A danger arises, however, in that types are not as interesting on the stage as individualized personalities. It may help to note that the authors have made them more than merely wooden stereotypes. Without losing their typicality, the roles have some individual characteristics which make them seem real and believable in performance. The actors should seize on and emphasize these individualizing characteristics in order to keep the drama effective.

THE MESSENGER: This role may be played either by a man or by a woman. The age of the person is unimportant. Dignity and poise are the prime requisites. See the notes for the Poet, p. 53, as these also apply to the Messenger in this play.

DEATH: The key word to the characterization of Death is flexibility. He assumes a different personality with each separate person. The actor play-

---

* These three paragraphs may serve as "program notes" for printed programs of performances. Permission to reprint for this purpose is herewith given.

ing this role should, therefore, be versatile. With some of the dying people he is friendly and kind; with others he is harsh and sarcastic; with still others he is filled with pain and pity at the necessity of performing his task. The actor may be of any age, but he should have a good strong voice. He need not be able to play the violin, as he merely pantomimes playing, but he should remember that Death is, above all else, a great and compelling musician. He must also be able to move without awkwardness.

THE EMPEROR: The Emperor is haughty and egotistical. He thinks only of power and of his own comfort. He has not ruled with wisdom, but he has ruled with military success. What he has not achieved with force, he has bought. He is horrified and shocked by dying since the thought of his own death has apparently never before entered his mind.

THE PRINCESS: The Princess is beautiful, but her beauty is the cold, vain, elegant kind. There is no real human warmth in her. She is regal and graceful in her movements. She meets her death with horrified despair.

THE YOUNG MAN: He is giddy, immature and fickle-hearted. Thinking only of the pleasures of the moment, he hopes to postpone repentance and salvation until his old age. He feels that he is being cheated and that it is very unfair to be taken at this time.

THE OLD WOMAN: She is very old, having outlived even her own children. She has always tried to lead a good life. Her primary characteristics are humility and selflessness. She is now lonely, tired and ill. She meets her death with happy relief. There is a strong lovable quality about her, and the audience should sympathize with her deeply.

THE JUDGE: He is not an honest judge. He has used his power and prestige to rule in favor of those who would do him the most good. He has learned how to ignore anything that does not directly affect his own comfort or wealth. He is terrified and cowardly when he discovers that he is to die.

THE NUN: She is dedicated to a life of holiness. At the present time, she suffers greatly from physical pain. She welcomes her death, for she knows she has sacrificed her life to prepare for it. She is gentle, sweet, and dignified in spite of her great suffering.

THE DOCTOR: The Doctor is kind and practical. He has become a physician for the motive of social service, not for money or professional prestige. He is familiar with death, and he knows from experience that it may be a great blessing. He meets it willingly.

THE BLIND WOMAN: She is nostalgic and dreamy. Her sense of hearing has sharpened since the time her sight was lost, and the music seems almost unbelievably beautiful to her. Death is welcome because she can appreciate the beauty of it. Through her, the playwright seems to make the point that compared with the greatness of eternal vision, earthly sight is little more than blindness.

THE RICH MAN: Wealthy in both land and investments, he has used his money only to make more money. He is greedy and miserly. He thinks of himself as a good man merely because he has been a successful man. When cornered, he tries to bribe Death with offers to spend huge amounts in philanthropic works, but even if it were not too late, his motives are wrong. He objects violently to dying.

THE MAIDEN: She has been shallow and coquettish. She thinks of little but dancing, looking pretty, and being admired. In spite of her fear of death and her dream, she has not wisely used her time since the warning. She has tried to get rid of death by not thinking of it. She is sad, depressed, and whimpering as she dies.

THE SOLDIER: He is an old, courageous fighter. He has always been pious and faithful to his ideals. He is glad to meet his death, and he has no fear of it. In fact, it is to him an old, familiar friend with whom he is thoroughly acquainted.

THE MOTHER: Her scene constitutes the emotional climax of the play, and her role must be played by a good actress. She is usually sweet, lovable, and good, but at the moment, her worry over her sick child drives her into unreasoning rebellion against the will of God. We must not blame her for this; in similar circumstances, most of us would undoubtedly behave more like her than like Abraham. She is real, and her suffering is sharp and intense. When her child dies, she blames herself because she has fallen asleep through sheer exhaustion. Then she tries to die herself. Eventually she will become resigned to her grief, but now her maternal instinct causes her to fight ferociously against the loss of her baby. She must be a thoroughly sympathetic character, or else the drama of this final episode will be lost.

Notes on the Properties

The PROP LIST comprises the following:

> violin and bow (carried by Death)
> sword (carried by the Emperor)
> ring (worn by the Emperor)
> black medical bag (carried by the Doctor)
> cane (carried by the Blind Woman)
> rose (carried by the Maiden)
> hand mirror (carried by the Maiden)
> baby (carried by the Mother)

The properties in this play constitute no serious problem. There are few of them. Also, each is the definite responsibility of a particular actor and can be carried on and off by him, and so no problem in keeping track of it is presented.

The most valuable property is, of course, the violin. It is not played, but it should obviously be as exquisite a violin as it is possible to find, not merely some battered old fiddle. Death should practice with it as many times as possible, as it will often be difficult to handle. He must have it constantly; he must often start playing quickly and gracefully; he must often stop playing in the same way; he must frequently do other things while carrying the violin and bow. Only through rehearsal can he handle the violin without awkwardness or without the audience feeling that he needs three hands.

The baby, who does not speak or move, is technically not a character but a prop. It might be possible and effective to use a real baby, but probably only if the actress playing the Mother is its mother in real life. Even then the child might cry and spoil the effect. If the performance is at night, it is also probable that the audience may feel the child ought to be home in bed, thus breaking the illusion for them. In most cases, therefore, the baby should be merely a small blanket wrapped up in such a way as to suggest that it contains a real baby. A doll should not be used unless it is either entirely covered up from the audience or extremely real looking. Audiences rarely get emotionally involved over an obvious doll.

The other props are relatively simple. The sword may be either real or constructed of wood. The ring should be big and flashy. The medical bag should be plain, simple, and dark in color. The cane should be white and sturdy but not elaborate. The rose may be either artificial or real, but it should be fairly large in order to be easily seen and identified by the audience as a rose. The hand mirror should be the large kind with a handle. If the lights flash in it so that beams may get in the faces of the audience, or if it casts distracting reflections around the church, it should probably be soaped slightly.

CHARACTERS

THE MESSENGER	THE NUN*
DEATH	THE DOCTOR*
THE EMPEROR	THE BLIND WOMAN
THE PRINCESS*	THE RICH MAN*
THE YOUNG MAN	THE MAIDEN
THE OLD WOMAN	THE SOLDIER
THE JUDGE	THE MOTHER

TIME: *Any time*
PLACE: *Any place*

[*As the play begins, strains of music are heard in the distance—*MUSIC CUE 1. *The* MESSENGER *enters from the left. He walks to the center rear of the acting area. As he begins to speak, he stands with arms outstretched, a position which he holds until he has finished speaking. The music fades away.*]

THE MESSENGER: E'er since dark
    Satan's evil act
In ancient Eden—Death was fact.
Now all Mankind's inheritance,
He forces all to do his dance.
For all he calls; not one he spares—
The rich, the poor, the unprepared.
He snatches from life's weary stage
The strong or weak at any age.

[*He takes a step or two forward and slightly to his right.*]

But still we have the Lord's commands
To rule our hearts and guide our
    hands;
All those with faith who live no lies
Shall enter heaven's paradise.

*Characters omitted in the shortened version.

[*He crosses to the exact center of the acting area and speaks earnestly and directly to the audience.*]

O Man, take heed whence you came,
Your present state, what you o'er-
    came;
Let deep reflection serve you all
Ere Death in God's own name shall
    call.

[*He moves to the left corner of the acting area nearest the audience.*]

Observe this mirror of the earth—
A show which brings you from your
    birth
To Death itself, o'er life's short road,
In hopes new thoughts may be be-
    stowed
Upon your hearts and minds laid
    bare—
Lest Death shall snatch you unaware!

[*At the word "Death,"* DEATH *enters suddenly from the right and stands menacingly just inside the entrance. He holds a violin.*]

95

DEATH: I conquer all in every land.
No one can stay my icy hand.

[DEATH *gestures imperatively to the* MESSENGER. *The* MESSENGER *quickly exits at the left.* MUSIC CUE 2.]

As flowers wither in the field,
So every man in time must yield
To do my dance, and thereupon
To pass into the world beyond.

[DEATH *disappears out right. A martial music sounds*—MUSIC CUE 3—*breaking up when the* EMPEROR *enters at the left.*]

EMPEROR: This empire great is mine
    alone;
No man can boast a grander throne.

[*He crosses to the center.*]

In battles great on foreign soil
I conquered all and reaped the spoil.
I brought back captives by the score
To serve and hail me Emperor.
Great kingdoms tremble at my name
And none on earth can match my fame!

[DEATH *enters from the right, walks quickly to the center, suddenly appearing before the* EMPEROR. *The* EMPEROR *draws himself up with offended dignity at this encounter.*]

DEATH: But I alone can conquer all,
And in my hand you're but a ball

MESSENGER

DEATH

Of simple clay returned to earth
From whence you came, of little worth.

[*The* EMPEROR, *highly indignant, tries
to go past* DEATH, *but* DEATH *steps
quickly forward and will not allow him
to pass.*]

You plundered, killed, and wrecked
    the lives
of many men, their babes and wives;
And in your drunken greed to rule
You've lost your very soul, you fool!

[*The* EMPEROR *draws his sword to
defend himself, but* DEATH *only raises
his hand and the* EMPEROR'S *sword
falls to the ground.*]

DEATH: Your sword is useless now,
    you see,

[*The* EMPEROR *begins to remove his
ring as if to offer it to* DEATH, *but*
DEATH *stops him with a negative gesture.*]

And so are bribes and trickery.
Your might of kingdoms, knights, and
    land
Is nothing,

[DEATH *picks up the sword from the
floor and returns it to the* EMPEROR.]

    and at my command
Your body, too—adorned with rings
And other tokens power brings—
Is helpless and must take its place
With slaves and serfs of every race
Who lie beneath the lowly sod
And wait the judgment of their God.

[DEATH *raises his violin and pantomimes playing it.* MUSIC CUE 4. *At
the first note the* EMPEROR *is forced
to move with the rhythm of the music
toward the door of eternity.* DEATH

EMPEROR

*moves backward toward the right at
first, the* EMPEROR *following. Then*
DEATH *stops, steps back out of the
way, and the* EMPEROR *continues going toward the right, speaking as he
goes.*]

EMPEROR: I lived in pow'r and maj-
    esty.
All men approached on bended knee.
Gold, jewels, furs and linens rare
Were mine, and must I all forbear?

[*The* EMPEROR *stops.* DEATH *momentarily stops playing the violin. The
music stops.*]

DEATH: The glories of the crown and state
Are only shadows, next to fate.
Your hoarded wealth and precious stones,
Your gold and furs cannot atone
For even one tear a wife has shed
For a husband through your evil dead.

[DEATH *takes up the violin again.*
MUSIC CUE 5. *The* EMPEROR *prepares to pass through the door.*]

EMPEROR: O fearful Death! Pity!

DEATH: Too late! True faith alone gives life.

[*The* EMPEROR *exits at the right, holding his sword aloft before him.* DEATH *returns, playing, to the center of the stage. He then stops playing.*]

All fame and pow'r and wealth untold
Could multiply a thousandfold
And still they could not add one day;
The time I choose naught can delay.

FOR SHORTENED VERSION,

CUT THE FOLLOWING SCENE

[DEATH *plays his violin again. Sweet and enticing music begins*—MUSIC CUE 6. *After a few moments the* PRINCESS *enters at the left, walking in the rhythm of the music.* DEATH *goes toward her, then puts down his violin. The music stops, and so does the* PRINCESS.]

DEATH: O Princess, I shall lead the way.
This dance is mine; make haste, I pray!
Your maids are gone. You are alone

And Death now claims you as his own.
The time for vanity is o'er.
I call; you dance; then dance no more.

[*He reaches out to her. The* PRINCESS *backs up two steps.*]

PRINCESS: Oh me! Must I with haste so wild
Leave land and subjects, man and child
And all with whom I used to smile?
O Death, go, spare me for a while!

[DEATH *lifts the violin again.* MUSIC CUE 7. *The* PRINCESS *is forced to walk*

PRINCESS

toward the door of eternity, at right, in
the rhythm of the music. DEATH *backs*
up before her until they reach the exit.]

PRINCESS: Now that I'm forced to such
  a dance
All things once prized lose elegance!
May God in heaven pity me,
Since I must like my partner be.

[DEATH, *who has accompanied her to*
the door of eternity, turns as the
PRINCESS *exits, crossing in front of*
him. The music stops as DEATH *lowers*
his violin. As he speaks, DEATH *crosses*
to the center.]

DEATH: So ends another life. Death
  maims
The beauty which the world acclaims;
For God counts only grace of mind—
The outward things are left behind.

SHORTENED VERSION
RESUMES HERE

[DEATH *turns and walks away from the*
audience, lifting his violin to play as
he goes. MUSIC CUE 8. *The* YOUNG
MAN, *as though attracted by the tune,*
enters from the left. He crosses to the
center, speaking as he goes.]

YOUNG MAN: From whence comes that
  enticing song?
Its mood might to my love belong.

[DEATH *whirls around, facing the audi-*
ence. He lowers the violin and the
music stops.]

I'll haste and take her in my arms;
Naught else can soothe me like her
  charms!

[DEATH, *drawing his cape about him-*

YOUNG MAN

self to hide his identity, steps forward
to block the YOUNG MAN'S *way*]

What do you want? Who are you?

[DEATH *throws back his cloak.*]

DEATH: The one whose likeness you
  shall take on.
Yes, look at me.

[*The* YOUNG MAN *takes a few steps*
backward.]

YOUNG MAN: Oh no, not death! I'm
  still so young
And life for me has just begun!
Must I give up wine, wife, and song
Before my prime? It seems so wrong!

[*He moves toward* DEATH, *pleading with him fervently.*]

O Death, pray spare me for a while.
I fear my soul I did defile,
For all my life was one grand feast—
I scoffed at God, lived like a beast.
I cannot die in such a way.

[*He kneels before* DEATH.]

O Death, grant me another stay!

DEATH: You fool, adept with wench
    and wine,
You trifler with the will divine—
Had you but paused to take account—
God gives all men strength to sur-
    mount
The evils done, both great and small;
But 'tis too late. You've heard Death's
    call.

[*The* YOUNG MAN *rises, turns and starts to run to the left corner away from the audience.* DEATH *lifts his violin and begins to play.* MUSIC CUE 9. *The* YOUNG MAN *stops. He is pulled backward a step or two. He seems to be struggling to go forward, but against his will he is pulled backward in rhythm with the music.*]

YOUNG MAN: Oh pangs of Death! Oh
    woeful end!
And none, alas, can help extend!

[*The* YOUNG MAN *is pulled backward toward the right as* DEATH *moves to the left, crossing behind him. At the center, the* YOUNG MAN *turns and is pulled forward to the right. At the exit, he turns again, hands upraised, and goes out backward.* DEATH *lowers his violin and moves swiftly to the center. The music stops.*]

OLD WOMAN

DEATH: Repentance must not be de-
    layed
If man would meet Death unafraid.

[*He begins to play again.* MUSIC CUE 10. *The* OLD WOMAN *enters slowly from the left. During her entire speech, she crosses slowly to the exit at the right, moving in front of* DEATH *and seeming not to see him. As she begins to speak, the music stops.*]

OLD WOMAN: My life is now all void
    and vain.
My last child's dead, and in my pain
I call to God to take me home.
I care no more this earth to roam
But long to be united there
With loved ones—joy beyond compare.
God grant that I may murmur not

But humbly bear my earthly lot
Until the time that deems Him best—
May it be soon!—to grant me rest.

[*She looks longingly out at the door right.* DEATH *walks to her, speaking as he goes.*]

DEATH: Good Mother, God has heard
    your prayers
And sends me now to end your cares.
No more alone, with those bemoaned
You'll kneel before His judgment
    throne.

[*She smiles at him gratefully and reaches out her hand to him. He touches her hand gently. Then he lifts the violin slowly and begins to play.* MUSIC CUE 11. *She turns, lifts her head high, and goes out at the right. As she goes, she lifts her arms toward whatever it is she sees.* DEATH *drops his violin and the music stops. He addresses the audience directly.*]

Oh blest is she who through the years
Her children carefully uprears;
For faithful souls who seek to serve
Their fellow man, though unobserved,
Are through their humble works of
    love
Brought closer to their home above.

[DEATH *lifts his violin, stepping out at the right as he does so.* MUSIC CUE 12. *The* JUDGE *enters from the left and crosses to the center. He stops with his back to the audience.* DEATH, *disguised as a beggar but still playing his violin, enters and crosses to him.* DEATH *stops playing. He plucks at the mantle of the* JUDGE. *Without turning to look at him, the* JUDGE *pushes* DEATH *away and speaks harshly.*]

JUDGE: Fool, let go! Out of my way!

[DEATH *plucks at his mantle again.*]

DEATH: Judge, justice! Justice is all I
    want!

[*The* JUDGE *pulls away from him, turns and comes toward the audience and the front left corner of the acting area. He darts a contemptuous look at* DEATH *but does not notice him very closely.*]

JUDGE: Oh, go your way and pay your
    debt!
I'm much too busy now to fret

JUDGE

About a simple beggar's case
Or anything so commonplace.
My interest lies in bigger things
With fees that might well ransom
    kings.

[DEATH *crosses a step or two toward
him, holding out his hand.*]

DEATH: Justice!

JUDGE: Begone, you fool, and cease
    your jest!
Of all low things, I most detest
A beggar who expects to buy
My aid with but a pleading eye!
For justice has its price tag too
And can't be bought by such as you.

[DEATH *crosses all the way to him and
plucks at his elbow.*]

DEATH: Justice!

[*The* JUDGE *gives him a severe shove.*
DEATH *is thrust momentarily back.*]

JUDGE: Out of my way! Leave me
    alone.

[*He begins to go toward the center,
but* DEATH, *throwing off his disguise,
stands erect before him. The* JUDGE
*sees him now, recognizes him, and falls
back, staggering.*]

DEATH: The justice you refused to do,
Oh judge, will now be done to you
With consequences far more dire
Than your warped justice would re-
    quire.
All the fees you bled from men
Have gone to plague mankind again.

[*The* JUDGE *kneels in terror.*]

Go, kneel before the judgment seat
For there true justice God doth mete.

JUDGE: O burning fate! I cannot bear

To be thus taken—unaware.

[*He rises.*]

For who will plead my hopeless case?
If I my guilt could but erase!
Is there no chance for an appeal?
I'd do what's just with anxious zeal!

DEATH: If you had taken seriously
Your grave responsibility
Instead of seeking earthly gain
While worthy causes you disdained,
You'd have no reason now to fear
The judgment which you soon shall
    hear.
You made your choice; you sealed
    your fate;
And now my dance you'll emulate.

[*The* JUDGE *raises clasped hands, but*
DEATH *starts to play. The* JUDGE
*passes before him and walks toward
the door of eternity.* MUSIC CUE 13.
The JUDGE *exits.* DEATH *returns to the
center and stops playing.*]

DEATH: From God doth law and truth
    proceed
As in the Bible all may read.
So man must strive from early youth
To hate deceit and love the truth.

FOR SHORTENED VERSION,

CUT THE FOLLOWING SCENE

[*He begins to play again.* MUSIC CUE
14. *The* NUN *enters. She walks a few
steps toward the right. Then* DEATH
*raises his hand. She stops. So does the
music.*]

NUN: I feel so strange! What can it be?
Can death be drawing nigh for me?
Alas! I'd hoped to learn still more—

Through knowledge better to adore
My blessed Maker, King of Kings,
From whom all joy and gladness
    springs.

[*She kneels.*]

My suff'ring mounts with every
    breath—
Blest Jesus, Saviour, send me death!
Oh guide me through this hour of
    need.
To heaven's peace. Make haste, I
    plead.

[DEATH *goes to her and makes the sign
of the cross over her. He speaks to her
comfortingly.*]

DEATH: Come, little sister, have no
    fear.
'Tis love divine that brings me here.
For Jesus Christ, your blessed Lord,
Now calls you home—'tis your re-
    ward—

[*At a signal from* DEATH, *the* NUN
rises.]

And waits for all who spend their days
In serving man, while God they praise.

[*He begins to play.* MUSIC CUE 15.
The NUN *crosses in front of him and
goes slowly out at the right.* DEATH
*looks after her as she goes and speaks
while playing.*]

DEATH: Oh blest the woman, blest the
    man
Who lives his life with clear cut plan,
Who lives each day as if it were
The last he'd know, and naught can
    blur
His visions of the joys he'll know
When he shall leave this earth below.

[DEATH *stops playing for a moment,*

then begins again—MUSIC CUE 16.
The DOCTOR *enters from the left. He
is in great pain. He carries a black bag.
As he starts to speak, the music stops.*]

DOCTOR: What is this clutching at my
    heart?
Oh, must my skill so soon depart
While oft for money, oft for naught
I helped the sick when I was sought?

[DEATH *crosses to him. The* DOCTOR
sets his bag down on the ground.]

DEATH: Good Doctor, you have served
    men well;
But life has taught you none can dwell
On earth except God give him breath.

NUN

Helped more for love's sake than for gain.
The God of mercy and of love
Will welcome you to joys above.

[DEATH *begins to play*—MUSIC CUE 17 —*and guides the* DOCTOR *toward the door of eternity. The* DOCTOR *goes out. Then* DEATH, *still playing, returns to the center of the stage.*]

SHORTENED VERSION

RESUMES HERE

[*The music continues for a while, and then the* BLIND WOMAN *enters from the*

DOCTOR

There grows no herb which conquers death.

DOCTOR: Ah yes, 'tis my end that I see.
A rich man had just called for me
That I might help him in his need
And now 'tis I who must concede.

[*He picks up his bag.*]

Good Death, lead on, for it's your case;
I know your pale but friendly face.
I go to lay a life of love
Before my Lord and God above.

DEATH: You kept God's laws and lightened pain,

BLIND WOMAN

left. She carries a cane. With it she feels her way to the right central portion of the stage, moving past DEATH *as she speaks.*]

BLIND WOMAN: Oh, what strange music bathes my ears!
The like of this, in all my years
Of sojourn through this world of woe,
Alone in dreams I e'er could know.
It is as though an angel-band
Had come to lead me by the hand
To the eternal paradise
Where blindness never shades my eyes.

[*She sits on the floor. The music pauses for a moment as* DEATH *lowers his violin.*]

Oh please play on, for when you do
I think of songs that I once knew
And sang upon my mother's knee.

[DEATH *begins to play again. She rises and begins to feel around for the location of* DEATH.]

Where are you, minstrel? I can't see!

[DEATH *steps over to her, touches her gently on the arm with his right elbow.*]

DEATH: Here at your side, for I have come
To lead you, Mother, to your home.

[*He crosses in front of her, and they begin to move slowly toward the right.*]

I'll take you where all Heaven resounds
The praise of Him whose grace abounds
And who will end your earthly night.
Behold your Lord's eternal light!

[*She raises her hands to her eyes, seeming to see, and then stretches out*

her arms to whatever she sees offstage right. She calls triumphantly.*]

BLIND WOMAN: I'm home!

[*She goes out.* DEATH *stops playing and speaks to the audience.*]

DEATH: Oh blessed, who in grief and pains
Through hope and faith the kingdom gains.

[*He disappears out at the right.*]

FOR SHORTENED VERSION,

CUT THE FOLLOWING SCENE

[MUSIC CUE 18. *The* RICH MAN *enters at the left. The music stops as he begins to speak.*]

RICH MAN: My harvest was so great this year
That, come what may, I need not fear.
I shall expand and grow and build
'Til all my wishes are fulfilled,

[*He crosses to the center.*]

And then I'll live a life of ease
While scores of debtors bend their knees
In work from early morn 'til night
To pay my fees, to my delight.
The days hereafter? I should care!

[DEATH *enters suddenly.*]

The main point is: I have my share!

DEATH: You usurer! You prince of fools!

[*The* RICH MAN *looks startled.*]

You thought of all your gains as tools
To serve your own small, selfish whims

RICH MAN

With ne'er a thought of prayer and
hymns

[*The* RICH MAN *kneels.*]

Of thanks to God who rules o'er all
And in whose Name you hear me call.
Now come before His judgment seat
And hear what justice deems is meet.

RICH MAN: Oh Death, please spare me
from your dance
For just a while! Give me a chance
To use my wealth as each man should
Not for myself—but common good.

[DEATH *turns his back on the* RICH
MAN *scornfully.*]

I'll build great churches, homes and
schools,
And see that only kindness rules
And all are cared for—young and
old—
I'll right my wrongs a thousandfold!
I'll strive for good and conquer
crime—
Just grant me still a little time!

[DEATH *turns and speaks to him angrily. He moves to the* RICH MAN.]

DEATH: You had your time. It is too
late
And just reprisals now await.
You planned the harvest when you
sowed
And now the harvest must be mowed.

[*In despair the* RICH MAN *rises. He
raises his hands, but* DEATH *has started
to play.* MUSIC CUE 19. DEATH *crosses
behind the* RICH MAN, *then turns and
begins to drive the* RICH MAN *before
him toward the right. The* RICH MAN
goes out at the right against his will.
DEATH *stops the music and addresses
the audience.*]

DEATH: None knows the day nor yet
the hour
When I shall break him by my pow'r.

[*He goes out at the right.*]

SHORTENED VERSION

RESUMES HERE

[MUSIC CUE 20. *The* MAIDEN *enters
from the left. She is carrying a rose
and a large hand mirror. She stops just
inside the entrance. As she begins to
speak, the music stops.*]

MAIDEN: That haunting dream I had
    last night
Cannot be lost by simple flight
No matter where I go or stay
It follows—much to my dismay.

[*She turns, looking out at the left.*
DEATH *enters at the right.*]

My breath is nearly stopped by fear,
I saw my body on the bier.
T'was robbed of beauty, naught but
    dust,
Deprived of life and joy and lust.

[DEATH *crosses to the left corner of
the stage behind her. She does not see
him. When he is there, she turns and
walks a step or two toward the right.*]

I have to overcome this fear
And so I go with heart-felt cheer
There to the garden where my friend
Is waiting for me to attend.

[*She tucks the rose in her hair and
looks in her mirror.* DEATH *moves up
quickly behind her. She sees him in
the mirror. She freezes suddenly with
alarm.*]

MAIDEN: Oh no! Not you! Not Death
    I pray!
I've fled from thoughts of you all day.
I'm still too young and lithe to die.
Such charm as mine you can't deny.

[DEATH, *still standing behind her, looks
into her mirror.*]

DEATH: Your worldly beauty's plain to
    see.

[*She turns suddenly, facing him.*]

Such shallowness means naught to me.

[DEATH *swings behind her and to the
right, seizing her mirror. He holds it*

*up before her and she turns to look
into it.*]

Alas, coquette, your beauty fades.

[*With horror, she watches this happening in the mirror.* DEATH *laughs.*]

I've put to naught your escapades.

[*She turns and runs to the left corner
away from the audience.* DEATH *runs
after her.*]

But, for a token, let us dance.

[*She shrinks from him. He lifts his
violin.*]

MAIDEN

Why shrink from me? Here is your
   chance!

[*He begins to play and to move backward.* MUSIC CUE 21. *She moves forward to the right in rhythm to the
music.*]

MAIDEN: Oh Death, how cruel you did
   come.
Now all my hope and joy are gone.

[DEATH *steps aside as they reach the
exit, and she goes out. He stops playing.*]

DEATH: All worldliness and vanity
Must fade before my majesty.

[*He returns to the rear center of the
stage and begins to play again.* MUSIC
CUE 22. *The* OLD SOLDIER *enters singing. He does not see* DEATH. *He crosses
to the front center of the stage, slightly
past* DEATH.]

SOLDIER: Grim death oft' rides as gen-
   eral
Midst rolling drums and cannon balls.
He grants parole and leads the way
Through bivouacs till the judgment
   day.
Nothing, nothing, nothing can remain.
Only, only God's will doth sustain.

[DEATH *walks forward and taps the*
SOLDIER *on the shoulder.*]

DEATH: Don't be alarmed. It is I.

[*The* SOLDIER *turns in surprise, but he
is not afraid.*]

SOLDIER: By Deuce! I almost felt
   alarmed!
It's you. And so I am disarmed.
I had no time to change a lot,
Yet God, my Lord, I ne'er forgot.

But since I never yield to fear
I'll not begin now that you're here.
Show me those comrades gone before;
God grant us peace forevermore.

[DEATH *crosses in front of him and
walks about three steps to the right as
he speaks.*]

DEATH: Eternal peace will soon be
   yours,
For this is what His grace assures
To all who trust Him 'til the end
And then their souls to Him commend.

[DEATH *begins to play.* MUSIC CUE 23.
*With his head, he motions to indicate
the door of eternity. The* SOLDIER
crosses right, moving in front of DEATH
and speaking as he goes.]

SOLDIER: Lead on, oh Death!
Farewell, my friend!

[*He goes out at the right.* DEATH *lowers
his violin. Then he lowers his head.
Solemnly he walks to the rear center
of the acting area. He looks straight
at the audience deliberately for a moment. Then he lifts his violin and begins to play.* MUSIC CUE 24. *A* MOTHER
*carrying her baby enters from the
right. She goes to the left corner of the
acting area nearest the audience. She
is extremely tired. The music continues
as she speaks.*]

MOTHER: I've lost so many hours of
   sleep.
A constant vigil I must keep
O'er you, my precious little one,
Or lose your life, so scarce begun.

[*She sits down on the edge of the acting area, her feet into the aisle.*]

But weariness o'ertakes me so
That I must rest before I go.

I'll just sit here a little while.
Oh, Lord, in mercy on us smile.

[*She puts the baby down beside her
and falls asleep.* DEATH *stops playing.
He walks slowly up to the child. Suddenly, as music begins*—MUSIC CUE
25—DEATH *kneels and picks up the
child. He holds it gently and lovingly.
The music fades away.*]

DEATH: O little one, you feel no fear—
No pity for your mother here
Who sleeps in blissful ignorance
While you succumb to do Death's
      dance.

[*He rises and begins to move backward very slowly.*]

You cannot question what is done—
Why death has come ere life's begun.
So sleep in peace. Your home above
Is yours because of God's great love.

[*The* MOTHER *awakens. She, looking
for her child, does not see it. She becomes frantic. She turns, and then sees
it in the arms of* DEATH.]

MOTHER: My baby! O cruel Death,
      you snatched my child
While I lay there with sleep beguiled.

[*She rises, runs toward him. Something
prevents her reaching him as if she had
run up against an invisible wall. She
falls to the floor and cries out.*]

Despite my pleading, prayers and pain,
You hear my cries with cold disdain.
Give back my child!

DEATH: You have lost it.

MOTHER: It is my child!

DEATH: It was.

MOTHER

MOTHER: What can I say? Oh, Lord of
      life,
I feel a pain as though a knife
Were thrust quite through my very
      heart.
Have I and child so soon to part?

[*She gets to her knees, facing him, her
back to the audience.*]

I kneel for you, oh sombre Death—
Pray, do restore my child's life breath!
I'll give you all I now possess,
Sing songs of joy if you'll say yes.

[DEATH *shakes his head slowly.*]

DEATH: That which I take will not return.

[*The* MOTHER *rises, walks angrily to the right.*]

MOTHER: Is cruelty then akin to God,
Can He trod under hearts, rough-shod?
Would He demand what He just gave
And thrust new life into the grave?
In deepest gratitude I bowed
And praised His holy name aloud,
As mother's love my heart o'erflowed
For Him, who had this gift bestowed,
And now He'd snatch it from my breast?
Is this how heavenly love's expressed?

[DEATH *walks a few steps toward her.*]

DEATH: His ways we cannot understand,
But all is grace that He commands.

[*The* MOTHER *turns and faces him.*]

MOTHER: How can you speak of grace?

DEATH: The human mind cannot foresee
The future with its deviltry,
But God's great wisdom foresees all
And in this wisdom He doth call.

[*The* MOTHER *starts toward the right.*]

MOTHER: Lies, lies as always! Spare your breath.

[*Then she turns, comes to* DEATH, *and cries out in anguish.*]

If you want prey, take me, O Death.
Take me! Spare the child!

[*She turns, runs to the door of eternity and tries to go out but something prevents her.* DEATH *speaks quickly as she struggles.*]

DEATH: Where is this mother's love you boast?
Would you leave those who need you most?
Your older children count for naught?
Think well—then answer as you ought!

[*She stops struggling, turns and comes slowly back as* DEATH *continues.*]

You cannot understand God's ways,
But trust Him now and sing His praise.
Resign yourself to God's decree;
Then time will heal your misery.

[*The* MOTHER *is weeping.* DEATH *crosses in front of her and moves slowly to the right, carrying the sick child.* MUSIC CUE 26. *As he goes past, the* MOTHER *looks lovingly at the child and strains toward it. The music, however, begins to take her backward slowly to the left.* DEATH *speaks tenderly to the child.*]

In heavenly glory and joy divine
I take you, and in the eternal shrine
The angels wait. Thy day is done.
Wake up, wake up, dear little one.

[DEATH *carries the child into eternity. The* MOTHER, *with an audible sob, buries her face in her hands and walks backward slowly out at the left.* MUSIC CUE 27 *plays in full. As it fades away the* MESSENGER *appears again at the left. As he speaks, he crosses to the center.*]

MESSENGER: So God doth judge the world aright.
Both young and old, both serf and knight,
Lie in the ground and none can tell
If life for them was ill or well.

But all of those who sleep in dust
Shall rise again. God says they must
Arise and at this judgment seat
Receive what for their work is meet:
Some life eternal, others grief
And endless pain without relief.
Those who are wise shall brightly shine
In heavenly light and joy divine.
And they who many souls have taught
And wand'rers back to God have
    brought,
Shall like the stars in glory be
Made bright to all eternity.

[*He walks directly toward the audience, getting as close to them as possible.*]

And you, who have now seen this play
Of life and death, go on your way.

Think, as you go, that like the wind
All life must pass and in death end.
But God is love and through His grace
We all may see Him face to face.
Go where you wish, do what you may,
But don't forget your harvest day.
That heaven's joys you'll some day
    know,

[*He raises one hand in prayer.*]

Amen!

[*He raises both hands.*]

God grant it may be so.

[*He bows his head.* MUSIC CUE 28. *The* MESSENGER *stands quietly for a moment or so as if praying. Then he goes quietly out at the left.*]

TOTENTANZ
MUSIC CUE 1

MUSIC CUE 2

MUSIC CUE 3

MUSIC CUE 4

MUSIC CUE 5: *Repeat Music Cue 4.*

MUSIC CUE 6

MUSIC CUE 7: *Repeat Music Cue 4.*

MUSIC CUE 8

MUSIC CUE 9: *Repeat Music Cue 4.*

MUSIC CUE 10

MUSIC CUE 11

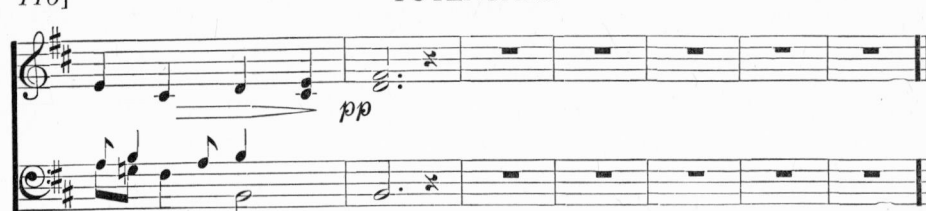

MUSIC CUE 12: *Repeat first six bars of Music Cue 11.*

MUSIC CUE 13: *Repeat Music Cue 4.*

MUSIC CUE 14

MUSIC CUE 15

MUSIC CUE 16   MUSIC CUE 17

MUSIC CUE 18

MUSIC CUE 19: *Repeat Music Cue 4.*

MUSIC CUE 20

MUSIC CUE 21: *Repeat Music* **Cue 4.**

MUSIC CUE 22

MUSIC CUE 23

ppp

Without Ped.

MUSIC CUE 24

pp

Ped.

MUSIC CUE 25

MUSIC CUE 26

TOTENTANZ

MUSIC CUE 27

MUSIC CUE 28: *Repeat Music Cue 27.*

EVERYMAN

AN ACTING VERSION IN MODERN ENGLISH BY ROBERT A. JOHNSTON

WITH ORIGINAL MUSIC BY THOMAS MATTHEWS

INTRODUCTION

Critics have long regarded the anonymous author of *Everyman,* the most famous of all English morality plays, as one of the world's finest dramatists. Written in the late fifteenth century, the play is less naive than the mystery and miracle plays that preceded it. And while they represent abstractions, its characters are more interesting and believable than those in most other moralities. Although Everyman is, as his name implies, a symbol for every man, he is also a real individualized human being whose character grows and develops during the course of the play.

Why has this play lived for so many centuries? Is it not because its basic theme has not changed over the years? Each person is still held accountable for his own life regardless of how many excuses, rationalizations, or criticisms of his environment or upbringing he may call forth to try to place the blame elsewhere. And many a man's reaction at the end is, to quote the most famous line in the play, "O Death, you come when I had you least in mind!" What theme could be more universal?

More than that, we hope it will help men today to face the difficult decisions of living with a more comforting assurance that the moral choice is always the wiser choice. For this play is not about men of the fifteenth century; it is about every man in every age, including the present.*

---

* These three paragraphs may serve as "program notes" for printed programs of productions. Permission to reprint is herewith given.

Notes on the Characters†

MESSENGER: See the notes on the Poet (p. 53). These also apply to the Messenger of this play. This role may be combined with that of the Doctor.

VOICE OF GOD: See the notes on the Voice of God (p. 5). These apply here except that in this play God is also identified with Jesus. God speaks in anger, hurt by the thoughtlessness of mankind, but the actor playing His voice must be careful not to make him sound cruel, harsh or unjust.

DEATH: Death, in this play, is a dark angel. He speaks in a hollow, ghostly tone of voice. He should be large physically and should be strong and commanding. He is stern and uncompromising.

EVERYMAN: Although he is basically a symbol for everybody in the world, he is also a well defined single individual. He is happy-go-lucky and young at heart, regardless of his real age. He is likeable and sincere. After Death's warning, he is greatly disturbed, and he goes through a series of varied and extreme emotions. The actor playing this role must be the most talented man in the group.

FELLOWSHIP: He has a warm and friendly personality. There is a hearty vitality in his every word and gesture, and he has a pleasant sense of humor. He gives the impression of unusual loyalty to his friends. These positive qualities must be emphasized or his refusal to accompany Everyman will

---

† Most of the characters represent abstractions. *See* Notes on Characters, p. 91.

not come as a shock. The refusal and subsequent uneasy backing out of his agreement must seem in contradiction with his character until we realize that much of his heartiness and loyalty are purely superficial. We should not realize this at first, however, or the effect will be spoiled, and so the actor should play him as sincerely loyal as possible. He may be of any age.

KINDRED: He is the kind of person who has genealogy and record-keeping of family relationships as hobbies. He has a stern sense of duty and family loyalty. He also has a sweetheart of whom he is tired. He keeps her only because he feels it is his duty, but he would like her to go away of her own accord. He professes loyalty to Everyman but refuses definitely to accompany him to the grave. He may be of any age.

COUSIN: Cousin is probably fat, younger than Kindred, and somewhat comic in appearance. He hates to refuse definitely and positively, but resorts to ruses and half-excuses to get out of going with Everyman. He is friendly and kind-hearted but weak. If played properly, he can be a rather amusing character.

GOODS: This role may be played either by a man or by a woman. The age is immaterial. Gross, sluggish, and insolent, this character suggests the power of great wealth. Note that this character is very intelligent and is not deceived about its own true values as Everyman is. There is a harsh, cold cruelty about Goods, and he seems to enjoy watching Everyman suffer. He moves slowly and heavily. The voice need not be kept realistic since the character does not represent a human being; it may take on exaggerated tones of sluggishness and insolence.

GOOD-DEEDS: This role may be played by a man by changing a few pronouns in the text, but it is much better to have it played by an attractive woman. She is delicate, pale, and gentle. In spite of this, she gradually reveals remarkable strength of purpose and loyalty. Note that she is the only one who goes with Everyman to death and beyond; she must be the most sympathetic character in the play. She is, in many ways, like a beautiful and good woman in love.

KNOWLEDGE: Less attractive physically than her sister, she is nevertheless a desirable woman. Her most obvious characteristics are wisdom and common sense. She is intellectual but not at all like the usual stereotyped notion of an intellectual. She is poised and dignified, and her voice is cultivated and mature. She is the kind of person one can always trust.

CONFESSION: He is an old priest. He is stern or kindly, depending on how one looks at him. There are character lines in his face indicating that he has lived long and has gained a great deal of religious wisdom during his long years of service. He is paternal and holy. The audience must have great respect for him.

DISCRETION: This role may be played either by a man or by a woman but preferably by a woman. She is quiet and circumspect. She walks on tiptoe. Her voice is pleasant and never harsh or angry. She is attractive, but there is a timid, tentative quality about her that keeps her from being strong. A favorite gesture of hers is to place one finger across her lips as if admonishing others to be silent.

STRENGTH: This may be either a

man or a woman, but it is better if it is a man. He should be huge and muscular: the body-builder type. There is a brusqueness about him which makes him either move suddenly in powerful movements or else stand perfectly still in motionless poses. That is, no movement should be small or tentative. He scowls a good deal. His voice is hard and commanding. He usually stands with his feet spread widely apart.

FIVE-WITS: This may be either a man or a woman. To even it up, perhaps it should be a man but it really makes little or no difference. Five-Wits, representing the five senses of man, is alert, open-eyed, open-eared, and observant in all ways. He is quick to respond to what is being said. He always seems to be eager and intelligent. The actor playing this role should have a good mobile face so as to show these qualities even more while listening than while speaking.

BEAUTY: This undoubtedly ought to be played by a woman and by a woman who can qualify for the name. Her beauty, however, is empty beauty compared with the deep beauty of Good-Deeds. She shows no great amount of perception or intelligence. In fact, she is more repelled by ideas of death, sickness, or anything ugly than an intelligent person would be. She must be able to act the emotion of terror well in the scene where she discovers the grave.

ANGEL: This role may easily be played by Death, and in fact, seems more logical that way. If so, the character remains the same but with additional elements of kindness and the promise of hope portrayed in it. Otherwise, if it is a separate Angel, it should probably be played by a woman. She should be firm, positive, maternal and kind.

DOCTOR: The play has better unity if this role is omitted and played by the Messenger. If it is desired to have more roles, however, it can be kept in. The playwright did originally write it as a separate role after all, and it can justifiably be played as such. In this case, the Doctor should be learned, dignified and instructive, with all the attributes of a good teacher.

Notes on the Properties

The PROP LIST comprises the following:

    large book of accounts (brought in
        by Good-Deeds)
    scourge (in Confession's inner
        pocket)
    long dark cloak (offstage right;
        later brought in by Knowledge)
    large wooden cross (offstage left;
        later brought in by Everyman)

Although there are only four props, each is very significant to the action of the play. The book of accounts should be large and interesting-looking. It can be covered with brown paper crinkled to look like leather and lettered with large words, "EVERYMAN'S LIFE," on it in gilt paint. Or any imaginative construction can be given it by someone creative in the group. The scourge is described in detail in the text of the play; it will probably have to be made because such religious objects are very rare nowadays. The cloak, which is the symbol of sorrow, should be appropriate to its meaning. The large cross can be made; it can be either of wood or of cardboard painted to look like wood.

CHARACTERS

MESSENGER	KNOWLEDGE
VOICE OF GOD	CONFESSION
DEATH	DISCRETION*
EVERYMAN	STRENGTH*
FELLOWSHIP	FIVE-WITS*
KINDRED	BEAUTY*
COUSIN	ANGEL†
GOODS	DOCTOR‡
GOOD-DEEDS	

PLACE: *Any place*
TIME: *Any time*

[*At the beginning, we hear music—* MUSIC CUE 1. *A* MESSENGER *enters from the left, walks to the center of the stage, faces the audience, pauses a moment, and then begins to speak. The music stops.*]

MESSENGER: I pray you all give audience
and hear this matter with reverence.
We intend to do a moral play.
It is called *The Summoning of Everyman,*
and it shows our living and our ending
and how transitory is our day.

The moral is: Man, in the beginning,
look well and think of your ending,
no matter how gay your life may be.
In the beginning you think sin sweet,
but at the ending your soul will weep
when your body is lying in clay.

Here you will see how Fellowship,
Jollity, Strength, Pleasure and Beauty
will fade away as the flowers of May,
and you will hear how heaven's King
calls Everyman to a general reckoning.
Give audience and hear what God will say.

[*Music suddenly bursts forth—*MUSIC CUE 2. *The* MESSENGER *walks slowly to the right and goes out. The music becomes softer; it continues behind the following speech. The* VOICE OF GOD *is heard from somewhere above or behind the audience. It is loud, resonant and powerful.*]

VOICE OF GOD: In my majesty, I do perceive
how humankind is unkind to Me.
Men live without dread in prosperity;
their minds are fixed only on worldly riches.
They are blind to the supernatural sight
and drowned in sin. They know Me not.

They forget the shedding of My red blood;

---

* Characters omitted in shortened version.
† May be combined with role of Death.
‡ May be combined with role of Messenger.

128

and though I offer a multitude of mercy,
there are few who ask Me for it.

Everyman lives only for his own private pleasure.
Everyman has no fear of Me.
Yet after his life there is nothing sure for him,
and with him I shall soon have a reckoning.

Where are you, Death, My mighty messenger?

[*The music stops. There is the sound of a whirring of wings*—MUSIC CUE 3. *Death enters suddenly from the right.*

MESSENGER

they forget that I hanged between the two;
to get them life I suffered death;
My head was hurt with the piercing thorns.
I could do no more to show My love,
and now my people are forsaking Me.

They practice the damnable seven sins
and thus leave the company of heavenly angels.
I see that the more I let them live,
the more wicked they become each year.
Charity, most of all, they all forget,

DEATH

He strides to the front and center, raises his great arms, and looks upward. He speaks in a hollow, ghostly tone of voice. The music stops.]

DEATH: Almighty God, I am here at Your will,
Your commandment to fulfill.

[*He drops his arms but continues to look up.* MUSIC CUE 4 *begins.*]

VOICE OF GOD: Go to Everyman and tell him
in My name that he must take
a pilgrimage which he cannot escape.
Tell him to bring a sure reckoning
without delay or any tarrying.

[*The music stops.*]

DEATH: Lord, I will run over all the world
and search out cruelly both great and small.
Every man who, like a beast, lives
away from God's laws I will smite.
Unless some goodness come to his rescue,
in hell he will dwell, world without end.

[*He drops his head and backs up three long steps.* MUSIC CUE 5, *light and airy, begins.*]

Lo, yonder I see Everyman walking.
Little does he think about my coming.

[EVERYMAN *enters from the left. He is happy and lighthearted. He saunters slowly toward the right.*]

His mind is on fleshly lusts and his treasure,
but he shall be caused to endure great pain

when he stands before the Lord Heaven King.

[DEATH *pauses while* EVERYMAN *crosses in front of him without seeing him. When* EVERYMAN *is a few steps past him,* DEATH *speaks suddenly to him in a harsh tone causing* EVERYMAN *to stop abruptly in surprise. At the same instant the music stops.*]

Everyman, stand still. Where are you going
so gaily? Have you forgotten your Maker?

[EVERYMAN *turns slowly to look at* DEATH.]

EVERYMAN: Why do you ask?
Do you want to know?

[DEATH *moves a step toward him.* EVERYMAN *scowls with faint distaste.*]

DEATH: Yes, sir. I will tell you why.
In great haste I am sent to you
from God in His majesty.

[EVERYMAN *looks at him suspiciously as though he does not believe him.*]

EVERYMAN: What, sent to me?
DEATH: Yes, certainly.
Though you here have forgotten Him,
He thinks of you in the heavenly sphere
as you shall soon learn as we go.

[EVERYMAN'S *worry is increasing.* DEATH *is calm, assured and a bit fierce in his manner.*]

EVERYMAN: What does God desire of me?

DEATH: God requires a reckoning
from you at once without delay.

[EVERYMAN *starts with surprise, then*

controls himself and speaks quickly.]

EVERYMAN: To give my God a reckoning,
give me the longer leisure I crave.
This sudden message blinds my wits.

[DEATH *glares at him.* EVERYMAN, *not able to meet* DEATH'S *eyes, drops his.*]

DEATH: You must take upon yourself a long journey;
therefore bring with you your book of accounts.
You shall answer before God and show
your many bad deeds, and only a few good.
How, in what way, have you spent your life?
Take some pains to think this out fully
for, as you well know, you shall have no mediator.

[EVERYMAN *looks up again.*]

EVERYMAN: I am not ready to give such a reckoning.
I do not know you.

[*There is a long pause. They look at one another.* EVERYMAN *grows more afraid. Suddenly, in quiet terror,* EVERYMAN *speaks.*]

What messenger are you?

[*At this question, the music gives out with a short "stinger"—*MUSIC CUE 6. DEATH *opens his eyes wide and lifts his arms. He speaks with quiet ferocity. At the word "Death,"* EVERYMAN *crouches in fear, his hands up before his eyes to shut out the dreaded sight.* DEATH *looks down at him in contempt and lowers his arms.*]

DEATH: I am *Death* that dreads no man;
for every man I wait and I spare no man.
It is God's supreme commandment
that all to me should be obedient.

[EVERYMAN *takes his hands from his eyes but remains crouching. He looks up at* DEATH *fearfully and speaks in great anguish.*]

EVERYMAN: O Death, you come when I had you least in mind!

[*He sinks to the floor and buries his*

EVERYMAN

*head in his hands. After a moment, he
controls himself and begins to think of
what to do. He gets an idea. He rises,
moves a step toward* DEATH, *and
speaks.*]

In your power, you could save me a
  while.
If you will be kind, I shall give you
  wealth.
Yes, a thousand pounds you shall have
if you will defer this matter till another
  day.

[DEATH *shakes his head slowly.*]

DEATH: Everyman, what you ask may
  never be.
I am not impressed by gold, silver or
  riches,
nor by emperor, king, duke or
  princes.
If I courted gifts, I might get all the
  world,
but my custom is contrary to bribery.
I give you no reprieve. Come. Do not
  tarry.

[EVERYMAN *turns suddenly and walks
swiftly to the extreme left, talking as
he goes.*]

EVERYMAN: Alas, shall I have no
  longer time?
I must say Death certainly gives no
  warning.

[*He stops, turns and speaks directly to*
DEATH.]

It makes my heart sick to think about
  you,
for all unready is my book of reckoning.

[*He moves a step in the direction of*
DEATH, *holding out his hands in sup-
plication.*]

I pray you, Death, for the mercy of
  God,
to spare me until I provide for my
  soul.

[DEATH *shakes his head again.*]

DEATH: It will not avail you to cry,
  weep or pray.
Make haste to get ready to go on your
  journey;
prove that your friends are your
  friends if you can.
For, as you well know, the tide waits
  for no man.
It is in the nature of each living crea-
  ture
in the world to die for the sin of
  Adam.

EVERYMAN: Death, if I should take
  this pilgrimage
and make my reckoning quickly and
  truly,
will you grant me, for the sake of Saint
  Charity,
to come back here again very shortly?

DEATH: No, Everyman. Once you are
  dead,
you may nevermore come here again,
  believe me.

[EVERYMAN *drops to his knees and begins to pray.*]

EVERYMAN: O gracious God, in the
  high seat celestial,
have mercy on me in this time of need.

[*He looks up at* DEATH.]

Shall I have no company from this vale
  terrestrial,
no acquaintance of mine to accompany
  me?

DEATH: Yes, if any friends will be so
    hardy
as to go with you and keep you com-
    pany.

[DEATH *moves to the right a few steps
as he speaks the next lines.*]

Now, come with me to God's magnifi-
    cence
to give your reckoning before His
    presence.
Did you think your life had been given
    to you?
And your worldly goods also?

EVERYMAN: Yes, I had thought so,
    verily.

[DEATH *stops, turns and looks solemnly
at* EVERYMAN.]

DEATH: No, they were only lent to you.
As soon as you go, the goods will go
    to another,
and from him to another, just as you
    got them.

[*He takes one short, quick step toward*
EVERYMAN.]

Everyman, you are mad; you have
    your five wits
and yet will not amend your life while
    alive,
and then suddenly I come.

[EVERYMAN *is still on his knees. He
clasps his hands in agony.*]

EVERYMAN: O wretched and wicked,
    where can I run
in order to escape this endless sorrow?

[*On his knees, he stumbles toward*
DEATH, *attempting to seize him by the
cloak.* DEATH *steps slowly back, thus
keeping just outside his reach.*]

Now, gentle Death, spare me till to-
    morrow
that I may amend myself
with this friendly warning.

[DEATH *raises his arm as if to strike.
He speaks violently.*]

DEATH: No, I will not consent to that.
No man gets a reprieve.
Suddenly I strike at the heart
without any warning.

[*Then he speaks more quietly—with
even a degree of kindness. His threatening gesture becomes almost a caress-
ing one.*]

Now I will disappear from your sight;
see that you get yourself ready shortly,
for you may say that this is the day
when no man living shall escape away.

[*He whirls suddenly and strides out at
the right.* MUSIC CUE 7 *begins; it dies
away a few moments after* DEATH *is
gone.* EVERYMAN *remains on his knees,
sobbing quietly with despair.*]

EVERYMAN: Alas, I must weep with
    the deepest of sighs,
for I have no manner of company
to help in my journey nor to be with
    me;
and also my book of accounts is way
    unready.
How can I get a good excuse quickly?
I wish to God I had never been born!

[*He rises to his feet, looks wildly
about.*]

My soul needs comfort and profit at
    once,
but now I fear pains to come, huge
    and great.

[*He pauses. Then he speaks franti-cally.*]

Time passes! Lord, help all whom
    Thou built.
Though I mourn, it is to no avail.

[*He pauses again and pounds his hands
together in despair.*]

The day passes! And it is almost gone!
I do not know what I ought best to do.

[*Suddenly he gets a bright idea and
seems cheered.* MUSIC CUE 8.]

What if I spoke to Fellowship about
    this?

FELLOWSHIP

For he is everything closest to me.
We have in this world on many a day
been jolly good friends in sport and in
    play.

[*Suddenly he sees* FELLOWSHIP *offstage
at the right. He is elated.*]

I see him yonder, certainly.
I trust that he will bear me company.

[FELLOWSHIP *enters at the right. The
music stops.*]

Well met, good Fellowship. Good
    morning to you.

[FELLOWSHIP *and* EVERYMAN *walk to
each other and clasp hands in a hearty
manner.* FELLOWSHIP *speaks with
cheery vitality.*]

FELLOWSHIP: Everyman, good morn-
    ing and good all day.
Sir, why are you looking so pitiful?
If anything is wrong, please tell me
    about it
so I may help to provide a remedy.

EVERYMAN: Yes, good Fellowship, yes.

[*He turns away from* FELLOWSHIP *and
walks a step toward the left as he
speaks.*]

I am in great jeopardy.

[*He stops, not facing* FELLOWSHIP.
FELLOWSHIP *moves to him.*]

FELLOWSHIP: My true friend, open
    your mind to me;
I will not forsake you to the end of my
    life
but will always give you good com-
    pany.

[EVERYMAN *turns and smiles gratefully
at* FELLOWSHIP.]

EVERYMAN: That was well spoken, and
lovingly.

[FELLOWSHIP *puts one hand on* EVERY-
MAN'S *shoulder as he speaks.*]

FELLOWSHIP: Sir, you must tell me of
your heaviness;
I feel pity to see you in any distress;
if any have wronged you, you shall be
revenged
even if I be killed on this very ground,
even if I know beforehand I must die
for you.

[EVERYMAN *smiles weakly. He pats*
FELLOWSHIP'S *hand which is still on
his shoulder.*]

EVERYMAN: Verily, Fellowship, thanks.
God give you mercy.

[FELLOWSHIP *removes his hand and
makes an impatient gesture.*]

FELLOWSHIP: Tush! By your thanks I
set not a straw.
Show me your grief and say no more.

[EVERYMAN *starts to speak, then stops
before he has said anything. A cloud
of doubt crosses over his face. He
speaks somewhat sadly.*]

EVERYMAN: If I should break open my
heart to you,
and then you should turn your mind
from me
and would not comfort me when you
hear me speak,
then I should be ten times sorrier than
I am now.

[FELLOWSHIP *speaks with earnest sincerity.*]

FELLOWSHIP: Sir, I will do in deed as
I say I will do.

EVERYMAN: Then be a good friend to
me in my hour of need:
I have always found you true before.

FELLOWSHIP: And I shall be true to
you evermore
for, in faith,

[*He crosses his heart and speaks more
fervently.*]

even if you went to hell,
I should never forsake you along the
way.

[EVERYMAN *sighs with relief.*]

EVERYMAN: You speak like a good
friend; I believe in you.
I shall tell you how it is.
I am commanded to go on a journey,
a long way, hard and dangerous,
to give a true account without delay
before the high judge, God.

[FELLOWSHIP *is surprised at this.*]

Therefore I ask you to bear me company,
as you have promised, in this journey.

[FELLOWSHIP *takes two steps backward. He shakes his head in consternation.*]

FELLOWSHIP: That is matter indeed!
Promise is duty,
but if I should take such a voyage
upon me,
I know very well it should be to my
pain.
Also I do not deny it makes me afraid.
But let us think this over as well as we
can,
for your words would make a strong
man afraid.

[EVERYMAN *frowns. He studies the
face of* FELLOWSHIP *closely.*]

EVERYMAN: Why, you said that if I had need,

you would never forsake me, alive or dead,

though it were to go to hell truly.

[FELLOWSHIP *nods his head in agreement.*]

FELLOWSHIP: So I said, certainly,

but so many pleasures would have to be set aside—

and also, if we took such a journey,

when should we come back here again?

[EVERYMAN *speaks sadly.*]

EVERYMAN: No, never again till the day of doom.

[FELLOWSHIP *makes a sudden decision. He speaks firmly and positively.*]

FELLOWSHIP: In faith, then I will not come there!

Who has brought such tidings to you?

EVERYMAN: Indeed, Death was here with me.

[FELLOWSHIP *starts suddenly in fright. He takes another step backward.*]

FELLOWSHIP: Now, by God Who has bought up everything,

if Death was the messenger,

I will not go on that loathsome journey

for any man that is living today—

not even for the father who begot me!

[EVERYMAN *speaks reproachfully.*]

EVERYMAN: You promised otherwise, my partner.

[FELLOWSHIP, *as if in great sympathy, moves a step toward* EVERYMAN.]

FELLOWSHIP: I know very well I said so. Truly I do.

If you had asked me to eat and drink and make good cheer,

or to hunt after women in lusty company,

I would never forsake you while the day is clear,

trust me verily!

[EVERYMAN *laughs sarcastically.*]

EVERYMAN: Yes, for that you would be ready.

To go to laughter, to solace, to play!

Your mind will sooner apply to these

than to bear me company in my long journey.

FELLOWSHIP: Now, in good faith, I will not go that way.

But even should you want to murder or hurt any man,

I would help you in that with all my will!

[*He crosses his heart again.* EVERYMAN *laughs sarcastically again.*]

EVERYMAN: O, that is simple advice indeed!

[*Suddenly he switches to desperate pleading. He drops on his knees before* FELLOWSHIP.]

Gentle Fellowship, help me in my necessity.

We have loved long, and now I need you.

Now, gentle Fellowship, remember me.

[FELLOWSHIP *turns away in embarrassment.*]

FELLOWSHIP: Whether you have loved me or not,

by Saint John, I will not go with you.

[EVERYMAN *becomes even more desperate.*]

EVERYMAN: Yet I pray you, take the time
and do this much for me:
to go with me, for Saint Charity's sake,
only as far as the edge of town.

FELLOWSHIP: No, even if I were dressed for it,
I would not go with you a foot.

[*He turns suddenly to face* EVERY-MAN.]

If you will stay here I will not leave your side,
but if you must go, God speed you on your trip.

[*He turns and walks quickly to the right.* EVERYMAN *rises.*]

EVERYMAN: Where are you going, Fellowship?
Will you forsake me?

FELLOWSHIP: Yes, friend.

[*He stops, turns back to face* EVERY-MAN, *raises his hand in blessing.*]

To God I commend you.

[EVERYMAN *rushes, sobbing, to* FEL-LOWSHIP. *He seizes his hand.*]

EVERYMAN: Farewell, good Fellowship; for this my heart is sore;
adieu forever; I shall see you no more.

[FELLOWSHIP *speaks with sincere affection.*]

FELLOWSHIP: In faith, Everyman, farewell now at the end;
for you I will remember that parting is mourning.

[*He removes his hand gently from* EVERYMAN'S *grasp and goes quickly out at the right.* MUSIC CUE 9 *begins*

as FELLOWSHIP *goes out.* EVERYMAN *looks after him forlornly. The music stops.*]

EVERYMAN: Alack! Shall our friends forsake us so fast indeed?
Fellowship leaves me when I need him the most.
He has given me great worlds of happiness,
but a little sorrow he will not undertake.
I have heard it said before that in prosperity you will find
friends that in adversity will prove to be unkind.

[*He rises and looks about him in bewilderment.*]

Where for comfort shall I flee
since Fellowship has abandoned me?
To my relatives I must apply,
praying them to help in my necessity.
I believe that they will do so, too,
for kin will creep where they may not go.

[MUSIC CUE 10. EVERYMAN *sees* KINDRED *and* COUSIN *offstage left. He speaks with renewed hope.*]

I will ask them, for yonder I see them.
Where are you now, my friends and kinsmen?

[KINDRED *and* COUSIN *enter at the left. The music stops.* KINDRED *walks over to* EVERYMAN, *speaking as he goes.*]

KINDRED: Here we are at your command.
Cousin, tell us what you want.

[*He shakes hands with* EVERYMAN. COUSIN *walks over to* EVERYMAN, *speaking as he goes. He crosses in*

front of KINDRED, *and as he does so,*
KINDRED *makes room for him by facing*
left and taking one step toward the
left, then turning right again.]

COUSIN: Yes, Everyman. Declare to
   us
if you are disposed to go anywhere,
for as you well know, we will live and
   die together.

[*He shakes hands with* EVERYMAN.]

KINDRED: In wealth and woe we will
   hold with you,
because a man's own family will do
   anything for him.

[EVERYMAN *smiles at them both grate-*
fully.]

EVERYMAN: God give you mercy, my
   kinsmen kind.
Let me tell you the grief in my mind.
I was commanded by a messenger
who is a high King's chief officer
to go on a pilgrimage far away
from which I may never come back
   again.

[*Both* KINSMAN *and* COUSIN *take a*
step backward in surprise.]

Also, I must give a straight reckoning,
or he will turn me over to

KINDRED

COUSIN

a great and powerful enemy who intends to do me harm.

[KINDRED *speaks suspiciously.*]

KINDRED: What account is this which you must render?
I must know this first.

EVERYMAN: I must show all my works, both bad and good;
how I have lived and spent my days;
how many ill deeds I have done
since life was first given as loan to me;
how many virtues I have refused.
Therefore I pray you to go with me
to testify for me, by Saint Charity.

[KINDRED and COUSIN *look at one another in dismay.*]

COUSIN: What, to go there? Is that the matter?

[*He goes to the left front corner of the acting area, crossing in front of* KINDRED. *He speaks as he goes.*]

No, Everyman, I would rather live on bread and water
for five years or more.

[EVERYMAN *cries out in offended despair.*]

EVERYMAN: Alas, that I was ever born!
For now I shall never be merry again
if even my family forsakes me.

[KINDRED *steps over to him, pats his shoulder encouragingly.*]

KINDRED: Ah, sir, don't take it that way. Do not moan,
for you have always been a jolly man.

[*His manner changes, becomes somewhat frightened. He does not back away from* EVERYMAN, *but he looks as if he would like to.*]

But one thing I warn you, by Saint Anne,
if you were counting on me, you shall go alone.

[EVERYMAN *crosses in front of* KINDRED *and goes to* COUSIN, *speaking as he goes.*]

EVERYMAN: My Cousin, will you not go with me?

[COUSIN *looks very startled as if he were thinking "To whom are you speaking? Me?". He suddenly develops a fake limp and crosses haltingly in front of* EVERYMAN *a step or two to the left.*]

COUSIN: No, by our Lady. I have the cramp in my toe.

[KINDRED *and* EVERYMAN *look at him in amazement.* COUSIN *looks back and forth from one to the other. Finally he speaks to* EVERYMAN *apologetically.*]

Do not look at me, for I swear to God I would be no good to you in your time of need.

[KINDRED, *catching on finally to* COUSIN'S *ruse, has a sudden bright idea. He crosses in front of* COUSIN *and speaks to* EVERYMAN. *He seizes* EVERYMAN *by the lapel of his robe.*]

KINDRED: Now, do not try to tempt us.
On the other hand, I do have a sweetheart.
I have had her for a long time.
She loves to dance and to feast and to travel.
I will give her permission to go along
if you can get her interested in your charms.

[EVERYMAN *pushes his hand away roughly and glares at him.*]

EVERYMAN: Now, tell me the truth
from the depths of your mind.
Will you go there with me or remain
here behind?

KINDRED: Remain behind? Well, yes, I
will if I may!

[EVERYMAN *turns away from him impatiently.*]

Therefore farewell until some other
day.

[KINDRED *hurries out at the left, crossing in front of* EVERYMAN *to do so.*
MUSIC CUE 11 *as he leaves.*]

EVERYMAN: How can I be merry or
glad?
All of them make fair promises to me,
but when I need them most, they forsake me.
I have been deceived: this is what
makes me sad.

[*He looks at* COUSIN *accusingly.*
COUSIN, *embarrassed, shuffles his feet.
He looks down, avoiding* EVERYMAN'S
eyes.]

COUSIN: Farewell now, cousin Everyman.
I do not believe I will be able to go
with you.
Besides, I have an unready accounting
of my own
which I must do something about
soon. I must hurry.
Well, God keep you well, and now I
must go.

[*He hurries out at the left, crossing in
front of* EVERYMAN. MUSIC CUE 12 *as
he goes.* EVERYMAN *walks slowly to
the right.*]

EVERYMAN: Ah Jesus, has it all come
to this?
Lo, fair words make fools be fooled,
and other fools will promise and do
nothing.
My kinsmen promised me faithfully
to stay with me steadfastly
and now as fast as they can they flee.
Fellowship, too, made promises to me.

[*He turns and walks slowly to the
extreme left.*]

What friend can I ever turn to now?
Oh, I waste my time to wait longer
here,
Yet in my mind a thing there is—
all my life I have loved riches.
If my Goods might help me in this
hour,
I could leave at least with a lighter
heart.

[*He turns, looks off toward the right.*]

I will speak to him in this distress.

[*He calls in a loud voice.*]

Where are you, my Goods and riches?

[MUSIC CUE 13. GOODS, *in a powerful
but slow and sluggish voice calls back
to* EVERYMAN *from offstage right. The
music continues.*]

GOODS: Who calls me? Everyman?
What is your hurry?
I lie here in corners, weighted down
and piled high.
In chests I am locked so fast
and in bags I am sacked so tightly,
you may see with your eyes I cannot
stir.
What do you want of me? Tell me and
let me lie.

[EVERYMAN *calls quickly and urgently. He crosses a step or two toward the center as he speaks.*]

EVERYMAN: Come here, good Goods,
    in all the haste you can make.
I desire some advice from you.

[GOODS, *slouching and grinning insolently, enters from the right. He stops just inside the entrance.*]

GOODS: Sir, if you have any trouble or
    adversity in this world,
I can help you to remedy it very
    shortly.

[*The music stops.* EVERYMAN *crosses to* GOODS *as he speaks.*]

EVERYMAN: In this world it is not, let
    me tell you.
I am being sent to another world.
All my life you have given me pleasure.
Therefore I pray you to go with me
    now,
for you may help me to clean and to
    purify
my record before the throne of almighty God.
For it is said among all men
that money makes right whatever was
    wrong.

[GOODS *has been smiling in smug satisfaction while* EVERYMAN *flattered him. Now he laughs scoffingly.*]

GOODS: No, Everyman, I sing a different song.
I follow no man in such voyages,
for if I went with you
you would fare even worse because of
    me.
Because on me you kept your mind
    too often,
now your account book is blotted and
    smeared.
Your account you will never be able
    to make,
and to think that you lived all your life
    for my sake!

[*He shakes his head in mock sympathy, going "Tsk! Tsk!" as* EVERYMAN *says his next lines.*]

EVERYMAN: If I must be ruined when
    I come to that answer,
you can be with me anyway to cheer
    me up.
Up, let us go together.

GOODS

[*He seizes* GOODS *by the arm.* GOODS *shakes him roughly off and speaks angrily.*]

GOODS: No, no, not so, I am too brittle. I would not endure.
I will follow no man one foot, of that you may be sure.

[EVERYMAN *turns sadly away.*]

EVERYMAN: Alas, I have loved you. I have had pleasure
all my life-days from treasure and goods.

[GOODS *speaks philosophically and with a touch of pity.*]

GOODS: That will go on the wrong side of the book,
for love of me is contrary to love everlasting.
But if you had loved me moderately
or if you had given part of me to the poor,
then you should not be in this state of sorrow.

[EVERYMAN *nods his head in agreement. He does not turn to face* GOODS.]

EVERYMAN: Lo, I was wrong. Why was I not aware
that I wasted the spending of all of my time?

GOODS: Did you think I belonged to you?

EVERYMAN: I had thought so.

GOODS: No, Everyman, I say no.
For a while only I was lent to you.
For a season you had me in prosperity.

[GOODS, *still essentially speaking to* EVERYMAN, *turns and looks at the audience, including them in the meaning of the following speech.*]

My condition is always to kill men's souls;
if I save one, a thousand I spill.
And could you think I would follow you?
No, from this world, that I cannot do.

EVERYMAN: I had thought otherwise.

[GOODS *continues to include the audience, looking now at them, now at* EVERYMAN.]

GOODS: To your soul, worldly Goods is always a thief,
for when you are dead—you are dying—my aim
is to deceive another in the same way
that I have deceived you and to ruin his soul.

[EVERYMAN *strides quickly to* GOODS *raises his fist as if to strike.* GOODS *is not frightened. The more fiercely* EVERYMAN *speaks, the more he laughs.*]

EVERYMAN: O false Goods, cursed may you be!
You traitor to God, you have deceived me
and caught me in your snare.

[EVERYMAN *apparently strikes* GOODS *with three hard blows.* GOODS, *unaffected, not moving, laughs good naturedly.*]

GOODS: This was your own fault. I am glad.
I must laugh at you now; I cannot be sad.

[EVERYMAN *drops on his knees, his face twisted in agony and frustration.*

EVERYMAN: Ah, Goods, you had long my heartly love;
I gave to you what should have been God's.
But will you not go with me indeed?

[*In contempt,* GOODS *pretends to spit upon* EVERYMAN.]

GOODS: No, and therefore, farewell. Have a good day.

[*He slouches out at the right.* MUSIC CUE 14 *as he goes.* EVERYMAN *comes toward the audience and speaks directly to them.*]

EVERYMAN: O, to whom shall I complain?
My friends have left me all alone.
They speak pleasant words about comfort and loyalty,
but all forsake me in the ending.

[*He looks out toward the right.*]

Of all of my friends, I loved Goods the best;
but of comfort from him, I have had the least.

[*He looks back at the audience and speaks confidentially and humbly.*]

I am very ashamed of myself.
I hate myself, as well I may.
I may as well go to my Good-Deeds,
but alas, she is so weak that she can neither speak to me nor walk.
Yet I will try.

[*He walks to the center, calls off somewhat timidly toward the left.*]

Good-Deeds, where are you?

MUSIC CUE 15, *beautiful but delicate and far away, begins. The voice of* GOOD-DEEDS *answers from offstage left;*

GOOD DEEDS

it is weak and far away but clear enough to be heard without difficulty. There is a strange, almost chanting quality to it.]

GOOD-DEEDS: Here I lie cold in the ground;
your sins have me so heavily bound that I cannot stir.

[EVERYMAN *calls to her.*]

EVERYMAN: O, Good-Deeds, I stand in fear.
I beg you to give me good advice,
for I must have help from somewhere.

[*The head and arms of* GOOD-DEEDS *appear on the ground at the left en-*

trance. *She reaches up her arms to*
EVERYMAN, *but she evidently cannot
rise. She speaks in the same strange,
sweet voice. The music continues.*]

GOOD-DEEDS: Everyman, I understand
  that you
are summoned to make your account
  to God.
My advice is to take me with you.

[*He walks to her, takes her hands and
tries to pull her up, but she is too
heavy.*]

EVERYMAN: I come to you humbly to
  plead with you
to go with me on this dread journey.

GOOD-DEEDS: I would if I could, but I
  cannot stand.

[*He stops trying to pull, scowls, looks
offstage to the left but apparently sees
nothing. The music stops.*]

EVERYMAN: Why, does something
  weight you down?

GOOD-DEEDS: Yes, and I may thank
  you for it all.
If you had ever gone cheerfully with
  me,
your book of accounts would be ready
  now.

[*She reaches behind her, gets a large
book, and brings it forward. With great
effort, she throws it to the center of
the stage where it falls with a heavy
thud.*]

Look in the book of your works and
  deeds
if you would see what weights me
  down.
It will weight your soul when you read
  what you know.

[EVERYMAN *rushes to the book, begins
to leaf frantically through its pages.*]

EVERYMAN: Our Lord Jesus, help me!
For one letter here I cannot see!

[*He drops the book, runs back to her.*]

Good-Deeds, I pray you, help me in
  this need,
or else I am damned forever indeed.
Therefore help me to make a reckoning.

GOOD-DEEDS: Everyman, I am sorry
  about your fall
and I would gladly help you if I were
  able.

[*She tries to lift herself again but cannot.*]

EVERYMAN: Good-Deeds, what counsel
  can you give me now?

GOOD-DEEDS: I can counsel you though
  I cannot move.
I have a sister who will go with you a
  while
to prepare you for the dreadful reckoning.
Her name is Knowledge.

[MUSIC CUE 16. KNOWLEDGE, *dignified
and upright, comes in at the left. She
stands back of* GOOD-DEEDS.]

KNOWLEDGE: Everyman, I will go with
  you and be your guide.
I will be by your side in your worst
  distress.

[*The music stops.* EVERYMAN *comes
to her, drops on his knees before her
and kisses the hem of her skirt.*]

EVERYMAN: I am wholly content with
  your company.
Thanked be God my Creator.

GOOD-DEEDS: And when God has brought you where
you may heal yourself of your self-wrought pain,
then with your reckoning and your Good-Deeds
together we shall go to the blessed Trinity.

[EVERYMAN *leans down and kisses her hair gently.* KNOWLEDGE *smiles maternally down upon them both.*]

EVERYMAN: God give you mercy, my sweet Good-Deeds;
I am well content with your loving words.

[GOOD-DEEDS *disappears off left.* KNOWLEDGE *takes* EVERYMAN'S *hand, helps him to his feet.*]

KNOWLEDGE: Let us go together lovingly
to Confession who dwells by the cleansing river.

[EVERYMAN *wipes his eyes with his hands.*]

EVERYMAN: I weep for joy; I wish we were there.
I pray you, tell me where he dwells, that holy man, Confession?

[*Together they begin to walk toward the right.* KNOWLEDGE *is leading and* EVERYMAN *is a step behind her.*]

KNOWLEDGE: In the house of salvation.
We shall find him there soon,
and he shall comfort us by the grace of God.

MUSIC CUE 17. CONFESSION *enters at the right.*]

Lo, this is Confession; kneel down and ask mercy,

for he is in good standing with almighty God.

[KNOWLEDGE *stops, leads* EVERYMAN *in front of her and then releases his hand.* EVERYMAN *kneels as soon as he has crossed in front of her. The music continues.*]

EVERYMAN: O glorious fountain that clarifies all uncleanness,
wash from me the spots of vices unclean
so that no sin may be seen upon me;
I come with Knowledge for my redemption,

KNOWLEDGE

repenting sincerely and full of contrition;
for I am commanded to take a pilgrimage
to make great accounts before my
God.

Now I pray you, Confession, father of
salvation,
to strengthen my good deeds and to
pity my sorrow.

[As EVERYMAN *kneels with bowed
head before* CONFESSION, CONFESSION
places his left hand upon EVERYMAN'S
head. The music continues. CONFES-
SION *speaks with infinite compassion.*]

CONFESSION

CONFESSION: I know your sorrow well
Everyman.
Because you come to me with Knowledge,
I will comfort you as well as I can
and I will give you a precious jewel
called penance to protect you from
adversity.
With it you must punish your body.

[*He takes his hand from* EVERYMAN'S
*head. From his cloak, he takes out a
small whip with several thongs to it. At
the end of each thong is a small bit of
metal. He lifts this up with his left
hand. He speaks more sternly. The
music stops.*]

Remembering that your Saviour was
scourged for you,
that He suffered it patiently, as you
must do,
you must take the scourge which is
penance strong,
and punish yourself painfully and endure it long.
Knowledge will stay by you in this
voyage,
and soon Good-Deeds, strengthened,
will join you.

[*He gives the scourge to* EVERYMAN.
EVERYMAN *looks up at him wonderingly but takes it.* CONFESSION *speaks
more kindly again.*]

Let this be your comfort: you may be
sure
of mercy, for you will be saved.
Ask God's mercy. It will always be
granted.
Your time comes soon but never too
late.
When man mutilates himself with the
scourge of penance,

he oil of forgiveness will be poured over him.

CONFESSION *looks at the audience significantly, turns and goes out at the right.* EVERYMAN, *looking closely at the scourge, rises and goes to the center, crossing in front of* KNOWL-EDGE. *He speaks as he moves. As he crosses, she turns to follow him with her eyes.*]

EVERYMAN: Thanked be God for His gracious work!

Now I will begin my penance.

This has rejoiced and lightened my heart,

but the pain of penance frightens me still.

KNOWLEDGE *takes one step toward him. As she begins to speak, he turns and listens to her respectfully.*]

KNOWLEDGE: Everyman, be sure to fulfill your penance,

no matter what pain it gives to you,

and I am Knowledge who will give to you

the words to make your last account clearly.

[*Comforted by her words,* EVERYMAN *nods slowly. He looks at the whip once more and touches the bits of metal wonderingly. Suddenly, in a rush of penitence, he drops to his knees, clasps his hands—with the scourge between them—and begins to pray. He is facing the audience.* MUSIC CUE 18 *begins and continues throughout his prayer.*]

EVERYMAN: O eternal God, O vision of good!

By his disobedience Adam caused man to fall,

but Thou descended into a virgin pure

because Thou wouldst redeem Thy Everyman.

I cry for mercy in Thy presence,

O blessed Godhead, elect and divine.

O Ransomer of the world, Mirror of joy,

Founder of mercy, Illuminator of heaven and earth,

hear my clamorous complaint, late though it be.

Receive my prayers; though I be unworthy

in this heavy life, sinner most abominable,

yet let my name be written in Moses' table.

O Mary, pray to the Maker of all things

to help me at my ending

and to save me from the power of my enemy.

Death is assailing me strongly;

And Lady, pray that I may partake this day

of Thy Son's glory, saved by His passion.

[*The music stops.* EVERYMAN *rises, looks at* KNOWLEDGE.]

Knowledge, I will begin if God will give me grace.

In the name of the Holy Trinity,

my body shall now be cruelly punished.

[KNOWLEDGE *nods approvingly.* MUSIC CUE 19 *begins. The self-flagellation which follows may be done in either of two ways. It is suggested that both ways be worked out in rehearsals and that the director then choose whichever version seems more effective with his particular actors and for his prospective audience. The first way is to have* EVERYMAN *turn his back to the audience and whip himself with the scourge all over the body and face as he speaks. Although he does not actually strike himself hard, he should flinch, writhe, and twist as if in great and ecstatic pain. If the actor playing* EVERYMAN *knows how to dance, this might be done choreographically rather than realistically. The second way, which should be used if the first way seems in the least awkward, comic, or revolting, is to have* EVERYMAN *go off-stage at the right, crossing in front of* KNOWLEDGE, *and say his speech from there. If this way is used, sound effects of whipping should be added to the music. The speech should be sincerely delivered, and little cries of pain may well be interspersed in between phrases.* KNOWLEDGE *looks offstage in great sympathy.*]

Take this, body, for the sin of being
    flesh.
You took delight in being comfortable,
in being clean and fresh. Take this.
Close to damnation you brought me,
and therefore suffer strokes and pun-
    ishing.
Penance is saving me from the sharp
    fire of hell.

[*This last line is spoken in an ecstatic wail. At the end, the music stops.* EVERYMAN *drops to the floor in exhaustion if the first way of staging is used; or he enters from the right in a state of exhaustion, crosses to the center in front of* KNOWLEDGE, *and drops to the floor if the second way is used. As soon as he is motionless,* MUSIC CUE 20 *begins and* GOOD-DEEDS *enters from the left. She is standing upright and her head is held high. She speaks as she enters and continues to speak as she walks over to* EVERYMAN *to stand beside him. She picks up the book of accounts, and it no longer seems heavy for her.*]

GOOD-DEEDS: I thank God. Now I can
    walk and go.
I am delivered of my sickness and woe.
Therefore with Everyman I will go
to help him declare his good works.

[KNOWLEDGE *comes up to* EVERYMAN *and stands on the other side of him. The music stops.*]

KNOWLEDGE: Now, Everyman, be
    merry and glad.
Here is your Good-Deeds, whole and
    sound
and walking upright over the ground.

[EVERYMAN *turns to face the audience, his face illuminated with gratitude.*]

EVERYMAN: My heart is light, and
    evermore it shall be.
Now I will strike faster than I did
    before.

[*He lifts the scourge as if to strike himself again, but* GOOD-DEEDS *gently reaches out and quickly takes it from him. She hands it to* KNOWLEDGE, *then touches his face soothingly and speaks to him lovingly.*]

GOOD-DEEDS: Everyman, pilgrim, my
    special friend,
may you be blessèd without end.
For you is prepared the eternal glory.
You have made me healthy and sound,
therefore I shall stand by you on every
    occasion.

EVERYMAN: Welcome, my Good-
    Deeds; now I hear your voice,

nd I weep for the very sweetness of
its love.

*He buries his face in his hands and
egins to sob.* KNOWLEDGE *goes off to
ne right as she speaks. She leaves the
courge offstage. Then she picks up a
ong dark cloak which she immediately
rings back onstage. She takes the
loak to* EVERYMAN.]

NOWLEDGE: Be sad no more but
always rejoice.
od will soon receive you at his throne.
ut on this garment which fits you
now.
t is wet with your tears.

He looks up at her.]

VERYMAN: Gentle Knowledge, what
cloak do you call this?

*She lifts the cloak high, gradually
ringing it lower and lower as she
peaks.*]

NOWLEDGE: It is the garment of
Sorrow.
t will save you from pain
ecause it wins forgiveness from God.

*She looks directly, significantly and
ympathetically at the audience as she
nys the next line.*]

od is pleased with those who wear
ne garment of Sorrow well.

*She places it in his hands. He is still
neeling.*]

OOD-DEEDS: Everyman, will you wear
it? It will heal your wounds.

She takes it from him. KNOWLEDGE
elps her place the cloak about his
houlders. MUSIC CUE 21 *begins as*

*the cloak is being put on. Then he
rises and the music stops.*]

EVERYMAN: Now blessed be Jesus,
Mary's son!
Now I have put on pure contrition.
Let us go now without tarrying.

*He starts off toward the right, cross-
ing in front of* KNOWLEDGE. *As soon as
he is past her, he stops, turns and
speaks to* GOOD-DEEDS.]

Good-Deeds, have we clear our reckoning?

*GOOD-DEEDS lifts up the book of ac-
counts so that he can see it.*]

GOOD-DEEDS: Yes, indeed, I have it
here.

EVERYMAN: Then I trust we need not
fear.

He takes one step toward them.]

Now, friends, do not part from me.

KNOWLEDGE: No, Everyman, that we
will certainly not do.

*GOOD-DEEDS puts the book on the floor
well back out of the way.*]

FOR SHORTENED VERSION,

CUT THE FOLLOWING SCENE

GOOD-DEEDS: Yet you must also take
along with you
four persons of great might.

*EVERYMAN is slightly surprised at this.
As he speaks, he crosses quickly in
front of* KNOWLEDGE *and addresses*
GOOD-DEEDS.]

EVERYMAN: Who are they?

GOOD-DEEDS: Discretion and Strength
two are called.
The others are Five-Wits and Beauty.

[*As* KNOWLEDGE *begins to speak, he turns slightly and listens to her.*]

KNOWLEDGE: You must call them all together,
and they will hear you undoubtedly.

[*He nods solemnly, turns, crosses in front of* GOOD-DEEDS, *and moves to the left side of the acting area. He calls off toward the left.*]

EVERYMAN: My friends, come here and be present.
Discretion, Strength, my Five-Wits, and Beauty.

[MUSIC CUE 22. *As he calls each name again,* DISCRETION, STRENGTH, FIVE-WITS *and* BEAUTY *enter one at a time from the left in a stately procession. They form into a group at the center as far back from the audience as possible.* KNOWLEDGE *and* GOOD-DEEDS *are now standing at the right.* EVERYMAN *is at the left.*]

EVERYMAN: Discretion. Strength. Five-Wits. Beauty.

[*As soon as the procession has stopped moving, the music stops.* BEAUTY *speaks.*]

BEAUTY: Here we are, ready for your will.
What would you like us to do?

GOOD-DEEDS: To go with Everyman and help him
in his voyage. Will you go or not?

STRENGTH: We will go along with him.
We will help him and comfort him.

DISCRETION: Together we will all g
with him.

[EVERYMAN *drops to his knees, clasp his hands in prayer and looks upward.*

EVERYMAN: Almighty God, be Tho
loved.
I praise Thee for letting me call

[*As he names each one, he indicate each with a gesture.*]

Strength, Discretion, Beauty and Five
Wits.
I lack nothing, since I have also
my Good-Deeds, and Knowledge clea
I desire nothing more.

[*He bows his head.* STRENGTH, *cross ing in front of the others, goes t* EVERYMAN *and stands at his righ* MUSIC CUE 23.]

STRENGTH: And I, Strength, will stan
by you in distress
even if you should fight from th
ground
in a battle.

[*He puts his left hand on* EVERYMAN *right shoulder. The music stops.* FIVE WITS *crosses in front of* BEAUTY STRENGTH, *and* EVERYMAN. *He turn naturally to his left as soon as he past* EVERYMAN *and stands at* EVERY MAN'S *left, placing his right hand o* EVERYMAN'S *left shoulder.* MUSIC CU 24.]

FIVE-WITS: And though you trav
around the world,
I, your Five-Wits, will not for swee
nor sour
depart from you.

[*The music stops.* BEAUTY *crosses be hind the group and stands directly b* hind EVERYMAN. *She places one hand on each of* EVERYMAN'S *shoulders.* MUSIC CUE 25.]

BEAUTY: Nor will I, whatever else happens to you,
up to the hour
of your death.

[*The music stops.* DISCRETION *crosses behind* STRENGTH, BEAUTY *and* EVERYMAN. *She comes directly behind* EVERYMAN *and slightly to his left.* BEAUTY *removes her hands from* EVERYMAN'S *shoulders, moves slightly to the right and replaces her left hand on his right shoulder.* DISCRETION *places her right hand on his left shoulder. Thus the entire group is formed into a symmetrical picture.* MUSIC CUE 26.]

DISCRETION: Everyman, consider everything well.
All shall be well
while we are with you.

[*There is a pause. Then the music stops.* EVERYMAN *speaks impulsively.*]

EVERYMAN: My friends, listen to what I shall tell you,
for I am about to make my testament
here before all who are present.

[*With his arms he indicates the audience.*]

Half my worldly goods I will give
with these two arms to the poor,
in charity and with good intent.
This I do in spite of the fiend of hell,
and I declare myself out of his peril
this day and ever after.

[MUSIC CUE 27. *Everyone on stage raises his or her arms and shouts with joy.*]

ALL: This day and ever after!

[*The music stops.* EVERYMAN *rises and crosses toward* KNOWLEDGE. *As he crosses, she crosses in front of* GOODDEEDS *about two or three steps. They meet a little right of center.*]

KNOWLEDGE: Everyman, listen to what I say.
Go to the priesthood, I advise you,
and receive the holy sacrament.
Then return to us. We will wait for you here.

[EVERYMAN *turns to look at the others for verification.* FIVE-WITS *crosses in front of* DISCRETION, BEAUTY *and* STRENGTH, *and goes to him.*]

FIVE-WITS: Yes, Everyman, go there at once.
There is no emperor, king, duke nor baron
that has so much commission from God
as has the least priest in the world.
The priest bears the keys of the sacraments;
he holds the cures for man's redemption.

[KNOWLEDGE *lifts one finger high and speaks as if lecturing on a very important topic. She addresses the audience as much as she does* EVERYMAN.]

KNOWLEDGE: There are seven of the blessed sacraments.
These are baptism, confirmation, ordination of priests,
the sacrament of God's precious flesh and blood,
marriage, the holy extreme unction, and penance.
It is good to remember these seven;

they are the gracious sacraments of high divinity.

EVERYMAN: I would like to receive into me that holy body,
and so to the holy father I will meekly go.

FIVE-WITS: Everyman, that is the best you can do.

[EVERYMAN *crosses in front of* KNOWLEDGE *and goes out at the right.* FIVE-WITS *turns slightly and addresses the audience directly.*]

FIVE-WITS: God's priests are above angels in degree,

for with five words they may consecrate
God's body in flesh and blood for the sacrament.
The priest handles his Maker between his hands;
and he binds and unbinds all heaven's bands.

[KNOWLEDGE *lifts her hand warningly, steps to the right side and halfway behind* FIVE-WITS. *She also addresses the audience directly.*]

KNOWLEDGE: When priests are good priests, that is so surely,
But when Jesus hanged upon the cross

DISCRETION

STRENGTH

He freely gave, out of His blessed
heart,
the same sacrament in great torment.
Jesus did not sell it to us.

[FIVE-WITS *half turns to look over his
shoulder at* KNOWLEDGE *with a slightly
shocked expression.*]

Therefore Saint Peter the apostle says
that all they who buy or sell their God
or who take money for service have
Jesus' curse.
Sinful priests give sinners bad examples.

[FIVE-WITS *turns to the audience again,
nodding his head in agreement but insisting firmly on his point of view.*]

FIVE-WITS: I trust to God no such may
we find;
therefore let us honor the priesthood
and follow their doctrine for the sake
of our souls.
They are the shepherds, and we the
sheep.

ALL THE OTHERS: Amen.

FIVE-WITS: Peace, for yonder I see
Everyman coming.

[*He points offstage right.* GOOD-DEEDS
*moves quickly to the extreme right,
speaking happily as she moves.*]

GOOD-DEEDS: It is Everyman indeed.

FIVE-WITS

BEAUTY

[EVERYMAN *enters. He is holding a large wooden cross. He moves just past* GOOD-DEEDS *and addresses all who are on the stage.*]

EVERYMAN: Now Jesus give you all prosperity.
I have received the sacrament and the extreme unction.
Blessed be they who counselled me to take it.
I thank you for waiting for me.
Now each of you set your hand on this cross
and follow me. God be our guide.

[*He faces the audience, holding out the cross. All move quickly to him and kneel before him, their backs to the audience. From right to left, they are in the following order:* GOOD-DEEDS, KNOWLEDGE, FIVE-WITS, STRENGTH, BEAUTY *and* DISCRETION. *Each places a hand upon the cross.*]

STRENGTH: Everyman, we will not leave you
until your voyage is done.

DISCRETION: I, Discretion, will be with you also.

KNOWLEDGE: And though this pilgrimage be long and difficult,
I will never part from you.
Everyman, I will be as true to you
as I was to Judas Maccabee.

[MUSIC CUE 28. *All take their hands from the cross.* EVERYMAN *steps forward between* FIVE-WITS *and* STRENGTH. *As he does, he grows weaker and stumbles slightly. Without looking at him,* STRENGTH *puts out an arm quickly to support him. Then* STRENGTH *rises, turns and assists him. The music stops suddenly.*]

EVERYMAN: Alas, I am so faint I may not stand;
my limbs fold under me.

[*He turns, stumbling, to the right. He is still holding the cross up. He goes to the right side of the stage.* STRENGTH *does not follow him. The others turn and look after him anxiously. He stops, buckling slightly at the knees, turns toward the audience and passes one hand over his brow.* MUSIC CUE 29, *suggesting a call from the grave, begins quietly and yearningly.* EVERYMAN, *as if dead tired, turns and looks at the others.*]

Friends, let us continue not on the earth,
for into this cave I must creep now
and turn to the earth and there to sleep.

[*He indicates a cave, which is apparently offstage at the right.* BEAUTY *runs quickly to the right, crossing in front of* STRENGTH, FIVE-WITS, KNOWLEDGE, GOOD-DEEDS *and* EVERYMAN. *As she sees the grave, she screams in terror. The music stops.*]

BEAUTY: What, into this grave? Alas!

[*She begins to run toward the left. As she passes* EVERYMAN, *he seizes her. She begins to sob, struggling with him. In the struggle, she falls on her knees. The others, except* GOOD-DEEDS *and* KNOWLEDGE, *look horrified.*]

EVERYMAN: Yes, there you, Beauty, shall be more loved and less.

[*She crouches before him, shivering with fright.*]

BEAUTY: But what—? I should smother there.

EVERYMAN: Yes, and nevermore appear above.
We shall live no longer in this world,
but only in heaven with the highest Lord.

[*She rises but he still holds her.*]

BEAUTY: Cross out everything I said;
adieu, by Saint John.
I take my cap in my lap and am gone.

[*She pulls away from him and runs to the left in front of all the others.*]

EVERYMAN: What, Beauty, where are you going?

[*She stops a moment before going out but she does not look behind her.*]

BEAUTY: Be still, I am deaf. I will not look behind me,
even if you were to give me all the gold in your chest.

[*She runs out at the left.* EVERYMAN *looks appealingly at the others. They look at one another in suspicion and distrust.*]

EVERYMAN: Alas, whom can I trust?
Beauty is running away, yet
she promised to live and die with me.

[STRENGTH *takes one step forward, lifts his chest and speaks firmly.*]

STRENGTH: Everyman, I must forsake you also.
I do not like this game at all.

[EVERYMAN *crosses in front of* GOOD-DEEDS, KNOWLEDGE *and* FIVE-WITS. *He clasps* STRENGTH *around the waist.*]

EVERYMAN: Will you all forsake me?
Strength, sweet Strength, tarry a little while.

[STRENGTH *shakes him loose easily.* EVERYMAN *falls to the ground.*]

STRENGTH: No, I will go from you fast
though you should weep until your heart breaks.

[EVERYMAN *looks up at* STRENGTH.]

EVERYMAN: You said you would always remain with me.

[STRENGTH *folds his arms and towers over* EVERYMAN. *He speaks as if to a small boy or a coward.*]

STRENGTH: I have brought you far enough.
You are old enough, I believe,
to take the rest of your journey by yourself.
I am sorry that I came so far.

EVERYMAN: Strength, I am to blame if you are displeased.
Will you break your promise to me?

[STRENGTH *laughs suddenly.*]

STRENGTH: Strength has never cared for promises.
You are but a fool to complain.
You spend your speech and waste your brain.
Go thrust yourself into the ground.

[*He stalks out at the left, crossing in front of* DISCRETION *to do so.* EVERYMAN, *without rising, faces the audience and addresses them directly.*]

EVERYMAN: I thought surely I had found Strength.
He that trusts in his own Strength
is deceived in the end.
Both Strength and Beauty forsake me,
yet both made me fair and loving promises.

[DISCRETION *tiptoes up to* EVERYMAN *and kneels behind him. She speaks gently.*]

DISCRETION: Everyman, after Strength is gone, I cannot stay.
As for me, I will leave you alone.

[EVERYMAN *looks up suddenly in renewed agony.*]

EVERYMAN: Why, Discretion, you will not forsake me?

[*She rises, looks off toward the left.*]

DISCRETION: Yes, I will go from you now,
for when Strength goes, Discretion always follows.

[*He turns, seizes her robe.*]

EVERYMAN: Yet, I pray you, for the love of the Trinity,
look in my grave once with one glance of pity.

[*He indicates the grave with a gesture. She shakes her head in gentle reproof. Then she takes his hand which is still clutching at her robe, loosens it carefully and steps back.*]

DISCRETION: No, so near a grave I never come. Farewell!

[*She glides out quickly at the left.* EVERYMAN *turns to address the audience again.*]

EVERYMAN: O, all things fail, save God alone.
Beauty, Strength, Discretion, all
run from me rapidly at last
when Death blows his final blast.

[*His voice growing fainter and fainter as he speaks,* FIVE-WITS *circles slowly around behind* EVERYMAN, *keeping a considerable distance from him.*]

FIVE-WITS: Everyman, even I must leave you now.
I follow the others. I forsake you here.

[*He pauses a moment at the left exit while* EVERYMAN *speaks in despair.*]

EVERYMAN: Alas! Then well may I weep.
I took you, Five-Wits, for my best friend.

[*He covers his face with his hands.*]

FIVE-WITS: I shall no longer keep you from Death.
Now farewell; this is the end of me.

[FIVE-WITS, *his voice dying away to nothingness, exits quickly at the left. There is a pause during which* EVERYMAN, *his body racked with audible sobs, is collapsed in hopeless despair. Suddenly he rises violently, throws his arms up and gives a great cry of anguish.*]

EVERYMAN: O Jesus, help, all have forsaken me!

[GOOD-DEEDS *crosses in front of* KNOWLEDGE *and speaks comfortingly to* EVERYMAN.]

GOOD-DEEDS: No, Everyman, I will stay with you.
I shall not forsake you.
You will find me a good friend in need.

[EVERYMAN *embraces her gratefully.*]

EVERYMAN: God give you mercy, Good-Deeds.
Now I know which friends are friends.
I loved them all better than I loved you.

He crosses in front of GOOD-DEEDS
and speaks to KNOWLEDGE.]

Knowledge, will you forsake me also?

SHORTENED VERSION

RESUMES HERE.

ADD ONE LINE BY EVERYMAN:

"Knowledge, you will not forsake me
at the end?"

KNOWLEDGE: Yes, Everyman, when
you come to the final moment,
but not yet no matter what the danger.

EVERYMAN: God give you mercy,
Knowledge, with all my heart.

KNOWLEDGE: I do not depart from
here
until I see where you go.

EVERYMAN: And I think that I must go
to make my reckoning and to pay my
debts,
for my time is nearly spent away.

He speaks directly to the audience.]

Take example from me, all you
who hear or see me in this play.
See how those I loved the best
forsake me, all except Good-Deeds.
Good-Deeds only remains with me.

*In the shortened version, he crosses in
front of* KNOWLEDGE *to* GOOD-DEEDS;
*in the regular version, he merely turns
to her. They smile at one another.
Then* GOOD-DEEDS *addresses the audience directly.*]

GOOD-DEEDS: All earthly things are but
vanity.
Beauty, Strength, Discretion always
forsake man.

Foolish friends and relatives speak fair
but always fly in opposite directions.

She speaks to EVERYMAN *again.*]

I, Good-Deeds, will never leave you
when you die.

He kneels and prays.]

EVERYMAN: Have mercy on me, God
most mighty;
and stand by me, Mother and Maid,
Holy Mary.

*She speaks to him reassuringly. Both
are looking up.*]

GOOD-DEEDS: Fear not. I will speak for
you.

A final sudden physical pain comes to
EVERYMAN. *He cries out.*]

EVERYMAN: I cry to God: mercy!

*She speaks soothingly. As she speaks,
his pain seems to subside.*]

GOOD-DEEDS: Our end is short; our
pain diminishes.
Let us go and never come again.

[MUSIC CUE 30. EVERYMAN *lifts up his
hands to God in quiet resignation. The
music continues softly behind his final
prayer.*]

EVERYMAN: Into Thy hands, Lord, I
commend my soul.
Receive it, Lord, that it be not lost.
As Thou bought me from sin, so defend me
and save me from the boast of the
fiend.
Let me appear with the blessed host
that shall be saved on the day of
doom.
Into Thy hands, I commend my spirit.

[*He rises, gripped with sudden and violent pains. He falls to the ground and dies. The music fades away gradually. When it has stopped,* KNOWLEDGE *addresses the audience directly.*]

KNOWLEDGE: Now he has suffered
    what we all shall endure.
Everyman has made his ending.

[MUSIC CUE 31 *begins.*]

I think I hear angels singing
and making great joy and melody
at the place where EVERYMAN'S soul is
    to be received.

[*She walks to the right, takes a long look at the grave, then turns slowly and goes out at the left, crossing in front of* GOOD-DEEDS *and the body of* EVERYMAN. *The music swells exultingly, and the* ANGEL *enters from the right. She stops just inside the entrance. The music diminishes as she begins to speak to* EVERYMAN.]

ANGEL: Come, elected and excellent
    spouse to Jesus,
come above with me because of your
    singular virtue.
I take your soul from your body;
your reckoning is crystal-clear.
Come with me into the heavenly
    sphere

[*The* ANGEL *turns and addresses the audience directly.*]

into which you all shall come
if you live life well before the day of
    doom.

[*She backs slowly offstage. The music becomes powerful, exultant, climactic: it tells of the resurrection of the soul.* EVERYMAN *rises slowly to his feet,* looks wonderingly about him, the* looks at GOOD-DEEDS *who smiles back at him reassuringly. She picks up th* book of accounts. They go out slowl* at the right. The* DOCTOR *enters from the left. The music stops as he begin* to speak.*]

DOCTOR: You listeners, old and young
    take this away:
this moral for all men as shown in ou*
    play.
Forsake pride, for he deceives you i*
    the end,
and remember that Beauty, Five-Wits
Fellowship, Strength and Discretion
forsake Everyman at the last.

[*He walks to the center.* MUSIC CU*
32 *begins softly.*]

Good-Deeds only can you take wit*
    you,
but if they are small and weak, yo*
    have no help at all.
There is no excuse for Everyman.
Alas, how shall he face living, then?
After death it is too late to mak*
    amends,
for mercy and pity forsake him then.

[*He walks to the right and looks off
stage.*]

If his reckoning is wrong when h*
    stands before God,
God will cast him downward for a*
    eternity,
but he that has his account complet*
    and sound
shall be crowned and placed high i*
    heaven;

[*The* DOCTOR *turns, comes back to th*
center, and faces the audience.*]

unto which place God bring us all
that we may live together body and
  soul.
May the Trinity help us in that!
Will the audience please say "Amen"
  to this

for the sake of Saint Charity?

AUDIENCE: Amen.

[*The* DOCTOR *goes out at the left. The
music swells to a great Amen and then
slowly dies away.*]

EVERYMAN
MUSIC CUE 1

MUSIC CUE 2

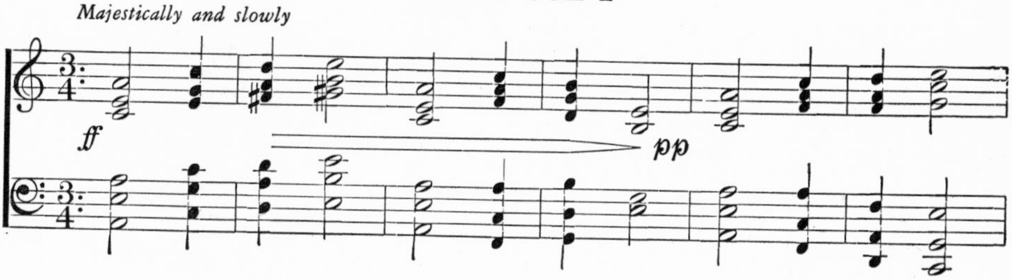

MUSIC CUE 3

MUSIC CUE 4

MUSIC CUE 5

EVERYMAN

MUSIC CUE 6: *Repeat Music Cue 3.*

MUSIC CUE 7

MUSIC CUE 8

MUSIC CUE 9

MUSIC CUE 10

MUSIC CUE 11

MUSIC CUE 12: *Repeat Music Cue 11.*

MUSIC CUE 13

MUSIC CUE 14

MUSIC CUE 15

EVERYMAN

MUSIC CUE 16

MUSIC CUE 17

MUSIC CUE 18

Slowly and with great feeling

Play twice

MUSIC CUE 19: *Repeat Music Cue 17.*

EVERYMAN

MUSIC CUE 20

MUSIC CUE 21

MUSIC CUE 22

MUSIC CUE 23

MUSIC CUE 24

MUSIC CUE 25

MUSIC CUE 26

MUSIC CUE 27: *Repeat Music Cue 26.*

MUSIC CUE 28

MUSIC CUE 29: *Last 11 measures of Music Cue 1.*

MUSIC CUE 30

MUSIC CUE 31: *Repeat twice slowly Music Cue 5.*

MUSIC CUE 32

Suggestions for the Director

Suggestions for the Director

Producing a good play is fun. But if the preparatory process and the rehearsals are not carefully organized, the fun soon turns into disappointment. There will be frayed nerves, temperamental outbursts, antagonisms where once friendships existed, and a painful kind of stagefright caused by embarrassing mistakes during the performance itself. On the other hand, if well handled, the rehearsal and presentation of a play can be one of the most rewarding of human experiences. This is especially true if the play is one with rich spiritual content, such as those in this volume. Socially, the undertaking can be an adventure the participants will always remember and cherish. Spiritually, it can lead to a deeper appreciation of the great truths of the Christian religion and to an insight into their application in our daily living. The suggestions that follow are designed to help the director who wishes to make sure that the performance of his group will be worth all the time and energy expended on it.

I. Planning the Production

STUDY THE PLAY THOROUGHLY FIRST

The first thing the director should do is to read the play as closely and as often as necessary to know it as well as if he had written it himself. This reading and rereading should be done before meeting the cast for the first rehearsal. In fact, most of it should be done even before selecting the cast.

This is not a dull task when the play has literary merit. On a cheap, inferior play, each successive rereading becomes more boring as the prospective director discovers the thinness and emptiness of it, but on a well written play, each successive rereading brings greater awareness of the depth of its values and more enthusiasm over the challenging prospect of bringing it to an audience.

A director may read each time with a different objective in his mind. In one reading, he will look at the play from the point of view of the story line. What is the basic story? Where is its climax? How does it build up to this? Since drama always has conflict, where is this conflict and how often does each opposing force get the upper hand? Which force finally wins out?

In another reading, the director may concentrate on character and character development. What are these people like individually? What effect do they have upon one another? What happens inside each one's mind as he says the lines given him by the playwright? Does each one change in any way during the course of the play, and if so, what causes this change?

In still another reading, the director may think of the audience reaction. Where will the audience find the "big moments" of the play? What parts will they find unclear and difficult to follow (and can something be done by the actors to help clarify these spots)? What should the audience carry away after the performance as the supreme thought or message of the play?

Through all these readings, the director should never forget his first reactions to the play during the initial reading. This may be, in some ways, the reaction most similar to that an audience will have. An audience will be hearing these particular words and seeing these particular actions for the first time. They must get as much as possible in one "exposure." A director should frequently, in his mind, compare his first reactions with his later ones. How can he help his actors retain the freshness and spontaneity of that first emotional impact? Also, how can the action of living performers bring out to an audience the values missed in his first "private reading" of the play from a book? The memory of his first reading will be a valuable tool not only in planning the production but also throughout the rehearsal period. In fact, the sincere director who wishes to perfect his craft will learn many valuable lessons for future productions from a comparative study of his first reading and the audience reaction to the performance itself.

CONFER WITH THE PROPER AUTHORITIES

As soon as a director or a group has decided to produce a play, arrangements should be made with the proper authorities. Although this seems an obvious step, it is surprising how often this is put off until it creates a problem of some sort, such as a conflict in scheduling. This, therefore, should be done as early as possible.

Many questions must be considered in this regard, and of course these will vary from group to group. Does permission to do the play need to be secured from higher authorities? This should be done first thing, of course. Then, will rehearsals need to be scheduled in the church, and if so, who should be seen to arrange for this? Will the church janitor need to be contacted to make arrangements for heating, lighting, keys to locked rooms, etc.? What arrangements will have to be made for scheduling the performance itself in the service? Exactly what will precede it? Exactly what will follow it? If printed programs are to be used, who is to prepare this program copy and to see it through the press? What will this person need to know? And how far in advance? A little foresight in arranging these matters will eliminate many problems that might become increasingly difficult to solve later on.

HAVE A TENTATIVE REHEARSAL SCHEDULE READY

Even before choosing the cast, it is well to have a tentative rehearsal schedule ready. It is easier to make slight changes in a planned schedule than it is to formulate one as you go along that will be satisfactory to everyone. If most people at try-outs are informed that a certain number of rehearsals will be required and that these will most likely be held on particular evenings, they will usually accept the schedule without quibbling. On the other hand, if you wait to "see what is best for everyone," you will probably find that each person has "nights he cannot come" and it may be an impossible job of coordination to find a schedule that will suit everyone.

The total number of rehearsals for any one of the plays in Book I should not be less than twelve. Each rehearsal should last approximately two hours. A shorter period may seem like wasted time for those who have to travel a considerable distance to get to the rehearsal. A longer period may lead to weariness and boredom.

It is actually better to schedule rehearsals on consecutive days immediately preceding the performance, but this is not always possible for non-professionals who have busy lives of their own and other commitments. The director will know the conditions in his own community best and should work out a schedule which will bring rehearsals as close together as possible without working undue hardships on his group. In any case, the final dress rehearsal should be arranged for the day or evening immediately before the performance. It should not be held on the same day as the performance, however, as this takes the edge off the freshness and vitality which a "rested" cast can give to a play.

II. *Casting*

INFORM THOSE INTERESTED
WELL IN ADVANCE

Announcements for the holding of try-outs should be made well in advance so that everyone interested will be notified. Last minute announcements may not reach some people at all; still others may be notified too late to change plans already made for those specific times. This may lead to feelings that the drama group is a closed clique open only to the immediate friends of the director. Such suspicions should be vigorously discouraged by announcing open try-outs to all interested persons well before they are held.

Occasionally a director will feel that for a first play, some already established small group should produce it and that try-outs should be limited to this special group which has already in some way indicated its interest in drama. This is all right for one production if it is the first time the church is attempting such a project, but it should not become the general policy. To discourage new talent because "old-timers always get the good parts anyway" is one of the quickest ways to foster the decline of a dramatics group. Snobbery, clique-forming, favoritism, or secrecy and haste in holding try-outs, are not only unsound artistically; they are also examples of the opposite kind of behavior it is hoped these plays with their Christian messages will promote. Everyone in the community who wants to try-out, talented or not, should at least be allowed to make the attempt.

Notice may be given by announcing try-outs on two successive Sundays before they are actually held. If mimeographed or printed brochures of the service are used, short announcements may be made in these on two successive Sundays. If the church sponsors any kind of bulletin or magazine, notice may be given in this way. If there is a bulletin board in a corridor or outside the church, notice may be posted there. Every available means of notifying the public should be used so that no one can complain that he was "deliberately left out" by not having been informed.

HOLD TRY-OUTS AT A
CENTRAL LOCATION

Probably the best place to hold try-outs is at the church itself. If a basement or separate room is available, it will probably be more satisfactory than the main part of the church as it will promote more informality and naturalness and will minimize the natural embarrassment of people trying out.

The tone or atmosphere set right at the beginning by the director or by those in charge is very important. A tactless, insensitive, or disorganized person can create additional embarrassment and confusion. A sympathetic but methodical person is best for taking charge of try-outs. Most people trying out are embarrassed anyway by feelings of inferiority, the desire "not to be first," or uneasy suspicions that they are making fools of themselves. The one who sets the atmosphere of the try-out session can dispel these fears or he can increase them. More work can be accomplished if the giggles, the coyness and the embarrassment can be eliminated.

It is wise to keep a record of everyone trying out. Names, addresses, telephone numbers, and any other information that might be needed should be entered on separate cards. During the readings, notes can be taken by the director on voice quality, ability to move without awkwardness, fitness for the role, or any other comments he may need in order to refresh his memory later when the time comes to make a final choice. These notes should not be shown to anyone during the try-out period.

There should be several copies of the play at the try-out session. It is usually better to read scenes, that is, to have people try out in groups rather than individually. This lessens embarrassment. More important, it allows the director to see how well people play together. It is best to ask them to stand while they read and even to have them suggest, if they will, a certain amount of basic movement (but not specific details or complicated actions such as falling on the floor which might at this point merely lead to awkwardness, embarrassment and unintentional humor).

Each person should be allowed to try out for several parts. The director should be careful not to indicate favoritism or any closing of his mind to future possibilities. Some of the group may request others to read certain roles, and this should certainly be allowed and encouraged. Everyone present should assist in the reading, even those who "merely came along to visit." Usually this is only an indication of shyness or a way of forestalling feelings of failure if they do not get a part. Sometimes, of course, they really do not want to be in the play. But in either case, it is well to ask them to help out by reading some part "not to try out for it but just to help someone else who is reading for another part."

No indication should be given at the end of the try-outs as to how the director is thinking. An inexperienced director can get into difficulty by "seeming to promise" certain roles to certain people; he will then be accused of "changing his mind afterward." Everyone should be thanked sincerely and warmly, even those who did not do well. They should be told that they will be informed of the final casting by a certain date.

THE DIRECTOR SHOULD HAVE THE FINAL WORD ON CASTING

Sometimes groups like to use a casting committee rather than to have the director make the selection. There are possible dangers in this system. Committee members may not agree. They may talk about their deliberations outside the committee meeting and cause feelings to be hurt. They may choose actors with whom the director will not be able to work well. If the committee system is used, the director should at least be a member of the committee and should be given final veto on the actors selected. It is probably better if such a committee thinks of itself merely as an advisory one.

The better system is probably to leave it entirely up to the director. Casting is a hard problem, full of many worries and conflicting desires, and weighted with the double responsibility of securing the best possible cast and of being fair to the people who want to act. If the director alone chooses the cast, he is solely responsible and cannot "pass the buck" if someone does not work out well. The chances are that, in his own private deliberations, the director will be able to choose a better cast with more fairness to everyone than if a group chooses the cast.

THOSE NOT CAST SHOULD BE INFORMED TACTFULLY

It is sometimes difficult to inform those who are not to receive a part, of this decision; but it is unfair not to do so. The director who lacks courage at this point and who allows those not cast to find out by indirect methods merely makes himself despicable. Most people respect the difficulty of the director's position and will be gracious about not getting a part if they are told directly and honestly.

They should always be thanked for trying out and encouraged to try again the next time a play is produced. It can usually be made clear to them that several people were competent for each part, that the director had a hard time making his decision, and that he finally had to choose only one person to play each part. The individual can then be asked to help the production by taking charge of props, making costumes, or merely with encouragement and good wishes. Sometimes the best and most reliable production workers will come from this group; sometimes the most enthusiastic supporters of the next proposal that a play be done will come from those who did not succeed in getting a part the first time.

THOSE CAST SHOULD BE INFORMED CAREFULLY

This task is as pleasant as the former is unpleasant, but there are dangers if it is not done right. When informing those cast, the director may reveal all the pride and enthusiasm he rightfully feels, but he must be careful not to encourage egotism or temperamental behavior. Each cast member should be given to understand that, although he was good at try-outs, he has yet to prove this to the audience. He will be expected to work hard, to learn his lines early, to attend all rehearsals on time, to put forth his best effort at each rehearsal (and not "save himself for the performance"), and to develop the best possible characterization for his part. In other words, the director should emphasize that he has great faith in the potentiality of his cast but that it is, at this point, only potentiality.

THE FINAL REHEARSAL SCHEDULE
SHOULD BE DISTRIBUTED

The tentative schedule should be shown to every cast member, and he should agree to attend all the rehearsals. If some problem arises, it should be ironed out at this point before the first rehearsal is held. The schedule may be changed if all agree to change it, but everyone in the cast should be given a chance to agree; and the final decision should be unanimous. If agreement cannot be reached, the original schedule should stand, and the person who cannot make a rehearsal should be thanked pleasantly but removed from the cast and replaced by someone else who can. It is better to have a "merely good" cast which is present at every rehearsal than to have a "perfect" cast with some members absent at rehearsals.

Each person should then have a written copy of the complete rehearsal schedule including time starting, time ending, and place. About halfway through at some definite rehearsal, the schedule should be marked, *"All lines learned at this point."* Each rehearsal should be devoted to accomplishing some specific objective such as blocking out action, working for characterization, or polishing up timing. (See below for a typical rehearsal schedule.)

III. *Conducting Rehearsals*

BE TACTFUL WITH THE ACTORS

Inexperienced directors sometimes use sarcasm or lose their tempers too frequently. Sarcasm is almost never effective, and anger is effective only if it is both justified and controlled. Actors are often sensitive and easily hurt, and the director should try to deal with them tactfully. This may sometime require self-control, but it is necessary in order to maintain a happy group and, therefore, an animated production.

BE WILLING TO MAKE DECISIONS

At the same time, no one likes a wishy-washy director. A good director like any good leader, is not afraid to assume authority. Although he does not abuse his authority, he knows how to be firm and decisive. He must sometimes arbitrate disagreements that arise among the actors without wasting time in pointless argument. When necessary, he must be firm in censuring lateness, laziness, and general "horsing around."

INSIST THAT THE ACTORS BE HEARD

This is probably the most important requirement of a performance. No matter how effective it may be in other ways, the play is a failure if the audience cannot hear the words. It is frequently necessary to remind the actors of this at rehearsals, for actors sometimes work only for realism in acting, and in real life people do not always talk loudly. In a play, however even whispering and mumbled talk must be heard. In other words, one thing that is never "lifelike" in a play is the additional projection of the voice so that people sitting at the back of the church can hear every word.

Inexperienced actors rarely project their voices properly until directors insist on it. If music teachers or speech teachers are available to show your cast how to breathe abdominally, this will help immeasurably. If not, you must simply do the best you can by insisting on clear enunciation and sufficient volume. It will help if, at several rehearsals, the director sits far back from the actors and stops them whenever they cannot be heard easily. He must remember also that he is used to the words in the play and so may sometimes have the illusion of hearing when projection is actually insufficient.

INSIST THAT THE ACTORS LISTEN
AND REACT APPROPRIATELY
WHILE NOT SPEAKING

Inexperienced actors sometimes get the notion that they are supposed to act only when they have lines to say. Thus they assume the roles while speaking and then drop out of character into their own personalities while someone else is speaking. The director must insist that they listen carefully each time to the words of the others and respond to these words as if they were actually the characters they represent.

A good play enables the audience to forget that "it is only a play" and to fall into the pleasant illusion that it is really happening. This cannot be achieved when actors drop out of character by giggling self-consciously, by looking bored, or by developing that glazed look which proves they are not really listening to the others.

Occasionally an actor will insist that

he need not remain in character at rehearsals, but that he will remain so at the performance itself. Experience does not bear this out. An actor who does not stay in character during rehearsals is even more likely to "break" (drop out of character) when actually before an audience. He must practice this difficult job of concentration at rehearsals.

DO NOT LET THE ACTORS
MOVE UNLESS THERE IS A
REASON TO MOVE

Inexperienced actors sometimes move about in tentative little movements, or they sway and teeter on their feet. They should be told to stand still when not moving and to move definitely and completely when they are supposed to move. No movement should be made without a reason. Reasons for movement include the demands of the plot, mental states or impulses of the characters, or merely mannerisms or traits of the characters.

A good production has movement, of course, and sometimes plays seem static and visually dull if actors just stand around and do not shift positions once in a while. Every movement must have some specific motivation, however, so that it will look natural and spontaneous.

KEEP THE ACTORS SINCERE
AND NATURAL

There are many approved styles of acting, but for inexperienced actors and for these particular plays, the best style is simple realism. This means being as sincere and natural as possible. All traces of "hamminess" or artificiality should be discouraged by the director. Be careful of the actor who seems to "listen to the sound of his own beautiful voice." Children act naturally when they play "let's pretend"; adults should act a play in the same way. They should relax, let themselves go, imagine what they would do and think if they were really the characters they are playing, and forget about showing off magnificent voices or accomplished acting techniques.

DO NOT LET THE ACTORS MAKE
THE VERSE SING-SONGY

The pronounced rhythm of these medieval plays does not need to be pushed or forced. The musical qualities of rhyme, meter, alliteration, assonance, hidden sound effects of various kinds, and other poetic devices are meant to be unobtrusive. If it helps the actors to avoid a sing-songy quality, they can be asked to think of it as if it were prose. The additional rhythmic pleasure afforded by the poetic form of these plays is effective only if subtle and hidden. Actors insult the intelligence of the audience if they seem to fear the audience will not know it is poetry and so push the rhythm in an obvious sing-songy delivery. The rhythms of normal, conversational talk will bring out the best poetic values of these plays.

CHECK ALWAYS TO MAKE SURE
THE AUDIENCE WILL BE ABLE TO
SEE AS CLEARLY AS POSSIBLE

Audiences want to see as well as to hear the play. Actors should not accidentally cover one another; that is, they should not stand between the audience and some other actor so that he is not seen clearly. If a large group is on stage, the actors normally should open up; that is, the characters closer to the audience should be placed at the sides so that every part of the total picture is clearly visible to as much of the audience as possible. This is also the reason for the old rule about not turning one's back to the audience. Although this is no longer a hard-and-fast rule, it must always be remembered by the director that each person in the audience, no matter where he sits, wants to see as much of the play as possible. Without sacrificing too much naturalness, then, the director should see that all important action in the play is clearly visible.

INSIST ON EARLY MEMORIZATION
OF LINES

Some amateurs apparently believe that lines should be learned by the evening of the performance. This is far too late. They should be learned well in advance, and at least half of the rehearsals should be held after all actors have memorized their lines. Learning lines well in advance will eliminate the possibility of prompting, that sure giveaway of amateurishness. It will also enable the actors to coordinate words and actions more efficiently and to grow in their roles at each rehearsal. Then the performance itself will be fluent, smooth, and polished.

PLAN EACH REHEARSAL CAREFULLY
AND KEEP TO YOUR SCHEDULE
SO AS NOT TO WASTE TIME

A typical rehearsal schedule might go as follows:

> Rehearsal 1: *Reading Rehearsal.*
> Read through the play from the
> books. Discuss the play but do

not try to act it out. Make sure everyone understands the content thoroughly. Measurements for costumes might also be taken at this session.

Rehearsal 2: *Blocking-out the Action.* Set up the rehearsal room approximately the way the playing area will be. Go through the basic action of the play along with the words. That is, entrances, exits, crosses, kneeling, etc., should be done. In this way, the actors memorize the actions along with the process of familiarizing themselves with the lines.

Rehearsal 3: *Developing Characterizations.* Although actions should be gone through at this and all subsequent rehearsals, the main concentration at this rehearsal should be on understanding the characters and on trying to assume the mental attitudes and specific thoughts of the characters.

Rehearsal 4: *Interpretation of Lines.* Although the director and actors will already have been working on this as a matter of course, it would be wise at this rehearsal to concentrate on meaning of lines. The director should make sure that the actors understand every word and every line clearly. Then he should make sure that they project this accurate interpretation to a listener. All details of line delivery should be worked out. Incidentally, imitating the director's tone of voice is a bad way to handle this. Actors should be made to get the right delivery by understanding what the lines mean. When they have the wrong inflection, the wrong stress, or the wrong pausing, it is usually because they do not understand the meaning correctly. Explanations are better than forced imitation of tone.

Rehearsal 5: *Coordination of Word and Action.* Have all lines learned by this rehearsal. At the first rehearsal without scripts, actors will probably stumble around and need to be prompted. This is only natural. It is a good idea to have a prompter available other than yourself to feed them lines when they forget. It is also good to have substitute props and suggestions of difficult costumes (such as capes) at this rehearsal, even though the actual props and costumes will undoubtedly not be available yet.

Rehearsal 6: *Projecting Characterizations.* At this rehearsal, all things worked on before should continue to be worked on if they need it. In addition, however, the director should see to it that the characterizations "come across." All facial expressions, gestures and bits of action should be large enough to be seen and understood clearly by the audience. Characterizations should be consistent and believable. Overly subtle interpretations may be lifelike, but if they will be unnoticed or a source of confusion to the audience, they should either be enlarged or omitted altogether.

Rehearsal 7: *Projecting Moods and Emotions*. At this rehearsal, the director should work to see that everyone stays in the mood of the play, concentrates on establishing the proper atmosphere, and re-creates the actual emotions of the characters insofar as they are able to do. At the same time, everything must be kept simple and convincing.

Rehearsal 8: *Rhythm and Tempo Rehearsal*. At this time, the director should check to see that the pace is neither too fast nor too slow. If it is too fast, it will be confusing for an audience to follow and so will actually seem to "drag." If it is too slow, it will seem dull and the illusion of reality will be spoiled by distractions in the minds of the audience members. Major and minor climaxes should also be carefully built up in intensity with periods of a more relaxed nature in between these "builds to climaxes."

Rehearsal 9: *Costume Session and Quick Run-Through*. At this meeting, all characters can try on their costumes for approval. Notes can be made of changes to be made. Following this, the show can be run through, quickly and without stopping, to give practice in continuity. This will also help establish the proper rhythm and tempo. During this rehearsal, the director can take critical notes, and afterward he can read these to the cast. If necessary, any weak spots can be repeated in rehearsal.

Rehearsal 10: *Polishing Rehearsal*. Use all the real props at this rehearsal. Work on all the details that need to be ironed out. During breaks and after the rehearsal, the costume people can check costume details.

Rehearsal 11: *First Dress Rehearsal*. All costumes, props, and music should be used at this rehearsal. Stops should be made frequently to iron out all the rough spots.

Rehearsal 12: *Final Dress Rehearsal*. This should run exactly like a performance without stopping. Transitions from the rest of the church service should be indicated before and after the play. The play should be timed by someone with a good watch. The director should take notes and read them afterward to the actors, the costume people, the props people, and the organist.

USE COMMON SENSE AND LEADERSHIP

If a director remembers all these things, he may still fail if he does not use the principles of good common sense. Many matters may come up which could never be foreseen by the editor of this book. Drama is a group art which thrives on common sense, ingenuity, and imagination. In fact, the qualities that make a good leader in any field are valuable attributes for a play director to apply.

IV. *Running the Performance*

BEFORE THE PERFORMANCE, BE CALM

If a play has been sufficiently rehearsed, and if the costumes and props are organized, there is no reason for anyone to be unduly nervous. A certain amount of excitement and stage-fright is only natural; it will, in fact, help make the performance vitalized. There is no sound reason, however, for the frantic behavior of some amateur directors and actors. See that everyone arrives well ahead of time. Give them a brief talk wishing them luck if you want to, but do not burden them with last minute instructions which merely increase their nervousness and which they will not remember at this point anyway. Above all, be calm. A confident attitude on the part of the director reassures the cast better than anything else. It proves to them that you have faith in their ability to do a good job.

DURING THE PERFORMANCE,
SIT OUT FRONT

In some amateurish productions, the director stays backstage and gets in everyone's way. The director's place is out front where he can observe the actors as if he were an average audience member. He can then judge his own work and theirs more accurately and objectively. He can also observe and analyze the audience reactions.

AFTER THE PERFORMANCE,
GO BACKSTAGE

It is customary for the director to go backstage after the performance, however, to let each actor know "how he did." If it is the final performance, the director should remember to thank individually the cast and those who worked on props, costumes, and music.

SHORTLY AFTER THE PERFORMANCE,
SEE THAT ALL PROPS AND COSTUMES
ARE DISPOSED OF PROPERLY

People often forget that after a performance, a play is not over. Props, if borrowed, should be returned with thanks. Costumes, if borrowed, should be sent to the cleaners first and then returned with thanks. If props and costumes belong to the group, they should be carefully stored away for possible future use.

FIND OUT THE AUDIENCE REACTIONS

Besides the reactions he notices at the performance itself, the director should, in the days after the performance, try to get frank opinions from those who have seen the play. He may consider such questions as the following: Was the play a success? What was weak about it? What was strong? Should another play be tried again next year? Could a play of this type become something of a tradition in our church?

Few things bring more happiness than looking back on a play which has been well planned, well cast, well rehearsed, and well produced. The more hard work put into it, the greater the satisfactions. It is sometimes difficult to get the first play through all four steps. Beginning directors may occasionally be a little discouraged by unforeseen problems, but once the play has been put on, the problems and difficulties are quickly forgotten. Only the glow of satisfaction remains. After a good play, it is never long before people are asking impatiently, "When are we going to put on the next one?"

V. *Scenery and Lighting**

There is considerable difference of opinion among theatre experts as to how these old plays should be staged. Some would have them done up like Broadway musicals with elaborate sets and intricate lighting effects. It is the opinion of others that since these plays are written with extreme simplicity, since they are meant to be performed in churches, and since in any case the visual emphasis should be on the actors, it is more artistic to do them without scenery. After weighing all the arguments on both sides, the editor is convinced that the latter group is right.

The best place to present these plays is in the church. This naturally fits in well with our proposed use of them as parts of actual services. If they are to be done elsewhere, some scenic touches might be used to suggest a churchlike atmosphere. Actual scenery and lighting, however, should be kept to a minimum. The lines spoken by the actors, the music, and the imagination of the audience can picture the various settings more effectively than flats and spotlights; notes in the printed program can always tell the audience where specific scenes are located.

The advantages of a production without scenery are, of course, obvious. Expense is saved; time is saved; emphasis is thrown sharply upon the actors and their words and actions. Another advantage is that the plays will fit in more effectively with the traditional services. It is our hope that each of these plays will find its greatest

use as a part—not the whole—of a religious service. If this is to be accomplished, it should not "steal the scene" away from other parts of the service. If an arch or other scenic "suggestion" is up throughout the whole evening, people will be curious about it at moments when they should not be thinking about the play. Yet if scenery is brought in at the beginning of the play, it will destroy the mood created by the earlier part of the service. The transitions between the service proper and the beginning of the play and then between the end of the play and the conclusion of the service should be smooth and unobtrusive, not awkwardly managed with scenery shifts or the manipulation of lights. It is well to keep in mind that medieval drama was taken out of the church when drama became more important for its own sake than for its religious function; this must not happen if these plays are to serve the purpose for which they are intended here.

Lighting is not too objectionable; in one play, the *Conversion of St. Paul,* it may definitely improve one of the dramatic effects. But too obviously visible spotlights, stage hands fussing with lights, etc., are definitely to be avoided. These plays can all be effectively produced without any lighting other than that naturally provided by the illumination available for the usual services. It will, of course, help some if the audience section can be dimmer or darker than the front where the actors are, but even this is not absolutely necessary for these particular plays.

No curtain need be used, as all characters enter and leave the stage. In

---

* Stage properties are discussed in detail after each individual play.

these plays no one is ever on stage either before the opening of a scene or after its close. The editor has provided stage directions which call for side entrances only, although groups with center entrances can certainly change these directions if they wish to provide more variety in entrances and exits. There should be some space off at the left and off at the right where the actors can be hidden from view when not on stage. This can be provided by screens if nothing else is available.

And so the energy and funds which a dramatic group might ordinarily put into scenery and lighting can be devoted entirely to costuming and to the play rehearsals themselves. The costuming, the make-up, the music, and the stage properties are the important elements of the technical production of these plays, and the usual big items of scenery and lighting can well be ignored.

VI. *Stage Make-up*

The first rule in using stage make-up for these plays is: *do not overdo it.* There is sometimes a tendency for enthusiastic but inexperienced people to make all the girls look like painted dolls and all the men look like girls. If the church is small, perhaps it will be better to use no make-up at all, except for beards. Certainly it is better to use too little make-up than too much. Too much will spoil the simplicity and naturalness demanded by these plays.

If it will help give a better appearance, the men may be powdered with a dark powder to give a tanner effect. Ordinary pancake make-up may be applied to give the same effect. If this is done, the powder or pancake make-up should also be applied to hands, bare legs, or any part of the body that shows to the audience. It will be ridiculous if the face is tan but the hands or legs are pale and sickly-looking.

A little dark rouge may be applied to the cheeks of the men, but it should be carefully blended in and softened so that it shows up merely as healthy cheeks and not as rouge. Dark lipstick should be used on the lips, but this should be done sparingly so that it does not show up as lipstick. Be careful to avoid making a "Cupid's bow" or anything which will tend to give an effeminate appearance.

Women usually know how to apply rouge and lipstick intelligently. Only a slightly greater amount than that used in tasteful street make-up should be used for these plays.

The eyes of both men and women should be outlined very carefully with an eyebrow pencil as close to the eyes as possible. A short line extending from the outer corners about a quarter of an inch should be drawn straight out (*not* up; *not* down). This will keep the eyes from seeming too small in proportion to the rest of the face, an illusion that distance sometimes gives them. The eyebrows should be darkened slightly with the same eyebrow pencil and then lengthened about a quarter of an inch to match up with the extended eyes.

Greater age can be suggested by drawing wrinkle lines on the forehead with the eyebrow pencil. These should be drawn evenly and continuously in natural curves across the forehead. Three little lines making "crowsfeet" can be put at the outer corners of the eyes. Lines around the mouth can give additional age. For more extreme old age, cheeks can be hollowed with a mixture of cold cream and eyebrow pencil. Eye sockets, hollows in the throat, and soft parts between the bones of the hands can also be made to look sunken by applying the same mixture. Again, be careful not to overdo these aging devices; it is wise to test them out a few times before the actual night of the production.

Beards are the most essential and the most difficult feature of some of these plays. A beard is usually made with crepe hair and fastened on with spirit gum. These can be bought at theatrical supply houses;* some drug stores carry them. The crepe hair is first combed out. Then it is applied to the face in tufts. Spirit gum is placed both on the tufts and on the face. Then each tuft is held in place with the hands until it definitely sticks. Be careful to get these tufts under the chin as well as on it. After all of the face is covered evenly, the whole thing is trimmed by someone with a little barbering ability. After the play, the whole beard can be ripped off quickly without too much difficulty. It is important that these beards be real-looking, and considerable time and practice should be spent on making them look authentic. Nothing can be so unwittingly funny as a badly applied beard.

If it is decided to use make-up, it should be tested at one or two of the rehearsals before the actual performance. The director or others should go out into the church and sit in different places to observe the make-up under the lighting that will actually be used for the play. Then when all make-up is approved, no significant changes should be made during the actual evening of the performance.

VII. *Costuming*

These plays may be done either in medieval English costumes or in Biblical costumes. We recommend Biblical costumes as being easier to make and more familiar to most groups, and so the sketches were drawn with this in mind. When the same kind of character appears in more than one play, a costume sketch is not always repeated. These sketches need not be followed slavishly, and each group should use its creative ingenuity to design and adapt its own costumes.

Costumes, of course, should fit. They should be tried on in advance and redone if necessary so that they will look well on the actors. Actors should rehearse in them for the last rehearsal or two in order to get used to wearing them without awkwardness or uneasiness.

They may be as colorful and elaborate as you wish. Since the plays are better without scenery and lighting, all the spectacle should be centered in the costuming. It is suggested, however, that costumes be made by the group rather than rented from theatrical costume houses. Many of the costume supply houses overcharge inexperienced groups, and a few are actually dishonest. Besides, the production is more your own if the ladies make the costumes. And if time and money do not permit much, there are always bed sheets, window draperies, and bed-

---

* If a group is not located near one of these, we can recommend Northwestern Theatre Associates, 1000 Foster Street, Evanston, Illinois. They will accept mail orders.

spreads that can be draped around the actors into the traditional Biblical costumes.

After the performance, the costumes should be cleaned and stored carefully away for use in later productions.

VIII. *The Music*

The music for these five plays will be found with each play. Note that the specific cues are already marked.

It is advisable for the organist to rehearse with the group at least once before the performance. If this is not possible, someone may have to be appointed to follow the script and give cues to the organist. This is done by lifting the hand in warning a few seconds before a cue is to start, then bringing the hand down sharply at the moment the cue is to begin. If the organist rehearses, of course, he can sense when to come in himself.

The music is important to the success of these plays, and it is imperative that it be well played. In some cases, it provides a significant part of the dramatic action; in others, it provides the climaxes; in still others, it underlines the action and creates the mood. Without this music, much of the effectiveness of these plays can be lost.

Book II
SELECTED CHORAL
READINGS

EDITED BY THEODORE MAC LEAN SWITZ

Introduction

The selected choral readings that follow are all much easier to produce than the plays in Book I. In selecting the materials for this volume, the editor has aimed to offer the large parish a variety of choices for different occasions, and yet to present some selections that would be well within the ability of even the smallest parish or mission. A number of these choral readings fulfill this latter requirement.

These selections, including those that are suitable as radio plays, although shorter and easier to produce than the plays in Book I, achieve a similar effect since they state great truths of the Christian faith and Christian life in a vivid, dramatic, and appealing manner. And because the Faith is far more than the bare logic of theological propositions or catechetical statements, the emotional depth and richness of these dramatic readings help to express its living complexity and reality.

Within recent years there has been a widespread development of interest in choral readings and the speaking choir. This has centered largely in the schools, especially as a means of communicating the enjoyment of poetry, but the speaking choir is ideal for church use, particularly in a liturgical setting. Poetry that might seem routine or monotonous if read by a single voice becomes vigorous and alive when presented by the constantly shifting tones and voices of a trained speech choir; meaning becomes clearer; and there is a keen sense of personal involvement.

Thus choral reading appears to be a wonderful tool for the Church to use in its divine mission to spread the Gospel and to teach the Faith. It is a particularly valuable means for teaching adults.

Its benefits, however, are not confined to the congregation to which the readings are presented. The members of the choir, studying and rehearsing together in order to give an artistic performance, gain a keener sense of Christian fellowship and are frequently awakened to a deeper and more faithful practice of the Christian life.

CHARACTERISTICS OF VARIOUS SELECTIONS

This section begins with "Four Apostles" by Hewitt B. Vinnedge. These four short plays were chosen from a number of similar dramas originally written for radio presentation. They are imaginative reconstructions of incidents from the lives of the apostles based on the Bible story and Church history.

Since they last only about 15 minutes, even with music, they may be presented in either of two ways: the cast can use the standard radio technique of reading them directly into a microphone connected with a loud speaker in the church, or the cast can record them in advance on tape for playing over a public address system. Either way we have a case of group "radio" listening; and in order to achieve maximum effect, it is best that most of the lights in the church be dimmed so that attention may focus upon the burning candles on the altar. Dimming the lights helps to put the congregation at ease while its members construct in imagination the scenes of the drama.

For five centuries *The Imitation of Christ* by Thomas à Kempis has been the most widely read devotional book, next to the Bible, in all countries both Catholic and Protestant. Naturally, it has been mainly used for personal devotional reading. The five selections presented here lift it out of this personal context and make it thoroughly suitable for group meditation or instruction within corporate worship. And to those who are familiar only with the prose translations of this work, the version here will come as a surprise.

One poem, "The Suffering of St. Mary," by one of the greatest modern French religious poets, Charles Péguy, is also presented. It states an old familiar story in such earthy and everyday language that it makes a fresh impact on the listener. It is also offered as an example of how other poems, such as the well-known "Hound of Heaven" by Francis Thompson, might be used.

The Oxford Book of Christian Verse is a splendid resource for great Christian poetry. Poems particularly suitable for speech choir use include "The Nativity" by Richard Crashaw, "Hymn: Crucifixus pro nobis" by Patrick Carey, "Christian Ethics" by Thomas Traherne, "O God Our Help" by Isaac Watts, "A Hymn of the Seasons" by James Thompson, "In Evil Long I Took Delight" by John Newton,

"Noel: Christmas Eve 1913" by Robert Bridges, and the following short poems by Christina Georgina Rossetti "Who shall deliver me?", "In the bleak mid-winter," "None other Lamb," "Paradise," "A Better Resurrection."

Book II concludes with "Christ Our Saviour" arranged by Frederick A. Schilling. In these biblical dialogues even the congregation takes part. Nothing could be more familiar to a church group than the Gospel of St. John, and yet the use of these dialogues presents their world-shaking message with so much power and vigor and freshness, and so much emotional involvement, that it seems as though we were hearing it for the first time.

VARIATIONS IN USE

All the selections in Book II were chosen to be suitable for use within a liturgical framework, that is, to take the place of a sermon in the offices of Morning or Evening Prayer. They are equally suitable, however, for presentation as a special feature at a mens' breakfast or dinner, or at a small or large meeting of The Woman's Auxiliary. In addition, some selections, particularly "The Royal Pathway" and "Christ Our Saviour," as well as the five plays in Book I, are excellent material for small reading and discussion groups. In a number of parishes there are small groups that like to read, as a group, novels, short stories, and plays and then discuss the Christian implications of these; these selections will fit very well into any such program.

FOUR APOSTLES

DRAMATIC READINGS BY HEWITT B. VINNEDGE

SUITABLE FOR CHURCH OR RADIO PRESENTATION

Reprinted by permission of Hewitt B. Vinnedge.

Thomas the Doubter

Within the company of Christ's apostles there was one who seemed to be possessed of a chronic spirit of doubt. Wherever in the New Testament narratives there is a record of his words or deeds, he gives evidence of this questioning attitude. "Doubting Thomas," as he has been called, was certainly not a willing unbeliever; but he was of a sceptical nature, and the grounds for his beliefs had to be positive and convincing.

CHARACTERS

NARRATOR
JONAS, father of Thomas
THOMAS, who becomes an apostle
LOIS, wife of Thomas
SOCRAPHON, father of Lois

PETER, an apostle
ANDREW, an apostle
JESUS
HARISHNU, a young Hindu boy

FIRST EPISODE

NARRATOR: *In a rather comfortable house in Capernaum, young Thomas is having a serious discussion with his father, Jonas. Thomas is deeply in love with a young Greek maiden, Lois. But since such a marriage is forbidden by Hebrew law, the matter is of serious concern to Jonas, who reminds Thomas:*

JONAS: But O my son, our holy law and faith
Forbid most clearly such a union with
The peoples of the Gentile tribes. Do not,
I pray you, Thomas, bring this grief on me
And on your mother.

THOMAS: It is quite in vain
For you to urge me thus. My will is fixed.

JONAS: Ours is a house of honor, ancient, proud.
Always have we adhered in strict accord
Unto the teaching of our sacred law.

THOMAS: I care but little for our "sacred law"!
And often have I had grave doubt of its
Reputed worth. At any rate, my will
Is fixed, and I shall wed the Grecian maid.

JONAS: But think, my son . . . Our house has ever been
Renowned for its devotion to the faith
Of Israel. In days of sore distress
One of our number always has been known
For zeal. When Jews were failing, on all sides,
To keep the law, and when our race was led
Into captivity, when this fair land
of Canaan was a pawn between the kings
Of Egypt and of Syria, and when
The Maccabees in valor smote the hordes
Of base idolaters who were infesting all
Our countryside, in every case our house
Stood true and steadfast in Jehovah's name,
To hold His covenant and keep His law.

THOMAS: And did their zeal and faithfulness avail
To keep the unbelievers from the land?
Nay, father, but look for yourself and see
How desolation stalks among our race!
The royal gods of ancient Egypt
The gods of Babylon and of Assyria,
The lordly gods of ever-conquering Rome
Outwitted our Jehovah in each case.
I can retain no longer faith in Him,
Or in His law. Besides, I love the maid,

Lois, the daughter of the Grecian sage:
And I will wed her in spite of you, and all
Our house, in spite of prophets and of law,
Yea, in spite of your Jehovah, even.

JONAS: My son, 'tis blasphemy that you have spoken.
You have abjured the faith of Abraham.
May God grant that I do not live to see
You follow after some new strange belief.

SECOND EPISODE

NARRATOR: *Thomas and Lois have been married for five years now and are living in Galilee. They have just finished their evening meal, and Thomas sits brooding, when Lois breaks in:*

LOIS: I should not be excited, were I you.
Remember, Thomas, how upset you were
Before our marriage in Jerusalem.

THOMAS: But, Lois, had you only seen His face,
The face, as 'twere, of God Himself, when He
Did stop me on the road and smiling spoke
His gentle order: "Thomas, follow Me!"

LOIS: But, surely, you are not the man to take
So weightily what every passerby
Might say to you. Besides, what do you know
Of this strange fellow, that is good? By all

Accounts he heralds some new strange
    belief
That is at variance with the sacred law
Of Israel. O Thomas, you do not
Forget how great a struggle once we
    had,
To keep you in the faith Jehovah gave.
Remember, years ago, that night when
    I
Was thinking on our love and of the
    day
When you should take me, Thomas,
    for your bride—
Remember how your father came in
    tears
And begged me to give up my Thomas,
    lest
A stain should fall upon his house by
    your
Taking to wife a Gentile maid. And I,
Rather than lose you, took your
    Hebrew faith,
With all its cold commandments, and
    became
A follower of all the Jewish law.

THOMAS: But He is learned in our law.
    'Tis said
He sits and teaches in the synagogues.

LOIS: Yet others say He rails against
    the priests
And has but small respect for all their
    words.
The Scribes and Pharisees themselves
    condemn
His acts and teachings. If you heed His
    call,
I fear that you will wander from the
    way
Of Hebrew faith which I have sacri-
    ficed
Already overmuch to keep you in.

NARRATOR: *There is a knock at the
outer door, and presently Socraphon,
the father of Lois, enters and says:*

SOCRAPHON: Greetings, my children
    both, how fares it now
With you, this splendid eve of Canaan's
    spring?

LOIS: Father, your coming is most
    opportune.
Thomas, I fear, is almost swept away
With some new teaching going round
    the land.

SOCRAPHON: And what is that, my son?

THOMAS: The Nazarene,
Jesus, of whom you doubtless have
    been told,
Spoke unto me today upon the broad
Highway and bade me follow after
    Him.

SOCRAPHON: I know not of the Man.
    What does He teach?

THOMAS: His teaching is so strange—
    his deeds yet more.
He is a man of learning, all agree.
Although the son of a poor carpenter,
He can confound the priests with their
    own books.
He teaches love for all mankind—a life
Of sacrifice and beauty is His goal.
No pride is in Him; with humility
And mild compassion He takes to His
    heart
The weak and suffering, the sinful and
The vile and destitute, and bids them
    all
Love one another. There is in His
    words
The morning song of hope for all that
    weep,
Life's springtime for the lowly of the
    earth.

SOCRAPHON: But why would He have
    you follow Him?

THOMAS: He has a group about Him
    who believe
That He is the Messiah, promised long
By all our prophets. And His fol-
    lowers
Practice His kind and gentle way of
    life.

SOCRAPHON: Then should I think that
    you would lose no time
In following His way of life. 'Tis thus
That our philosophers of old did teach
In Greece. Yet were they shunned by
    all the crowd,
And ridiculed and made to suffer, or
To drink the fatal hemlock. But we
    know
Today that those men were the very
    flower
And fragrant essence of the spirit of
Our race. Today the wise ones honor
    them.

LOIS: But father, can you not see how
    a course
Such as you recommend, would take
    away
My husband from the tenets of his
    faith?

SOCRAPHON: My daughter, I am old, a
    little wise;
And if your Thomas can but gain the
    rich
And varied beauty such a life would
    seem
To promise, little does it matter if
He break the shackles of a narrow
    creed.

LOIS: But he would have to follow
    through the land
That curious fellow, and leave me
    alone.

SOCRAPHON: And even this would I
    have him do

If he might aid in bringing to the world
The radiancy of such a glorious dream.

THOMAS: I thank you, father, for your
    words of help.
They have removed my doubts. And
    now shall I
Link to the lowly Nazarene's my life,
And follow whither He may summon
    me.

THIRD EPISODE

NARRATOR: *Two years later in the
upper chamber of a house in Jerusalem, eleven men are gathered and talking quietly together when Thomas, one
of their number, boldly speaks out his
objection:*

THOMAS: Yet I will say, it cannot be.
    With my
Own eyes I saw Him nailed unto the
    cross.
With my own eyes I saw the Roman
    dog
Thrust in His side a spear. With my
    own ears
I heard Him cry, as He gave up the
    ghost.
And I did see Him laid within the
    tomb
Like any other man that has been
    killed.

PETER: But, Thomas, I am not a liar,
    nor
My brother Andrew. Will you not be-
    lieve?

THOMAS: Except I see the nail-prints
    in his hands
And put therein my fingers, and except
I thrust my hand into His side, I'll not!

ANDREW: But here are James and John
    to testify;

Verily I believe that you are but
A little better than the one who did
Betray him.

THOMAS: That, you know, is false, for I
Was faithful to the Lord until the last.

PETER: Nay, you are now no longer
fit to be
One of our brotherhood. And we shall
cast
You out as though you were Iscariot.

THOMAS: You will not and you cannot,
Stony Heart.

PETER: We can, and we shall straight-
way do this thing.

NARRATOR: *And as the discussion continues, tempers shorten: angry voices
now side with Peter, now with Thomas.
Then suddenly a blinding light fills the
room. And Thomas exclaims:*

THOMAS: That light! Whence comes it?

JESUS: Peace be unto you.

PETER: Master, we have a doubter in
our midst.
Should we not cast him from our
brotherhood?

JESUS: Thomas, come unto Me. . . .
Put hither in
These prints of nails your fingers, and
thrust in
My side your hand. . . . And be not
faithless but
Believe in Me.

THOMAS: My Lord, my God!

JESUS: Because
You have beheld, you have believed.
Blessed
Are they that have not seen and yet
believed.

THOMAS: O help my unbelief, my Lord,
my God!

FOURTH EPISODE

NARRATOR: *Forty-five years have passed
since that gathering in the upper room.
And the preaching mission of Thomas
has taken him to India, to the lower
Ganges. And now, an old man, he lies
upon a bed of straw in a poor peasant
hut. Thomas is dying. His breath is
labored; his countenance troubled.
Finally, he speaks:*

THOMAS: Why should I doubt after
these years? Have I
Not labored long to spread the Mas-
ter's faith?
Have I not spent my years on these hot
plains,
In these cruel hills of India, to teach
The doctrine of the Lord of life? Then
why
At this last hour should all the words
of those
Wise men of India come to my mind?
Why should the learned Brahmins
shake my faith
At this moment when day by day they
strove
In vain to reason me away from my
Belief? And why should all the sayings
of
The wise who follow in the way of
Buddha
Crowd fast upon my heart and rob me
of
My peace and solace in the hour of
death?

[*For a moment Thomas remains quiet,
and then the silence is suddenly broken
by an agonized cry.*]

Lord, I believe; O help my unbelief!

NARRATOR: *Opening the door, a little Hindu boy, his cheeks tear stained, quietly enters. His name is Harishnu, and to Thomas he says:*

HARISHNU: Good master Thomas, are
    you very sick?
You will not leave us? . . . No? . . .
    You will not go?
My mother told me you were going far
Away . . . To see the gentle Lord
    that died
Upon the cross. And if you see Him,
    will
You tell Him something for me? . . .
    Tell Him I,
The little Harishnu, will see Him by
And by. Tell Him I love Him and will
    come
To see Him, too.

[*While the lad has been speaking, the troubled look has gradually receded from the face of Thomas. In its place there has come one of peace and assurance. Brokenly, but confidently, he speaks.*]

THOMAS: Blessed be your faith, my
    child,
Because you have not seen and yet be-
    lieved.
This evening when I see the Master, I
Will tell Him. Go in peace.

HARISHNU: Good-bye. Do not
Forget to tell the Lord.

NARRATOR [*very softly*]: *Harishnu then kisses the wrinkled face of the Apostle and runs from the room. A new power seems to come into the dying body of Thomas. With one last effort he lifts himself up and stands for a second at his full height, imperious, bold, fearless. He raises his hands on high—*

THOMAS: My Lord! My God!

John the Beloved

St. John was one of the most appealing and lovable characters in the company of our Lord's disciples. He was perhaps the youngest of the group, and it was, no doubt, somewhat difficult for him to appreciate the seriousness of the call, for he was a first cousin of Jesus, their mothers being sisters. It is always difficult to realize that one's own close relative may be a man of destiny, and certainly it must have required considerable mental struggle to believe that one's cousin could be the Eternal Son of God.

CHARACTERS

JOHN, a fisherman, younger brother of James
JAMES, a fisherman
ANDREW, friend and partner of John

MARY, the mother of Jesus
POLYCARP, a young disciple of John; later Bishop of Ephesus

FIRST EPISODE

NARRATOR: *On the shore of the Sea of Galilee, two young fishermen are earnestly talking together as they mend their nets. They are stirred by the word that has come to them about the preaching, in Judea, of their distant kinsman, John the Baptist. The younger fisherman, John, a lad in his late 'teens, speaks:*

JOHN: I wonder if our father, Zebedee,
Could spare us for two days, or three, for I

Am eager to learn more about the man.

JAMES: And so am I. This John, with his baptizing,
Is stirring up the province of Judea
With his new teaching. Then, the fact that he
Is one of our own kinsmen pleases me.
I hardly think he is Messiah. Yet
We cannot be too sure.

JOHN: I wonder how
He got his name. It is the same as mine;
Yet in that portion of the family

There's no one else that bears the
name.

JAMES: I used
To puzzle over it myself, until
One day I asked our mother, and she
said
It was because of some prophetic word.
She did
Not seem to know the full details; but
there's
Enough of mystery in it, so that I
Have wondered all the more. You see,
if John
The Baptist is a prophet, then it is
Our duty as his relatives to go
And give him our support. Then, too,
if he
Should be Messiah, I should like to be
Beside him when he sets up power.
We, as
His kinsmen, might expect a place of
trust
And honor in his kingdom.

JOHN: Yes, I've thought
Of that myself. I will admit that I
Have been ashamed of thinking of it.
We,
Like all good Hebrews, should support
the man
Jehovah will set up to reign. But, still,
I could not but be proud, if it should
be
One of our relatives; and I'm afraid
That I would hope to share his glory,
too.

JAMES: I think that you should hardly
be ashamed
To feel like that. Remember, it is for
The glory of our Israel that we
Would serve the king . . . But is
there any point
To all this dreaming? First, we must
find out

The truth about this John. Without a
doubt,
He is a prophet of the Lord, and that
Is a great honor in itself. But I
Cannot be satisfied with rumors. I
Agree with you, that we should get
away
From business a few days. I do believe
Our father would consent to let us go.

JOHN: I think so, too. Only this week
we made
A catch of fish beyond our greatest
hopes;
The market, too, was good. Let's go
and ask
Him now.

JAMES: Agreed! And if he will consent
We shall set out to-morrow.

JOHN: James, I feel
That this will be a journey we shall
not
Forget. I cannot help but think that we
Shall learn of plans and hopes and
dreams,
That will affect our lives: your life and
mine,
Perhaps the lives of all our family,
Perhaps, too, of all Israel.

JAMES: Come on;
We must be getting back. But do not
raise
Your hopes too high. Remember we
have not
A thing but hearsay yet to build upon.

SECOND EPISODE

NARRATOR: *With his friend Andrew,
John journeys to the half-desert region
of northeastern Judea. And there, by
the River Jordan, they join the crowd
intently listening to John the Baptist,*

who is exhorting his listeners to peni-
tence and urging them to be baptized.
As the two eagerly listen, Andrew
whispers to John:

ANDREW: You say he is your kinsman?

JOHN: Distantly.
His mother was Elizabeth, and she
Was distant cousin unto Salome,
My mother.

JOHN THE BAPTIST [*from a distance*]:
O repent ye all! . . . God's king-
   dom—
It is at hand!

ANDREW: He is a prophet—no
Mistaking that. You do not think
   perhaps
He could be the Messiah?

JOHN: I do not
Know what to think. He seems to make
   no claim
To great position. Yet there is a power
Within his words that moves one
   deeply . . . I
Was baptized yesterday by him; so I
Am his disciple now.

ANDREW: Were you indeed?
I also was. And did you tell him of
Your kinship?

JOHN: Yes, I tried to mention it.
But he paid little heed. With his stern
   gaze
Fixed on my eyes he said: "Brother,
   repent,
The kingdom is at hand!"

ANDREW: The kingdom! That
Most surely sounds like the Messiah. . . .

JOHN: Look!

[*In the midst of the chatter of the*
crowd, may be heard questions like,
"Are you Messiah?" "Are you the
prophet that is to come?" "Are you
the Christ?"]

JOHN: There are some people asking
   questions. Let
Us hear his answers.

JOHN THE BAPTIST [*from a distance*]:
                  No, friends; I am not
Elias, nor that prophet. Not the Christ.

ANDREW: You hear him? He is not
   Messiah.

JOHN: No;
That much is settled. Listen!

JOHN THE BAPTIST [*from a distance*]:
                        I am but
The voice that cries: "Repent! Make
   straight
A highway in the desert for the Lord.
I do indeed baptize with water, but
There stands a Man among you Whom
   you do
Not know. He is preferred before me.
   I
Am all unworthy to unloose his shoes.
Behold!

JOHN: Whom does he mean? Can you
   see where
His hand is pointing?

ANDREW: No, not yet . . . Yes . . .
   now
I see the One he means . . . John! Is
   that not
Your Cousin from the town of Nazareth?

JOHN: It looks like Him from here
   . . . But, no; there must
Be some mistake. . . .

JOHN THE BAPTIST [*from a distance*]:
          Behold, the Lamb of God!
He that shall take away the sins of all
The world!

JOHN: 'Tis past belief! I did not know
That Jesus had intended to come down
Into Judea also. . . . Andrew, how
Can this great prophet be mistaken?

ANDREW: But
I thought you all suspected Mary's Son
Would be a prophet some day.

JOHN: Yes, but not
Messiah. He has not the force, the
will,
To lead men into battle.

ANDREW: Yet it seems
The prophet is quite sure. He even
hails
Him as the One Who shall baptize
mankind
With God's own Spirit . . . Listen
. . . Now he calls
Him Son of God!

JOHN: I cannot understand
What he may mean.

ANDREW: But listen, John! Both you
And I have felt the prophet's strength,
the truth,
Sincerity, and wisdom of his words.
Let us not think he is mistaken now
Only because he hails a Man whom
you
Have known for long.

JOHN: But Andrew, don't you see . . .

ANDREW: No, John; I don't but I intend to learn
What all this means. . . . So let us
now approach
Your Cousin Whom the prophet just
has hailed

As Lamb of God.

JOHN: We shall find out where He
Is staying here. Then we shall spend
the day
With Him, and try to learn what this
can mean.

NARRATOR: *And "they came and saw
where He dwelt, and abode with Him
that day, for it was about the tenth
hour. One of the two that heard John
the Baptist speak. . . . Andrew, Simon Peter's brother . . . findeth his
brother . . . and saith unto him, 'We
have found the Messiah,' which is,
being interpreted, the Christ. And he
brought him to Jesus" (John 1:39-42).
Then John also sought out his own
brother, James, and brought him unto
the Lord. And so it was that these
four, Andrew and Peter, John and
James, became the first disciples of
Christ.*

THIRD EPISODE

NARRATOR: *As time went on, John
with Peter and his brother James entered the inner circle that witnessed
the great acts of Christ and enjoyed
His confidence. John's following Christ
leads him to the very foot of the Cross
where now he stands with Salome, his
mother, and Mary Magdalene, and
"the other Mary." The little group is
attempting to comfort Mary, the
mother of Jesus, when the solemn hush
that has fallen on the tragic and holy
hill of Calvary is pierced first by the
jeers and taunts of the multitude, and
then, after some moments of silence,
by the solemn words of Him on the
cross, as He entrusts His mother to the
care and love of John. Turning to
Salome, Mary, Jesus' mother, says:*

MARY: O Salome, my sister, it has
   come!
His mind is going. He no longer knows
One from the other. Did you hear Him
   call
Your John my son? Ah, well; perhaps
   'tis best . . .
He will not feel the pain so keenly.

JOHN: No;
You do mistake His meaning. He
   knows well
Enough who we all are. I think He
   meant
That I should care for you when He
   is gone.
Look, Mary! O, my blessed aunt, He
   hears
What we are saying! . . . See him
   nod? Then I
Was right, you see.

MARY: But John, that cannot be.
You must not feel responsible for me.
I shall but burden you.

JOHN: You burden me?
Do we not love each other? Do we not
Love Him above all else? Then must
   we not
Obey His word to us?

MARY: We must. . . . O yes . . .
It will not be for long . . . God will
   not let
Me long survive this awful day. He
   whom
My soul has magnified—the Holy One
In whom my spirit has rejoiced, will
   soon
Take me away from this so bitter
   world
That slays my Son, and drives deep in
   my heart
This sword of anguish.

JOHN: Yet perhaps it is

His will that you should still live on,
   and tell
The wonders of our Jesus to mankind,
And bring men closer unto Him.

MARY: Perhaps . . .
But how? . . . How shall I ever speak
   His Name?
O John! . . . And yet . . . perhaps
   I may . . . The grace
Of God may fill me once again, and
   cause
Impossibilities to come to pass . . .
Yes, John . . . perhaps you're right
   . . . You know His love,
The miracles that it can bring . . .
   That night
When He was born—it was the mira-
   cle
Of Jesus' love that brought me through
   that hour
Of trial and weariness in Bethlehem,
After the long and dangerous journey
   . . . I . . .
I wish you might have seen Him then
   . . . His head—
I never saw a baby's head so
   formed . . .
Forgive me, sister Salome; I know
Your John's was perfect, too . . .

JOHN: Do not
Remember all these things just now.

MARY: O yes!
Let me recall them, John—for it is
   love
That brings these memories forth, and
   He would not
Gainsay my love . . . He was my
   Baby, John—
My Baby, listening to His mother's
   song
Of love and praise . . . He was my
   little Boy

That played about the shop in Nazareth . . .

He used to play with nails and ham-
mer . . . Nails!

O, God in Heaven! See those nails that
pierce

His hands and feet! . . . He drove
me to despair

That time we lost Him in Jerusalem . . .

And now, here in Jerusalem, I lose

Him once again . . . Take me away!
. . . O take

Me home! . . . I can no longer see
my Son

In torture hanging there!

JOHN: Your Son . . . is gone.

MARY: My Son . . . is gone? . . .
What are you saying?

JOHN: Look.

His Spirit He has yielded up . . . He
has

Laid down His life for us . . . for
Israel.

MARY: For all mankind . . . Take me
away, John . . . home!

FOURTH EPISODE

NARRATOR: *According to tradition,
John remained by the side of Mary,
the mother of Jesus, during the rest of
her earthly life. And afterwards, without benefit of her company, he con-
tinued his preaching of the Good
News, the gospel of love. And finally,
when an old man, he settled, as bishop,
at Ephesus where now we find him,
seated in his home and talking with
Polycarp, his disciple and companion.
John is informing Polycarp that he has
chosen him to be his successor and
that soon he will consecrate him*

*Bishop of Ephesus. Polycarp, deeply
moved by this news, interposes in all
humility:*

POLYCARP: You do me too much
honor, Father John.

How can I hope to fill the place that
you

Have occupied in Ephesus?

JOHN: My son,

I have observed your work and patience, and

Your zeal and labor for the Lord. I
know

My choice has not been wrong. My
eyes are dim,

But I can see things with my heart
and I

Have felt the Holy Spirit guiding me

To choose you for my place in Ephesus.

POLYCARP: But why? I have not seen
the Lord, as you

Have done. His glory as Incarnate God

Have I not known.

JOHN: No, Polycarp, and there
Are very few remaining now who saw

The everlasting Word of God revealed

In flesh. There are but few who have
beheld

The glory of the only Son of God.

Remember, son, I am the last of all

The Twelve. But now the time has
come when you,

Who have beheld Him only with the
eyes

Of faith, must do His work—must
make men see

In faith His Way of love and righteousness.

POLYCARP: But how am I to teach His
Way? And how

Can I be sure that I am able to
Direct His flock?

JOHN: Do you not love these folk?

POLYCARP: Of course, but . . .

JOHN: Therein is the only test;
For God Himself is love. And if we
    love
The brethren of His Son, then are we
    sons
Of God; then is His love perfected in
Ourselves. And if we love God's chil-
    dren, then
We do but manifest our love of God.
We can but keep His word and bear
    the yoke
That He may lay upon us. So, as sons
    of God,
We overcome the world through Him
    —through love.

POLYCARP: If I must take this burden,
    then I wish
That you, who knew the Master
    closely, would
Reveal more of your life with Him,
    more of

Those years when, with His blessed
    mother, you
Proclaimed His Gospel here in Asia.

JOHN: There
Is little to reveal. He loved us all,
And we loved Him. I loved His
    mother, and
In love we brought His message to the
    men
Of Asia.

POLYCARP: Yes; but what am I to
    teach
After you go? To me these Christian
    folk
Will look for guidance.

JOHN: Well, the message is
Quite simple. They will be your chil-
    dren in
The Lord. Tell them that God loved
    us, and sent
His Son to expiate our sins. Tell them
The simple rule of life that they must
    follow—
Just: "Little children, love ye one an-
    other."

Andrew the Summoner

St. Andrew was not a conspicuous member of the apostolic band. He frequently appears as a somewhat steadying influence in the life of his more brilliant, but impulsive, elder brother, Peter. St. Andrew has sometimes been called the first missionary, for his first act upon learning of the Christ was to bring his brother to the Lord. It is, perhaps, for this that the X-shaped cross of St. Andrew is frequently used as a missionary symbol.

CHARACTERS

PETER, later the apostle
ANDREW, younger brother of Peter
PAUL, the apostle
MATTHEW, the apostle
THE VOICE OF JESUS
DION, a young convert of Andrew's

FIRST EPISODE

NARRATOR: *In a small fishing boat on the lake shore near the Galilean town of Bethsaida, two young fishermen are disputing the disposal of their catch as they ready it for delivery. Peter, with some impatience, demands:*

PETER: Why do you have to be so hidebound?

ANDREW: I
Am not. It only seems to me that we
Should carry our agreement out.

PETER: But why
Just now? I will admit that we agreed

To furnish one full net of fish each
    day,
But you should not forget that yesterday
We furnished more; also two days last
    week
We did the same. Our quota is complete;
We can afford to take things easy, just
To-day.

ANDREW: O Simon, how you always
    try
To put the best appearance on your
    whims!
When Zebedee and his two sons agreed

To underwrite our labor with a price
That seemed quite fair, we both with
eagerness
Accepted. Well, they always have been
just;
And James has widened out the market far
Beyond what we expected. And when
he
Could get a price above the contract
rate,
He always turned the difference in to
us.
So how have we a right to idle for a
day
Because we furnished extra fish last
week?

PETER: But listen to the singing of the
birds,
And see the wild flowers blooming
there. Why man,
It's spring again! You know a day like
this
Was never meant for work.

ANDREW: Ah, now I see
The reason why you want to get away.
That maiden in Capernaum is on
Your mind again, but work comes
first.

PETER: But she
Needs cheering up. Her mother has
been sick
Almost the winter through. She has not
been
Outside the house for nearly seven
weeks.

ANDREW: Exactly, Simon; that is just
the point.
You see, she had a job to do, and did
Not try to get away from it. I know
That girl. She would not welcome you
up there

To-day, if for a moment she had cause
To think you were neglecting anything
In order to be with her.

PETER: There you go!
Always exaggerating things. You might
Suppose that I was asking you to do
The work of both of us to-day.

ANDREW: And that
Is what I shall do, if I find a boy
That I can hire to help me with the
net.

PETER: Well, go ahead and be a mar-
tyr.

ANDREW: No;
I hardly call it martyrdom to do
What I have promised.

PETER: Well; I shall be off.

ANDREW: Have a good time, my
brother. Don't forget
To tell them of the extra price we got
Last week because of James, and that
good deal
He made across the lake. I know that
it
Will please them when they hear that
we
Have been so fortunate.

PETER: Here, take the net!

ANDREW: What are you doing?

PETER: Never mind. Just take
The net while I launch forth . . .
Now Andrew—for
A haul of fish beyond their wildest
dream!

SECOND EPISODE

NARRATOR: *Three years later, Andrew
and Peter with their partners James
and John travel down into Judea to*

*hear for themselves the new prophet,
John the Baptist. They find him, at
last, in a small Judean village, and
eagerly they join the circle of his listeners. But Peter, who has made this
journey only with reluctance, wanders
off. When Andrew finds him, he says
to Peter, in great excitement:*

ANDREW: O Simon, I am glad I found
    you. I
Have searched the town, looked every-
    where for you.

PETER: Well, here I am—but why the
    breathless rush?
For days I could not get you far
    enough
Away from that baptizing fellow, to
Inform you I was eager to go home.

ANDREW: But now I had to see you
    . . . I have news.

PETER: I hope it's good news.

ANDREW: O, it is . . .

PETER: I'm glad.
When shall we go back home?

ANDREW: Back home?

PETER: Why, yes;
You said the news was good. The only
    news
That could seem good to me would be
    for you
To say that we return at once unto
Bethsaida.

ANDREW: No, Simon; it is not
That sort of news. . . . To-day the
    prophet . . .

PETER: O,
So that is it! . . . Well, Andrew, I
    care not
To hear about your prophet. . . .

ANDREW: No, but wait.
The news is not of him. It is about
The Christ . . . Messiah. . . .

PETER: What?

ANDREW: Yes, Simon; it
Is true. To-day the prophet pointed
    out
The Man Who shall redeem our peo-
    ple.

PETER: O,
My brother! All this madness must
    have got
Into your head. Now let us just go
    back
To business in Bethsaida, for we
Have been away too long.

ANDREW: We shall go back,
Of course. But first you must come
    with me.

PETER: No
You still are young enough to be im-
    pressed
By all this shouting and excitement
    but
You must be practical. Our work is
    there
At home awaiting us.

ANDREW: Now, Simon, you
Cannot take this big-brother attitude
With me. I did not beg you to remain
Beside the Jordan listening to John.
I felt it was your own concern if you
Did not perceive his righteous power
    But this
Is something different. Once I saw the
    Man
The prophet pointed out, and talked
    with Him.
I knew I must come straight to you
    and bring
You unto Him.

PETER: You listen, Andrew, now.
I had no wish to come down here with
    you.
This is a busy season. James and John
Came off on this wild notion, and your
    heart
Was set on coming, too. And so I
    came
To keep you company. Since we ar-
    rived,
You have spent all your time with that
    queer crowd
Around this preacher on the Jordan's
    banks.
I let you listen to his nonsense, but
It has been going on quite long
    enough.
The time has come to say good-bye to
    this
Emotional debauch. We're going home.

ANDREW: Not yet. . . . We are not
    going home just now.

PETER: What are you saying? I won't
    have . . .

ANDREW: You come
With me. My brother, I have found the
    Man
Who can transform your life.

PETER: Transform?
My life is not so bad. I'm satisfied.

ANDREW: No . . . you are not. Not
    any living man
Can say that he is satisfied . . . not
    you . . .
Not I . . . not anyone we know. But
    now
I know that I have found the Man to
    bring
New purpose into lives like ours. . . .
    So, come.

PETER: What has come over you?

ANDREW: A power, a grace
That I cannot explain. . . . But all I
    know
Is that it must be shared with you. I do
Not wish to keep this to myself. So
    you,
My brother, must come with me now,
    and let
Me bring you unto Him.

PETER: Well. I shall go
And see this Paragon of yours. But I
Am warning you: I will not be im-
    pressed.
I'll go and see Him, if you wish; but
    then
I shall go home, with or without you.

ANDREW: Come.

THIRD EPISODE

NARRATOR: *Some twenty years have
passed. And once more at the lakeside
near Bethsaida, there are gathered
Andrew and Peter with Matthew, who
also had been an apostle, and Paul,
who is a recent convert. Together, they
are earnestly discussing the persecution
that is confronting their company of
believers, when Peter says:*

PETER: I'm glad we all could meet
    together here.
This region has so many memories
For most of us.

PAUL: Sometimes I envy you
Those years you spent in Galilee with
    Him.

ANDREW: You need not, Paul. It was a
    harder thing
For you to follow the Apostle's way
Than for the rest of us. I sometimes
    think
We have it very easy—we who knew

The Lord, and talked with Him, as man to man.

PETER: But some of us have found it rather hard
To keep things going smoothly. That is why
I wanted us to talk things over here.

MATTHEW: What is your problem, Peter?

PETER: Well, I fear
I can no longer stand the pace at which
I have been working. Then, my funds are low,
And at my age I have to think of that.
Now it has come to pass that an old friend
Has just inherited a fishing business,
Equipment all complete, good trade established
Up in Capernaum. Now if I should
Return to my old business, I am sure
That working five days every week, I could
Make a good living—maybe more than that.
Then I would have my week-ends free to preach
The Gospel in the cities round the lake.
It is not just what I would like, of course,
But then in times like these . . .

ANDREW: O Peter, have
You not become unduly frightened?

PAUL: No—
I do not think so. I can see good sense
In such a plan. My situation is
Not greatly different. I have two good friends
In Ephesus that deal in my old trade,

Tent making. They have recently proposed
To open up a branch in Corinth, and
Put me in charge of all their interests in
Both Greece and Macedonia. This work
Is to my liking, and would be so much
Less difficult than is my present care
Of all the churches. And I still would have
Some time in which to do the Master's work.
The times are growing worse; I feel that we
Should try to be prepared for them.

ANDREW: But Paul
That day on the Damascus road . .

MATTHEW: O, let's
Be practical. We ought not to allow
Our judgments to be ruled by sentiment.
I understand what Paul and Peter mean.
I, too, have been concerned over the way
In which affairs have gone of late
Now I
Just recently have had a chance to go
Back in the revenue employ. It is
A business that pays well, you know, and if
I take this offer, I can make enough
To keep myself in comfort, and to care
For all the rest of you, if need should come.
Besides, this work would give me leisure and
Enable me to write more widely of
The life and works of Jesus. I believe
That I could help the Cause more in that way
Than any other.

ANDREW: You do not believe
What you are saying, Matthew; and
the rest
Of you are trying to convince your-
selves.
O Paul, my faithful friend, when
Christ appeared
In blinding glory unto you that day
On the Damascus highway, did you
think
That He was calling you to spare-time
work?

PAUL: Well . . . no . . .

ANDREW: And Matthew . . . there
around that bend
Of shore Capernaum is lying. There
The Master called you from the taxing
trade
To follow Him. In all those years we
spent
In His blest company, did you once
think
Of failing to obey the call? Did you
Once dream that ever you'd go back
unto
The money changers' tables?

MATTHEW: Well . . . not when
You put it that way . . .

ANDREW: Peter—O my well
Beloved brother!—Look at that wide
stretch
Of sand where I am pointing . . .
there beside
The lake . . . it's just a little way
from where
We four are sitting now . . . Does
not that spot
Recall what happened there so long
ago?
O, Peter . . . that is where we beached
our boat

After that miracle of fish, when we
Had toiled all night in vain. You say
you fear
You can no longer stand the pace at
which
You have been working . . . Peter,
that is where
Our Lord said: "Fear not; henceforth
you shall be
A fisher of"—what was it, Peter?—
"Men!"
That spot is where we quit the fishing
trade.
How long a time is "henceforth,"
Peter?

PETER: Why,
For always, I suppose, but . . .

PAUL: Brothers, I . . .
I think we have no need for further
talk
About these matters . . . Let us pray
. . . and then
Perhaps the Holy Spirit will direct
Us all. . . . Lord, what wilt Thou
have us to do?

VOICE [coming as from the depth of
the lake]: Behold, I show you
what great things you must
Endure for My sake . . . Go, launch
out into
The deep . . . let down your nets
. . . catch men . . . fear not,
Fishers of men henceforth . . . Fear
not! Behold,
I shall be with you always—till the end
Of time . . . henceforth, until the
world shall end.

PAUL: Good-bye. . . . I'm going back
to Ephesus . . .
And not to tents in Corinth.

MATTHEW: Andrew . . . God

Be with you . . . I shall go to Egypt, then
Perhaps as far as Ethiopia.

PETER: My brother . . . once again I needed you
To summon me from weakness . . . Now I go
To Rome. . . . It's far, I know . . . but I must go
And tell that wicked city of the Lord . . .
We may not meet for many years. . . . It is
So far away. . . .

ANDREW: Go, Peter, go!

PETER: Yes . . . I . . .
O, Andrew . . .

ANDREW: Go!

PETER: Good-bye.

ANDREW: Good-bye . . . Thank God!

FOURTH EPISODE

NARRATOR: *It is twenty-five years later. And Achia, the Roman proconsul, has sentenced Andrew to death—to death on the cross. But Andrew is not nailed thereto, instead he is bound by ropes that his death may be the more painful, the more lingering. Thousands in curiosity have come to this seaside place to behold him on his cross, to witness his lingering death; and to them Andrew still speaks out the Good News, the Gospel of salvation. At this moment, he is close to death, and one of his new converts, Dion, stepping forward, says to him:*

DION: This never should have been, good master. Why
Did you insist on preaching to the wife
Of the Proconsul? If you had not won
Her to your faith, the tyranny of Rome
Would not have brought you to this cross.

ANDREW: And what
Of her? Did I not have to summon her
Unto the Lord? . . . And what of you, my child?

DION: I? . . . What have I to do with this injustice?

ANDREW: For two days I have hung upon this cross,
And all the countryside has come to hear me.
This cross of pain is rich in blessing . . . What
Of you, had I not been here?

DION: Yes . . . of course . . .
I never would have heard your message, if
I had not come in curiosity
To see you on this cross.

ANDREW: And so—it has
Not been a cross of tyranny alone.
It is a cross of blessing, for our Lord
Has brought some thousands unto me out here,
That I might bring them unto Him . . . that I
Might summon them to everlasting life.

James the Thunderer

The two sons of Zebedee, James and John, were among the first of Christ's disciples. They seem to have been young men of positive convictions and outspoken attitudes; it was, doubtless, because of this that Jesus referred to them as *Boanerges,* which means "sons of thunder."

CHARACTERS

ZEBEDEE, the father of James and John
JOHN, a younger son
           (of about 18 years)
JAMES, an older son
           (of about 25 years)

SALOME, wife of Zebedee and mother
    of James and John
JUDAS, a disciple
IBERUS, a young Spanish Christian
PETER, an apostle

FIRST EPISODE

NARRATOR: *In Bethsaida, a lakeshore town in Galilee, live Zebedee and Salome with their two sons, James, the elder, who is twenty-five years of age, and John, who is a lad of eighteen years. Their home is a comfortable one, and the family have just finished their evening meal when Zebedee speaks:*

ZEBEDEE: We certainly have done quite well this year.

With Simon and his brother working now

With us, I think we'll soon control the trade

Throughout this region. O, we cannot take

All credit to ourselves. The fish have run

Surprisingly, and thanks for that are due

Jehovah. Yet you boys deserve much praise.

JOHN: Oh no, not much; yours was
the whole idea.

ZEBEDEE: Of course, but if you had
not made such friends
Of Andrew and of Simon, why, I
doubt
If we could have them working on our
side;
And they'd be difficult competitors.
And you, too, James; had you not
stormed the towns
Around the lake, to get good contracts,
we
Would certainly not be where we are
now.
I thought that you were pushing things
too fast,
With too much lightning speed, when
you sought out
The contract with the Roman garrison.
I was afraid the quartermaster might
Think you were thundering at him
night and day,
But how successfully your plan has
worked!

JAMES: I knew it would. As long as
we shall deal
In fish, it seems to me that we must try
To have first place. None else will sat-
isfy
The house of Zebedee.

SALOME: That's right, my son.
I always want my boys to be the first
In every way, in all they undertake;
Just as I want my sister Mary's boy
To have first place as Prophet. We
must watch
His progress. O, I hope that He will
not
Antagonize the ones who best can
help.
I hope that He will listen to advice.

He speaks so beautifully; it is a large
And eager following that seems about
To follow Him. And yet I fear He is
A little too outspoken now and then.

JOHN: I wonder, though . . . Perhaps
His way is right.

SECOND EPISODE

NARRATOR: *Through the outskirts of a*
village in Samaria, thirteen weary men
are slowly making their way toward
the open country. Their leader, though
as tired and worn as his followers,
calmly pushes on to the disgust of one
Judas, who angrily questions:

JUDAS: Why does He not declare Himself right now?
How long must we endure this wandering
Around the countryside? How long
will He
Put up with insults from these heretics?

JAMES: I tell you, Judas—well, it
made me boil
Within, to see how these Samaritans
Bade us move on, as if we beggars
were,
Or vagrants, tramps. And all because
they saw
That we were headed for Jerusalem!

JUDAS: Where else would Jews be go-
ing when they plan
To worship? Certainly not to this
Mount
Of Gerezim, which these Samaritans
And heretics revere!

JOHN: O, Judas, now—
The Master would not have us speak
so harsh
Of these misguided folk.

JAMES: The time has come

For harshness. Let Him strike them
down
With bolts from heaven, and crush
their unbelief.

JOHN: No, James; let us not make yet
more mistakes.
Remember how we fared before . . .
that day
When our dear mother took us to the
Lord
And asked that we be given the high-
est place
Within His kingdom. . . . Do you not
recall
The just rebuke He gave to us all
three?
No, let us not attempt to put our
views
Against His own. Perhaps His way is
right.

JAMES: Now listen, John. I do not
give myself
The credit for this act I'd have Him
do.
I shall but quote the Scriptures to
Him, and
You surely must agree that they are
right.

JOHN: How do you mean?

JAMES: I'll tell you, John. He knows
Elijah well. Why, it was but last week
That you and I were on the mount
with Him
When Moses and Elijah came and
talked
To Him. . . . When Ahaziah was the
King
Of Israel, Elijah called down fire
From heaven to consume his enemies
Sent by the king. Now why cannot the
Lord
Do likewise?

JOHN: Well perhaps . . . I had not
thought
Of that, and since so recently He saw
Elijah . . . James! Perhaps it was for
this
Elijah came and talked with Him! We
must
Remind the Lord.

JAMES: Yes, let us waste no time.
O Master . . .

JESUS: Yes, my cousin James; say on.

JAMES: Well . . . Master . . . I . . .
we wondered . . . John and I . . .
You tell him, John.

JOHN: Well . . . Master . . . in the
Book
Of Kings we read of what God's
prophet did . . .
Elijah . . . You remember how he
called
Fire down from heaven to blast his
enemies . . .
It seemed to us that now it might be
well . . .
If You could see our way . . . we
thought it might
Be well . . .

JAMES: To burn these low Samaritans!

[*Gasps and murmurs from the company.*]

JESUS: Is that your spirit? Well, it is
not Mine.
I came not that I might destroy men's
lives,
But save them. . . . Now, let us be
going on
To other towns . . . You brave, misguided sons
Of thunder . . . You have much, so
much, to learn!

THIRD EPISODE

NARRATOR: *Fourteen years have passed, and James is now in Spain preaching the Gospel. At this moment he is talking with Iberus, a young Spanish Christian, who addresses him:*

IBERUS: But Father James, it seems so needless, such
A waste of time and purpose for you now
To go to Palestine. What benefit
Can come of this long journey? And what if
You find that you cannot return to us?

JAMES: I have no answer for your questions, son:
For all I know is that my brethren there
In Palestine have need of me. Last night
I felt the Holy Spirit's prompting voice
Urging that I return. I know my work
Here, in your Spain, cannot be called complete.
Iberus, did I ever tell you how
The Lord would call my brother John and me
"The sons of thunder"? Well, perhaps that's it.
Herod Agrippa, knave son of a knave,
Is reigning in Jerusalem. Reports
Have come that he is harrying the Church.
My brethren, the Apostles, have gone on
To other fields, and few are left at home.
Peter is there, of course, my brother John,
And James, the brother of the Lord, who was
Not of our company before His death.

Perhaps Matthias is on hand, but most
Are far away: Thomas in India;
And Matthew has dropped out of sight
To write his book, and that is right, for he
Can do it best. Simon is in the West
Somewhere. I'd hoped to see him here some day.
And so you see, Iberus, I must be
In Palestine, where lightning strikes just now.
The sons of thunder must not be too far
From where the sparks are flying!

IBERUS: John is there.

JAMES: Ah, yes . . . and that's another thing. Do you
Remember that I told you how one day
The Lord took three of us upon a hill,
And there He was transfigured in our sight? . . .
I, James, was one of them; my brother John
Another; Peter was the third—or first,
Perhaps . . . Iberus, now it seems the Church
Will need our witness. We three were the ones
Who saw the Lord as King of glory. We
Must thunder out His glory to the Church,
And drown the sounds of wails and bitterness.

IBERUS: But what is to become of us? The church
Is tender here, and needs your guiding hand.

JAMES: So tender that she will be let alone

To grow in peace for years to come.
 By then
She will be able to resist assaults
From anywhere. But now in Palestine,
Where she is strongest, is the need
 most great;
For there she is most bitterly attacked.

IBERUS: You're right, of course . . .
 The Holy Spirit could
Not err. But we shall miss you; we
 shall be
Bewildered, longing for your word to
 tell
Us more of truth.

JAMES: Yes; that I understand.
It grieves me now to go. But let us
 hope;
Let us hold fast the Faith. You are a
 man,
My son; you are a soldier of the Lord.
I know how hard it was for you to
 leave
The army, with promotions on the
 way.
As Caesar's soldier you were going far,
But as the soldier of the Lord you'll go
Much farther—to behold the King of
 kings,
Not share an earthly Caesar's triumph.
 And
You'll lead an army; as our Blessed
 Lord's
Commander here in Spain, a host will
 come
And follow you to His eternal camp.
You are in charge of God's great
 work, till I
Return again.

IBERUS: And if . . . you do not
 come?

JAMES: And if . . . why, then you
 but remain in charge

Till death . . . How I have loved my
 people here!
It is with sorrow that I leave . . .
 And yet
I feel that this is not a last good-bye.
In life or death I shall return to Spain.
Here may my body rest among the
 folk
That I have loved and taught; and
 may it here
Await the resurrection of the dead.

FOURTH EPISODE

NARRATOR: *After this James returned
to Jerusalem where, in the year 44,
King Herod Agrippa is attempting to
crush what he regards as the dangerous, new Christian sect. He has
thrown the leaders, Peter and James,
into jail. In their prison cell, not far
from the Temple, Peter and James are
discussing their situation. James re-
marks:*

JAMES: To-day is Friday, Peter.

PETER: Yes, three days
Until the Easter anniversary. Well,
The resurrection now has been pro-
 claimed
Throughout much of the world. This
 year there'll be
A joyous celebration everywhere
Among the brethren.

JAMES: But this day He died.
And, Peter, we were all so shaken. I
Cannot forget how on that final night
We all forsook Him.

PETER: Yes . . . and I . . . O, I . . .
As if last night . . .

JAMES: Hush, Peter; I forgot.

Forgive my mentioning . . . You were
    no worse
Than all the rest of us that fatal
    night . . .
I often think how John and I thought
    we
Should have the highest places in His
    realm.
Do you remember how incensed you
    were,
You and the others, when we asked
    that we
Might sit, one on the right, one on the
    left
Of Jesus in His Kingdom? . . . We
    had much
To learn.

PETER: We all did, James. It seems so
    long . . .
And yet but yesterday, when He was
    here.
O, How the blessed years have
    smoothed out all
The jealousies and pride that warped
    us then!
O James, my brother, it was good of
    you
To come to Palestine. We needed you.
You've strengthened us in these dark
    days . . . But why
Must you have come for this? Your
    work in Spain
Will now be all in vain.

JAMES: No, Peter, no.
The Master's work can never be in
    vain.
And do not grieve. Do you remember
    when
He told me I would one day be bap-
    tized
With His own baptism. . . . Well, it
    has come.
And I am glad that I am going first

Of all the Twelve. I shall but sooner
    see
The Lord in glory . . . Peter, now I
    seem
To feel the surging splendor that we
    knew
The day He took us to the mountain,
    and
Was there transfigured . . . Well, I
    soon shall see
The living Christ as He appeared that
    day.

PETER: We have some blessed memo-
    ries—you and John
And I . . . we three. . . . Has John
    been here to-day?

JAMES: No, Peter; not to-day. I said
    good-bye
To him last evening . . . I asked him
    to stay
Close by our aunt, the holy Mother,
    for
She seemed to feel great sorrow over
    me,
As if Agrippa's sword would pierce her
    heart.
Do you suppose that she will have this
    grief
To bear, when each of us shall go?

PETER: Perhaps. . .
And yet not always thus. You are the
    son
Of her beloved sister. That makes it
More poignant in your case . . . And
    then, the day . . .
It's Friday, as you said . . . and that
    recalls . . .

JAMES: I know . . . Of course it
    would . . . Well, Peter, now
The time is almost here . . . This is
    good-bye,

Old friend. We've often said good-bye
    before . . .
As boys, there in Bethsaida, when we
Would separate, each to his home,
    from play. . . .
And when we said good-bye to fishing
    boats
The day the Master called us . . . and
    when we
Were sent out two by two in Galilee

Before they killed the Lord . . . and
    when I went
To Spain just after Pentecost . . .
    Well, this
Should not be greatly different . . .
    So, good-bye . . .
God bless your labors, Peter . . .
    everywhere . . .
Pray for the work in Spain . . . Look
    after John. . . .

THE ROYAL PATHWAY

READINGS FROM *THE IMITATION OF CHRIST* BY THOMAS À KEMPIS

TRANSLATED BY HENRY PARRY LIDDON

ARRANGED FOR A SPEAKING CHOIR BY THEODORE M. SWITZ

WITH ORIGINAL MUSIC BY THOMAS MATTHEWS

Note: The speaking choir should have a minimum of four, or a maximum of eight, voices; half should be male, and half female, voices. At least one male, and one female, voice should be powerful enough for solo parts. The speaking choir may wear robes identical with those of the regular choir, or the men may wear cassocks and cottas. The choir, with its leader in front, stands facing the congregation.

THE ROYAL PATHWAY OF THE HOLY CROSS

Chapter 12, Book Two, of
THE IMITATION OF CHRIST.

[MUSIC CUE 1.]

SOLO VOICE (*male*): This seems to many a hard saying,

MEN: "Deny thyself,
Take up thy cross,
And follow Jesus."

SOLO VOICE (*male*): But far harder will it be to hear that word at last,

MEN: "Depart from me, ye cursed, to everlasting fire";

SOLO VOICE (*male*): For those who gladly hear the word given by the Cross, and follow it,
They will not fear to hear
Eternal condemnation.

WOMEN: This sign—the Cross—shall be in heaven
When the Lord shall come to judge.
Then all the servants of the Cross, who lived as did the Crucified
Shall come to Christ the Judge quite trustful.
Why then fear to take it up?
By it you win your way into the kingdom.

[MUSIC CUE 2.]

FIRST MAN: In the Cross is safety,

FIRST WOMAN: In the Cross is life,

SECOND MAN: In the Cross protection from our foes,

SECOND WOMAN: In the Cross is sweetness
Poured on us from above:

THIRD MAN: In the Cross is spiritual joy,

THIRD WOMAN: In the Cross the sum of virtues;

FIRST WOMAN: In the Cross is holiness in perfect beauty.

ALL: There is no safety to the soul,
No hope of life eternal,
Save in the Cross.

MEN: Take then your Cross and follow Jesus,
And your path shall lead to everlasting life.
He went His way before you,
Carrying the burden for Himself.
He died for you upon it,
That you might take your own
And die upon it too.
But if you die with Him,
Even so with Him you live:
And if you are the comrade of His pain,
You shall share His glory too.

[*A brief pause.*]

SOLO VOICE (*female*): See—in the Cross all lies,
In death upon it all consists;

ALL: And there is none other road
That leads to life and to true peace of soul;

SOLO VOICE (*female*): None other save the holy Cross,
The daily killing of our sins.
Walk where you will,
Seek what you will,
And you will never find a higher road above,

Nor surer road below,
Than in the pathway of the Holy Cross.

[MUSIC CUE 3.]

ALL: Arrange and order everything to
     suit your will, to suit the pleasure
     of the eye,
And you will always find—a cross;
For either in your body you will meet
     with pain,
Or in your soul will have to bear
     trouble of spirit.

WOMEN: Now and again God leaves
     you;
Now and again your nearest friend will
     anger you;
And more—you will be grievous to
     yourself;
And you will not be able to be quit of
     it,
Or make it lighter
By any remedy or solace,
So long as God wills you to bear it.

MEN: His pleasure is that you should
     learn to suffer care uncomforted,
Wholly subjecting you to Him,
Getting a humbler spirit from your
     trials.
Christ's sufferings are by none so really
     felt
As by the man who has to bear the
     like.

[MUSIC CUE 4.]

SOLO VOICE (*male*): Therefore the
     Cross is always ready,
And at every turn awaits you.
Run where you please,
You cannot shun it;
For everywhere you take yourself
     along with you,
And you shall always find yourself;

WOMEN: You shall always find the
     cross,—
Above, below, within, without,
Turn where you will.

MEN: And you must needs be patient
If you would have peace within
And gain the everlasting crown.

[MUSIC CUE 5.]

WOMEN: Bear the cross willingly
And it will carry you,
And lead you to the longed-for goal,
Where there shall be an end of suffer-
     ing—
Though it will not be here.

MEN: Bear it unwillingly,
You make a burden for yourself,
Loading yourself the more—
And you must bear it still.

WOMEN: Throw it away,
And surely you will find another,
Perhaps a heavier one.

ALL: Think you to escape
What mortal men can never be with-
     out?

SOLO VOICE (*male*): What saint upon
     the earth has ever lived apart
     from cross and care?

SOLO VOICE (*female*): Why, even
     Jesus Christ our Lord was not
     even for one hour free from His
     Passion's pain.
"Christ," says He, "needs must suffer,
Rising from the dead,
And enter thus upon His glory."

SOLO VOICE (*male*): And how do *you*
     ask for another road
Than this—the Royal Pathway of the
     Holy Cross?

All His life meant cross and martyrdom,
And do *you* seek peace and joy?

ALL: Wrong, wrong, if you seek anything but to suffer tribulation;

SOLO VOICE (*male*): For all this mortal life of yours
Is full of misery,
Dotted round with crosses.
The higher anyone advances in the spirit,
The heavier are the crosses he will find;
For as his love grows greater, so there grows the punishment—his exile on the earth.

[MUSIC CUE 6.]

WOMEN: Yet though man be tried by manifold afflictions,
He has comfort wherewith to raise him;
For from the very suffering of the Cross he feels great good accrue to him.
He makes his will bow down unto himself,
And all the burden of his cares is turned to trust in comfort from on high.

MEN: The more the flesh is worn by suffering,
The more the mind is strengthened by the grace within;
And now and then the man becomes so strong (in love of tribulation and adversity),
Longing to make his cross like His,
That he would not be free from pain and care.
The more acceptable to God he deems himself,
The worse the trials and the heavier the cares

That he can bear for Him.

SOLO VOICE (*female*): This is not man's virtue, but Christ's kindness,
Which can do and which does so much in man's frail flesh,
That what by nature flesh abhors and flees from,
It gets to love and tries to gain through this fervent mental fire.
'Tis not man's way to bear a cross,
To love a cross,

MEN: To beat the body and to keep it down in slavery,

WOMEN: To flee from honours,
Willingly to bear contempt,

MEN: To look down upon himself,
To love that others should look down on him,
Suffering adversity and loss,
And sighing for no prosperous days.

ALL: Look to yourself,—
You will be able to do none of these;
But trusting in the Lord,
There shall be given you strength from heaven,
The world and flesh being brought low beneath your power.
Nor will you fear your enemy the devil,
If you be armed with faith, marked with the Cross of Christ.

[MUSIC CUE 7.]

MEN: Then take your station as Christ's good and faithful servant,
To bear your Lord's Cross like a man,
The Cross of Him that out of love to you was crucified.

ALL: Be ready to endure much that will go against you,

And many things you will not like here
in this life of misery;

WOMEN: For it will be with you,
where'er you are.
Hide yourself where you will,
You will find it so indeed.
It must be so;
There is no way to shun the grief and
ills that troubles bring,
But by bearing with yourself.
Drink lovingly the chalice of the Lord,
If you would be His friend and have a
part with Him.
Leave consolation unto God;
With such things let Him act as seems
Him good.

SOLO VOICE (*male*): But you, take up
your station to withstand all woes,
and think them only as great comforts,
"For the sufferings of this time are not
worthy to compare"—
No, not though you alone could suffer
all the sufferings in the world—
"With the glory in the days to come."

[MUSIC CUE 8.]

SOLO VOICE (*male*): When you have
come to this, that cares are sweet,
and, borne for Christ, taste pleasantly,
Then think it well with you;
For you have found an Eden on the
earth.

ALL: So long as it is hard to suffer and
you try to shun it,
So long will you be ill at ease,
And everywhere the cross you shun
shall follow you.

SOLO VOICE (*male*): If you set yourself
to what you should,—
I mean, to suffer and to die,—

ALL: Things will get better soon, and
you will find your peace.

SOLO VOICE (*male*): Though you be
rapt to the third heaven with Paul,
You are not, therefore, sure that you
will never suffer things that go
against you.
Saith Jesus, "I will show him
What he must suffer for My sake."
Suffering then will stay by you.
If you would love Him, and for ever
be His slave.

MEN: O would that you were worthy
to endure for Jesus' name.
How loud would be the shout among
the saints of God;
How large the progress in your neigh-
bour's life;
For all praise suffering,
Though few can bear it.
But it were only reason that you
should suffer for Christ a little,
When many suffer worse things for the
world.

[MUSIC CUE 9.]

WOMEN: Be sure of this,
That you must lead a dying life.
The more a man dies to himself,
The more will he begin to live to God.

MEN: No one is fit to understand the
things of heaven,
Unless He brings himself to bear ad-
versity for Christ.
Nothing is dearer unto God,
Nothing more wholesome in this life,
Than willing suffering for Christ.

WOMEN: And if you had to make your
choice,
You should choose rather woe for
Christ

Than the refreshment that many com-
   forts bring;
For you would be nearer Him,
More like to all the saints.

ALL: Our merit and our onward way
   lie not in comfort nor in much
   delight,
But rather in great troubles and in
   suffering many a care.

WOMEN: If there were anything for
   human safety better, more useful
   than endurance,

Christ would have shown it in His
   words and life;
For He cheers on His followers in
   plain words,
And all who would come after Him,
To bear the Cross, and says,

ALL: "If any would come after Me,
Let him deny himself,
And take his cross and follow Me."

[MUSIC CUE 10.]

THE ROYAL PATHWAY

MUSIC CUE 1

MUSIC CUE 2

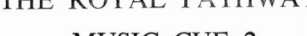

MUSIC CUE 3

MUSIC CUE 4

MUSIC CUE 5

MUSIC CUE 6

MUSIC CUE 7

MUSIC CUE 8

MUSIC CUE 9

MUSIC CUE 10

HOW TO GAIN PEACE AMID
TEMPTATION AND ADVERSITY

*Chapters 11, 12 and 13, Book One,
of* THE IMITATION OF CHRIST.

[MUSIC CUE 1.]

SOLO VOICE (*male*): We might have
    peace, great peace,
If we would not load ourselves with
    others' words and works,
And with what concerns us not.
How can he be long at rest
Who meddles in another's cares,
And looks for matters out of his own
    path,
And only now and then gathers his
    thoughts within him?
    Blest are the simple-minded;
Peace in abundance shall be theirs.

WOMEN: Why were certain of the
    saints so good in life, so deep
    in thought?
Because they tried to make themselves
    as dead to all the longings of
    the world,
And thus with all the marrow of their
    hearts they clave to God,
And could find time to muse upon
    themselves.

ALL (*slowly*): We are too busy with
    the sufferings of our lives;
We are too careful of the transitory
    world;
We rarely utterly defeat one sin;
We do not burn to hurry forward on
    our daily road;
So we stay lukewarm—or else, cold.

MEN: If we were wholly dead unto
    ourselves,

And if our inner life were less en-
    meshed,
We then could taste the gifts of God,
And catch some glimpses of the sight
    of heaven.
    Our whole, our greatest hindrance,
    this:
We are not free from passions and
    from lusts,
Nor do we try to enter on the footsteps
    of the saints.
For when a little trouble faces us
We are too soon cast down,
And turn for comfort to our fellow-
    men.

[MUSIC CUE 2.]

WOMEN: But if we strove to stand in
    battle line like soldiers true,
Above us we should see God's help
    descending from the sky.
Ready is He to help all those that fight,
And build their hopes upon His kindli-
    ness.
He *makes* for us chances to fight—that
    we may win.

    If we but mark our path by all those
    outward rules we keep,
Soon will our devotion find its goal.
But let us "lay the axe unto the root,"
To purge ourselves from passion, and
    to gain the treasure of a mind
    at peace.

MEN: If every year we would root out
    one fault,
Soon we should be perfect men.
But often it is just the opposite. We
    find
That we were better, purer men when
    we set out towards God,
Than when for many a year we had
    professed our love.

Our steps should daily further go,
    our love should brighter burn;
But now we think it a great thing
If any one can keep a spark of the first
    fire.

SOLO VOICE (*female*): If at the first
    we would but be a little hard
    upon our sins,
Then we could master everything in
    after days
With ease and cheerfulness of heart.
Hard is it to throw off our custom's
    chain,
And harder still to go against our
    wishes.
Yet if you vanquish not the slight and
    little sins,
When will you overcome the greater
    ones?
Unlearn the evil habit,
Stand up against your bent at first,
Lest the little greater grow, and make
    things harder for you still.
    I fancy you would be more eager on
    your heavenly path,
Did you but think what rest to your
    own life,
What joy to others you would bring
By a firm hold upon yourself.

[MUSIC CUE 3.]

MEN: Useful it is for man sometimes
    to meet trouble and care op-
    posing him,
Calling him back to his own heart,
That he may know himself a stranger
    in the land,
That he may place no hope in aught
    upon the earth.
    Useful it is for man to suffer contra-
    diction
(Though he does well, means well),

When men think ill of him, or know
    but half the truth.
These are the guides that lead to low-
    liness,
That shield him from vainglory;
For then, when outwardly men hold
    us cheap,
When they will hear no good of us,
Clearer we look towards God, the
    inner Witness of our deeds.
A man should root himself in God—
    so fixedly
As not to need consoling words from
    men.

SOLO VOICE (*female*): A man (who
    means to do so well),
When scourged by evil thoughts, har-
    rowed and tried,
Can see more clearly that *he must have
    God,*
Can grasp that without God he can do
    nothing good.

    Then he is sad, he moans, he prays,
By reason of his misery.
Weary of longer life,
He sighs for death to come,
To be dissolved and be with Christ.
And then he fully learns
That in the passing world full peace
    and perfect safety cannot long
    abide.

[MUSIC CUE 4.]

SOLO VOICE (*male*): So long as in this
    world we live,
We cannot be untempted and un-
    scourged;
Wherefore in Job we read
That life of man upon the earth means
    trial.
So every man should in his prayers
    keep watch

To meet temptations that he knows
    are his,
For fear the devil, never slumbering,
But going up and down in quest of
    men he may devour,
Find a weak place to cheat him in.
None so holy, none so good,
As not to meet temptation now and
    then;
We cannot quite be free.

SOLO VOICE (*female*): Yet there are
    trials (hard and troublesome,
    may be)
Very useful unto men;
For, meeting them,
We are brought low, made pure, made
    wise.
    All saints have gone through many
        a trouble—many a harrowing
        care—
Gone through with gain;
And those that could not bear them—
They have deserted God, and failed.

WOMEN: No order is so holy, and no
    spot so hidden,
That troubles and temptations may not
    come.
Long as he lives, man is not safe from
    them,
Because the root whence the tempta-
    tion comes lies in himself.
For we were born in lust.
One trial or one sorrow ebbs away;
    another takes its place;
And we shall always find something to
    bear,
Since man has lost the blessing of his
    happy state.

[MUSIC CUE 5.]

SOLO VOICE (*male*): Fire proves the
    iron,
And trial proves the good.

Often we know not what our powers
    may be,
But trial shows us what we really are.
    Yet must we keep a careful watch to
        meet the first approach,
For then an enemy is vanquished with
    more ease;
If we will give no entrance at the gate-
    way of the mind,
But meet him at his knock beyond the
    lintel of the door.
And one has said,
"Withstand disease's onslaught at the
    gate,
The leech's after-thought may be too
    late."
For first upon the mind the simple
    thought beats in,
Then comes the stronger picture of the
    sin,
Then comes delight in it, and then
We basely meet it and we yield.
And thus by slow degrees the wicked
    foe gets in with all his power,
If at the first he finds no enemy;
And he who lazily puts off the fight
    becomes
Weaker and weaker every day;
Stronger and stronger is his foe.

WOMEN: Some meet their heaviest
    trials at the first
Along the pathway of their road to
    God,
Some at the ending of the way.
Some too are visited, it seems, through
    all their lives,
Some lightly tried enough,
As God in wisdom and in justice
    wills,
Who weighs what each man is, what
    each deserves,
And from of old ordains all things that
    work the safety of His own.

ALL: Therefore we ought not to despair
    when tried,
But raise a brighter flame of prayer
    continually to God,
That He will deign to help us in all
    our harrowing cares,
For, in the words of Paul, He "will
    provide
Along with trial, an escape
To make it possible for us to bear
    it."

MEN: Humble your souls then 'neath
    the hand of God
In every trial and in every woe.

The lowly-minded He will raise—will
    save.
In trials and in cares the progress of
    the man is shown;
In them his greater merit lies,
In them his virtue shows itself the
    clearer.
And it is nothing much,
If we be holy, if we burn in love, when
    there is no trouble at the heart;
But if a man bears up when things are
    all against him,
There will be hope that he has made
    great steps upon the road.

[MUSIC CUE 6.]

THE ROYAL PATHWAY

MUSIC CUE 1

MUSIC CUE 2

MUSIC CUE 3

MUSIC CUE 4

MUSIC CUE 5

MUSIC CUE 6: *Repeat Music Cue 1*

FOLLOWERS OF CHRIST

Chapters 1-3, Book One, of
THE IMITATION OF CHRIST.

[MUSIC CUE 1.]

WOMEN: "He that followeth after Me
walks not in the darkness; Thus
saith the Lord.
These are Christ's words, and by them
we are told
How far to imitate His life and ways,
If we would be truly filled with light,
And from all blindness of our hearts be
set at liberty.
Therefore our study above all must be
Upon the life of Jesus Christ to ponder.

SOLO VOICE (*male*): "His teaching
passes all the teaching of the
saints,
And he who has the spirit of Christ
Would find the manna hidden there.
But it is thus, that many a man,
Hearing the Gospel ever and again,
Feels for it little longing,
Because the spirit of Christ is none of
his.
Yet he who would in all their fulness
Taste and know the words of Christ,
Must study to make all his life like in
its beauty unto His.

SOLO VOICE (*female*): What boots it
deeply of the Holy Three to talk,
If, lacking humbleness, you grieve that
Holy Three?
Deep words make no man just and
holy,
But lives of virtue make men dear to
God.
Far rather had I feel a sorrow for my
sin,

Than know the definition of the feel-
ing;
For if in the mere letter you should
know the Bible through,
And all the sayings of the wise,
What—without love of God, without
His gracious touch—would all be
worth to you?

SOLO VOICE (*male*): "Vanity of vani-
ties, and all is vanity,"
Save loving God and serving Him
alone.
That is the best philosophy,

SECOND MAN: To scorn the world and
strive to gain the kingdom in the
skies.
Therefore it is but vanity to seek the
riches that will fail,
And to build hopes on them.

THIRD MAN: It is but vanity to look for
offices of state.
It is but vanity to raise oneself on high.
It is but vanity to follow longings of
the flesh,
Panting for what must bring us heavy
punishment in days to be.

ALL (*slowly*): It is but vanity to wish
for life that shall be long,
And care but little for its being good.
It is but vanity to think alone upon the
life we lead,
And not look forward to the things
which are to come.
It is but vanity to love what with all
speed is passing by,
And not to hasten there where joys
eternal dwell.

[MUSIC CUE 2.]

WOMEN: If you think you know much
and comprehend things well,

Reflect that there is much you do not know.

Be not high-minded,

But confess your ignorance.

Why would you put yourself before another?

Many may be found more skilled than you,

Many more learned in the law;

But if you would learn something that will profit you,

Love to be all unknown, and to be held as nothing.

MEN: The deepest lesson for a man to learn is this, and the most gainful too:

Truly to know—ay and to scorn himself.

Great wisdom is it, and it makes a man far better,

To put no price upon himself,

And to think highly of his neighbour with a kindly mind.

For if you saw another sin some open sin,

Or do some grievous deed,

Think not the better of yourself for that.

ALL: How long can you stand straight? You cannot tell.

We all are frail;

But this must be your thought—

'None is more frail than I."

MUSIC CUE 3.]

WOMEN: Happy the man taught by the truth itself;

Not by the shapes and sounds that pass across his life,

But by the very truth.

Our thoughts and senses often lead us wrong;

They see one side alone.

SOLO VOICE (female): The man to whom the Word Eternal speaks

Is loosened from the bonds of many theories;

For from one Word come all things,

And all things speak—one Word.

This Word is the beginning.

It also speaks to us.

Without this Word, no one can judge or think aright;

But he to whom all things are One,

And who to One brings all his questions,

And in One sees all his answers,

Steadfast-hearted will he be,

And rest at peace in God.

MEN: O God of truth,

Make me one with Thee in eternal love.

Oft am I weary, reading, listening,

But all I wish and long for is in Thee.

Then silent be all teachers, hushed be all creation at the sight of Thee:

Speak Thou to me, alone.

[Brief pause.]

SOLO VOICE (male): The more a man is one within himself, and simple in his inner life,

The deeper and the more he understands—yet without toil.

For down from heaven there comes to him the light that brings intelligence.

A spirit simple, pure, and firm, is never wasted in a multitude of business,

Because its business is in all to honour God.

It strives to be at rest within itself from all self-seeking thoughts.

Who troubles you? Who hinders you?

Naught but your heart's affection—yet unkilled.

The good and pious soul first maps out
    in his heart
His business in the world,
Nor does his work e'er draw him off
    into the longings of a wicked
    mind.
He bends it all to listen to his rea-
    son,—
Reason, the holy witness of his life.—

ALL: Who fights a braver fight
Than he who strives to win a battle
    o'er himself?
This, this should be our ceaseless work,

ALL: To crush the enemy within our-
    selves,—
Daily to get a braver hold on him,
And win some ground upon the better
    path.

[MUSIC CUE 4.]

MEN: All our ideal life upon the earth
Has something unideal that clings to it,
And no deep thoughts of ours are free
    from some dark mists.
The humble knowledge of yourself
Will be a surer road to God
Than a deep searching into knowledge
    of the world.

SOLO VOICE (*female*): Yet knowledge
    is not to be blamed,
Nor any simple grasping of a thing.
Nay, in itself considered, it is good,
And is of God ordained,
But a good conscience and a virtuous
    life are ever put before it.
Still, because many rather strive to
    know
And not to live in holiness,
They often err,
And bring forth little fruit, if any at all.

    O, if they used the care they spend
      upon their questions,

In rooting out their vices and in sow-
    ing seeds of virtue,
There would not be such scandals and
    such evils in the world,
Such careless ways within the cloister
    walls.

MEN: But, when the day of judgment
    comes, we shall be asked
What we have done,—and not what
    we have read;
How holy were our lives,—and not
    how fine our words.

SOLO VOICE (*female*): Where now may
    all those lords and masters be
Whom you knew well
While on the earth they lived,
And while they flourished in their
    learning?
Their office others hold;
I cannot tell if they think once of them
In life it seemed that they were some-
    thing great,
And now none speaks of them.

SOLO VOICE (*male*): How fast, how
    fast the glory of the world flits by
I would their lives had balanced with
    their knowledge;
Then good had been their studies and
    their books.
How many perish by vain learning in
    the world,
That care too little for the service of
    their God.
Because they make their choice for
    greatness, not for lowliness of
    mind,—
And vanish into shadows, while they
    meditate.

WOMEN: Truly great is he,
Who has great charity.

MEN: Who in himself is small,
And holds as naught all heights of
    honour.

WOMEN: Truly wise is he,
Who deems all earthly things as dung,
That he may win the prize of Christ.

MEN: Truly learned too is he,
Who does God's will,
Letting his own will go.

[MUSIC CUE 5.]

THE ROYAL PATHWAY

MUSIC CUE 1

MUSIC CUE 2

MUSIC CUE 3

MUSIC CUE 4

MUSIC CUE 5

GOOD THOUGHTS IN SOLITUDE
AND SILENCE

Chapters 20-22, Book One, of
THE IMITATION OF CHRIST.

[MUSIC CUE 1.]

SOLO VOICE (*male*): Seek a fit time to
be at leisure for yourself,
And often think on the kind deeds of
God.

SECOND MAN: Leave your curious
questionings;
Read and re-read the things that bring
no busy thoughts,
But sorrow for your sins.

WOMEN: If you can tear yourself away
from useless talk,
And idly going here and there,
From hearing all the gossip and the
news,
You will find time enough, and time
well-fitted too,
To muse on what is good.

MEN: The greatest saints avoided,
when they could,
Solace from men,
And chose to serve God in the cell.

WOMEN: And one has said,
"Often as I walked with men,
Less of a man did I return."
Again and yet again we see,
When we keep chattering,
That it is easier wholly to be dumb
Than not to step beyond the line in
talk;
That it is easier to stay quietly at home
Than to keep guard over ourselves
abroad.

ALL: He then who would attain the
inner holier life
Must draw away, as Jesus did, a little
from the crowd.

[MUSIC CUE 2.]

SECOND MAN: No man is safe walking
abroad,
Unless he loves obscurity at home.

THIRD MAN: No man is safe in speech,
Unless he loves the quiet tongue.

FOURTH MAN: No man is safe in
power,
Unless he loves the lower place.

SECOND MAN: No man is safe in places
of command,
Unless the lesson of obedience is
learnt.

THIRD MAN: No man is safe in joy,
Unless he have within a conscience that
is good,
The witness of his life.

SOLO VOICE (*male*): Yet mark. This
safety of the saints existed not
Without a thorough fear of God,
And no less anxious, no less humble,
were they in themselves
For all the shining glory of their virtues
and their grace.
But for the fancied safety of the bad,
It springs from self-conceit and pride,
And at the last it turns and proves,
Even to itself, how false it is.

SOLO VOICE (*female*): O if a man
would never seek the joys that
pass quickly by,
If he would never worry with the
world,
How good his inward heart would be;
If he would cut but clean and deep

Into the wound of empty cares,—
If he would only think of what is
wholesome
And of what comes from heaven,—
If he would lay the corner-stone of all
his life in God,
How great would be the treasure of
his peaceful rest.

WOMEN: No one deserves comfort
from heaven
Unless he diligently practises a holy
sorrow for his sin.
Then if you would be sorry in your
heart,
In with you to your room;
Bar out the tumult of the world:
As it is written,
"At your bedside bemoan your sin."

[MUSIC CUE 3.]

SOLO VOICE (*male*): Better to live a
hidden life
And to take thought about oneself,
Than to work miracles and leave one-
self untended.
To go abroad but now and then,
To shun publicity,—
Ay, even not to wish to see the face of
man,
All this is to be praised in one who
takes the vows.
Why wish to see
What one must not have?
The world goes by, and all the lust for
it.
The wishes of our sensual nature draw
us on to roam abroad,
But when the hour is gone,
What can we carry back?
A conscience heavy and a heart dis-
turbed.

MEN: The merry visit often brings the
sad return,

The merry watch kept up till late
makes the morning dark.
So every fleshly job comes with a
smiling face,
But at the last it bites and kills.

SOLO VOICE (*male*): Then lift your
eyes unto your God on high,
And pray against your sins and all
you leave undone.
Throw vanity to vanity,
But, as for you, mind you the precepts
of your God.
Go in and bar your door
And call upon your loved one, "Jesus,
come to me."
Stay in your room with Him;
Elsewhere you will not find such rest.
Had you not left your room,
Had you not heard a whisper from the
gossip of the world,
You would have been more restful;
But if you love now and again to hear
the talk of men,
Your heart will have to bear its stormy
hour.

[MUSIC CUE 4.]

WOMEN: Where'er you are, where'er
you turn, you are but miserable,
Save when you turn to God.

MEN: Why so dismayed
When things succeed not with you as
you dearly wish?
Who is there that has all things just to
suit his will?
Not I, not you,
Nor any living man.
No one without some grievous care
and some distress lives in the
passing world,
King though he be or Pope.
Who has the better lot?

The man who can bear anything for
    God.

SOLO VOICE (*female*): It is the talk of
    poor weak-minded souls to say,
"See you that man? How good his life,
How rich, how great, how high, how
    strong."
But turn your eyes to what is rich in
    heaven.
And you will see that all this trash of
    time is naught,
Quite unsafe, and only burdensome;
For it is never held apart from anxious
    thought and care.
Man's happiness does not consist
In the abundance of the things of time;
A little is enough for him.

SOLO VOICE (*male*): Life on the earth
    is misery indeed.
The more a man longs for a higher
    life,
The greater is the bitterness of this,—
More clearly does he see, more plainly
    feel,
The want and the corruption of hu-
    manity.
We eat, we drink,
We sleep, we watch,
We rest, we work,
We yield to all the other debts that
    nature makes us pay
All this is misery and sorrow to the
    pious soul,
Who longs to be quite free, untram-
    melled by a sin.
His inward heart is much disturbed
By all the body's needs here in the
    world;
Whence comes the prophet's pious
    prayer
To be far from them as he may:
"Tear me away from my necessities, O
    Lord."

[MUSIC CUE 5.]

SOLO VOICE (*female*): But woe to
    them that know not their own
    misery;
And woe, worse woe to those who love
    this life,
So wretched, and so ready to decay;
For some hug life to them so close,
That, could they scarcely get enough
    to eat
By begging or by work,
If they could only live on here for ever,
They would care nothing for God's
    kingdom.
Fools and faithless in your hearts,
So deeply sunk in earthly things,
That you taste nothing save the flesh;
But at the last you wretched men will
    feel it heavily,
How cheap and worthless are the
    things that you have loved.

But saints of God and all the pious
    friends of Christ
Cared not for all that pleased the flesh,
Cared not for all that flourished in this
    passing time,
But all their thoughts and all their
    hopes panted for the everlasting
    good,
All their desires were lifted up, high
    up to what lasts long, to what
    men cannot see.

MEN: My brother, lose not heart, in
    going on upon your spiritual
    path;
There still is time: you have an hour,
Why will you so put off your plans for
    good?
Rise and at once begin,
And say,
"Now is the time to act,
Now is the time to fight,

Now is the time to make myself a better man."

WOMEN: When you are in trouble and
in woe,
Then is the time to win your crown;
Through fire and water you must pass,
Till you come out into a cooler land;
And, save you act with violence,
You will not crush your sin.

ALL: As long as we have with us this
weak mortal frame
Sinless we cannot be,

Nor can we live apart from weariness
and pain.
We would so gladly be at rest from all
our trouble,
But, as by sin we lost our sinless state,
We lost as well our blessedness.
So we must needs be patient
Waiting for God's pity,
Till "this iniquity be overpast,
And our mortality be swallowed up by
life."

[MUSIC CUE 6.]

THE ROYAL PATHWAY

MUSIC CUE 1

MUSIC CUE 2

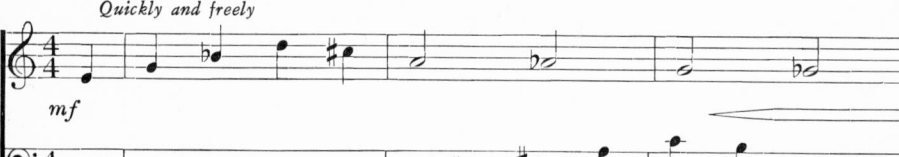

MUSIC CUE 3

MUSIC CUE 4

MUSIC CUE 5

MUSIC CUE 6: *Repeat Music Cue 1*

OUR PREPARATION FOR
THE FUTURE

Chapters 23 and 24, Book One, of
THE IMITATION OF CHRIST.

[MUSIC CUE 1.]

WOMEN: Soon, so soon, it will be over
with you here;
Think how it may be with you—there.
Man lives today,
Tomorrow he is gone,
And when he passes from the eyes of
men,
Even so soon he passes from the mind.

SOLO VOICE (*male*): How dull, how
hard the heart of man;
He muses only on the things that are,
And does not raise his eyes to what
must come.
Therefore in every deed and thought
you ought to act
As though you were to die today.
If your conscience were but good
You would not have much fear of
death.
Better it were to guard against your
sins
Than nurse this fear.
If today you are not ready,
Will you be tomorrow?
And tomorrow is a day you must not
count on;
How do you know that you will have
the morrow for your own?

WOMEN: What is the use of living long,
When our improvement is so slow?
But, ah, a long life does not always
make us good;
It often only makes our guilt the
greater.

Oh, would to God that in this world
we had spent *one day* well.
Many count up the years since first
they turned to God,
But often there is little fruit to show
of life made holier.
If it be terrible to die,
Perhaps the living on and on will be
more dangerous still.

SOLO VOICE (*female*): Happy the man
who ever holds before his eyes his
hour of death,
And every day makes himself ready
for the end.
If you have ever seen a death,
Think that you too must cross by the
same road,
And in the morning say,
"I shall not see the evening of the
day";
And at the eventide,
"I dare not promise morning to my-
self."

MEN: Therefore be ready,
And live so
That death may never take you un-
awares.
Many die suddenly and unexpectedly,
For "in an hour when you think not,
The Son of man will come."
And when that last hour does come
on you,
Then you will begin to feel so differ-
ently
Concerning all your life that has gone
by;
And you will grieve and grieve that
you were so remiss,
And that you left so much undone.

[MUSIC CUE 2.]

WOMEN: How happy he, and prudent,
Who tries in this life to be such a man

As he would be found in death.
Perfect scorn of all the world,
And burning longing to get on upon
the virtuous path,
Love of self-discipline,
And penitential work,
Quickness to listen,
And self-sacrifice,
And readiness to bear whatever goes
against him
For love of Christ,
Will make a man sure of a happy
death.

MEN: Try then so on earth to live
That in the hour of death you may be
glad, not frightened.
Learn your lesson now; die to the
world,
That you may then begin to live with
Christ.
Learn your lesson now; scorn all,
That you may then be free to go to
Him.
Chasten your body now by penance,
That then your confidence may be
more sure.

SOLO VOICE (*male*): Ah, fool, why
think you you will live so long?
For you have no day sure to you.
How many are deceived,
Torn from the body unexpectedly.
Have you not ever and again heard
people say,

SOLO VOICE (*female*): "He was pierced
through with the sword,

SECOND WOMAN: Another drowned,

THIRD WOMAN: Another killed by falling from a height,

SOLO VOICE (*male*): One stiffened into
death as he was eating,

SOLO VOICE (*female*): Another in his
play,

SECOND MAN: Fire took another,

SOLO VOICE (*female*): Or the steel,

SECOND WOMAN: The plague,

THIRD WOMAN: The robbers on the
road."

SOLO VOICE (*male*): And thus is death
the end of all,
And human life is like a shadow
swiftly passing by.
Who will regard you after death,
And who will pray for you?

[MUSIC CUE 3.]

ALL: Ever gaze upon the end,
And think how you will stand before
the awful Judge,
Whose eye sees all,
Who smiles not on your bribes,
Who takes not your excuses,
Judging with a judgment that is just.

SOLO VOICE (*male*): O sinful one, fool-
ish and wretched,
You who now and then are trembling
at the face of angry man,
What answer have you for your God
Who knows your evil deeds?
Why not provide yourself with some-
thing on the judgment day, when
none will by another's word be
shielded, none excused;
But every man will be a burden to
himself,
Heavy enough to bear?
Then will your present toil bear fruit,
Then will your tearful prayers be
heard,
Your groans will reach His ear,
Your grief will cleanse you and will
satisfy your God.

SOLO VOICE (*female*): A patient man
    that when receiving wrong
Grieves more about another's evil
    thoughts
Than for the hurt unto himself,
Loving to pray for those who are op-
    posing him,
Not slack in asking pardon of other
    men,
Readier for pity than for rage,
Often hard upon himself,
And trying in all to bring the flesh
    below the soul,
He has a faithful medicine that will
    purify his life.

MEN: Better it is upon the earth to
    purge our sins,
And cut away our faults,
Than if we keep them to be purged in
    days to come.
In truth we cheat ourselves
By our unending love unto the flesh.
What else shall be the fuel of that fire
If it be not your sins?
The more you spare yourself in life,
The more you follow in the body's
    steps,
The harder will the reckoning be,
The more the food you keep to feed
    that blazing flame.

[MUSIC CUE 4.]

SOLO VOICE (*female*): The sins
    wherein the man has sinned,
In them shall he be punished with the
    greater pain;
For *there* the lazy shall be driven with
    burning goads,
There the greedy shall be tortured with
    a thirst and hunger infinite,
There the wanton and the lovers of de-
    lightsome things

In burning pitch and in foul brimstone
    shall be bathed;
And like mad dogs
The envious men shall howl for grief.
No sin,
That shall not meet its own peculiar
    torment.
There shall the proud
Be covered with the blushes of confu-
    sion.
There the miser
Shall with most miserable poverty be
    fettered.

SOLO VOICE (*male*): And *there* one
    hour shall in its punishment far
    heavier be
Than fivescore years on earth
In strictest penance spent.
On earth from time to time
There *is* a rest from toil.
And here we now and then enjoy the
    comfort of our friends.
There is no rest,
No comfort for the lost.

ALL: Be anxious now, be woeful now
Over your sins,
That in the judgment-day you may be
    safe among the blest.

[MUSIC CUE 5.]

WOMEN: Obedience, plain obedience
    shall then higher stand
Than all the cunning of the passing
    ages.

SOLO VOICE (*male*): A conscience fine
    and good shall make a man more
    glad
Than studied learning deep.

WOMEN: Then shall the scorn of
    wealth weigh heavier in the scale
Than all the treasures of the sons of
    men.

SECOND MAN: Then you shall get more comfort from your holy prayers
Than from your dainty fare.

WOMEN: Then you shall be far more joyful for the silence you have kept
Than for long tattling tales.

THIRD MAN: Then shall your holy deeds be worth
More than your lovely words.

MEN: Then shall your penance stern and rule of life delight you
More than all the pleasures of the earth.

SOLO VOICE (*male*): So train yourself in little things to suffer,
That in the day to come you may be freed from heavier woe.
Try first on earth
What you can do hereafter.
If now you can endure so little,
How will you bear a torture that must last for ever?

If now the little suffering makes you so impatient,
What will gehenna make you then?

MEN: Behold the truth—the two you cannot have,
Here in the world to pass delightful days,
And afterwards to reign a king with Christ.

SOLO VOICE (*male*): And had you lived even till today in power and pleasure,
What would it all have done for you,
If in this instant 'twas your doom to die?

ALL: So, all is vanity
Save loving God and serving Him alone;
For he who loves his God with all his heart
Fears neither death nor punishment.

[MUSIC CUE 6.]

THE ROYAL PATHWAY

MUSIC CUE 1

MUSIC CUE 2

MUSIC CUE 3

MUSIC CUE 4

MUSIC CUE 5

MUSIC CUE 6

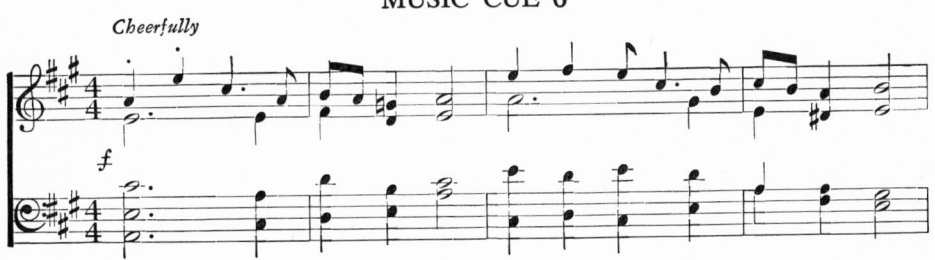

The Suffering of
ST. MARY

BY CHARLES PÉGUY

TRANSLATED FROM THE FRENCH BY JULIAN GREEN

ARRANGED FOR THREE READERS BY THEODORE M. SWITZ

FIRST READER: It was their fault. It must have been their fault.

They had always been too proud of him.

Joseph and she, they had been too proud of him.

It was bound to end badly.

You mustn't be so proud.

You mustn't be as proud as that.—

SECOND READER: Weren't they pleased

On the day when that old fellow Simeon

Sang that hymn to the Lord,

Which will be sung forever and ever. Amen.

And then there was that old woman in the temple.

THIRD READER: Weren't they proud!

Too proud.

FIRST READER: And that other time, too.

The time when he shone among the doctors.

At first they got quite a jolt,

When they came home

And he wasn't with them,

All of a sudden he wasn't with them.

They thought they had forgotten him somewhere.

Mary was all taken aback.

They thought they had lost him.—

That was no joke. It made her tremble.

It wasn't something that happened every day

To lose a twelve year old boy.

A big twelve year old boy.

THIRD READER: Fortunately they found him in the temple in the midst of the doctors.

Sitting in the midst of the doctors.

And the doctors listening religiously.

He was teaching, at the age of twelve, he was teaching in the midst of the doctors.

How proud they had felt.

Too proud.

SECOND READER: Just the same, he ought to have been careful, that day.

He had really been too brilliant, he shone too much in the midst of the doctors.

Too much for the doctors.

He was too great among the doctors.

For the doctors.

He had let it be seen too clearly.

He had let it be seen too much.

He had made it known too manifestly that he was God.

Doctors don't like that.

He ought to have been more careful. People like that have good memories.

It is even because they have such good memories that they are doctors.

He surely hurt their feelings that day.

And doctors have a good memory.

Doctors have a memory that goes way back.

FIRST READER: He ought to have been more careful. Those people have a memory that goes back a good deal.

And then they always stick together.

They uphold each other.

Doctors have a memory that goes way back.

He surely hurt their feelings that day.

When he was twelve.

FIRST, SECOND, and THIRD READERS: And when he was thirty-three, they got him.

And this time they wouldn't let him
　　off.　　　　　　　　　　[*Slowly*]
It meant death.

SECOND READER: They had him.
They got him.
When he was thirty-three they caught
　　him.
Doctors have a memory that goes way
　　back.—

FIRST READER: He had been a good
　　son to his father and mother.
Until the day when he began his mis-
　　sion.—
He was generally liked.
Everybody liked him.
Until the day when he began his mis-
　　sion.
His comrades, his friends, his com-
　　panions, the authorities,
The citizens,
His father and mother,
They all thought what he did was all
　　right.
Until the day when he began his mis-
　　sion.—

THIRD READER: The authorities thought
　　what he did was all right.
Until the day when he began his mis-
　　sion.
The authorities considered he was a
　　man of order.
A serious young man.
A quiet young man.
A young man with good habits.
Easy to govern.
Giving back to Caesar what was Cae-
　　sar's.
Until the day when he had begun dis-
　　order.
Introduced disorder.
The greatest disorder in the world.
The greatest there ever was in the
　　world.

The greatest order there had been in
　　the world.

FIRST, SECOND, THIRD READERS: The
　　only order.
There had ever been in the world.—

SECOND READER: He was a good son
　　to his father and mother.
He was a good son to his mother
　　Mary.
And his father and mother thought
　　everything was all right.
His mother Mary thought it was all
　　right.
She was happy, she was proud of hav-
　　ing such a son.
Of being the mother of such a son.—
And she gloried perhaps a little in her-
　　self, and she magnified God.
Magnificat anima mea.
Dominum.
Et exultavit spiritus meus.
Magnificat. Magnificat.
Until the day when he had begun his
　　mission.—
Perhaps she no longer said Magnificat
　　then.
For the last three days
　　she wept.
She wept and wept　　　*Slowly*
As no other woman　　　*Emphatically*
　　has ever wept.—
No boy had ever cost his mother so
　　many tears.
No boy had ever made his mother
　　weep as much.
And that is what he had done to his
　　mother
Since he had begun his mission.—

FIRST READER: For the past three days
　　she had been wandering, and fol-
　　lowing.
She followed the people.
She followed the events.

She seemed to be following a funeral.
But it was a living man's funeral.—
She followed like a follower.
Like a servant.
Like a weeper at a Roman funeral.—
As if it had been her only occupation.
To weep.—   [*Pause*]
That is what he had done to his
    mother.
Since the day when he had begun his
    mission.—
You saw her everywhere.
With the people and a little apart from
    the people.
Under the porticoes, under the ar-
    cades, in drafty places.
In the temples, in the palaces.
In the streets.
In the yards and in the back-yards.
And she had also gone
    up to Calvary.   *Slower*
She too had climbed up   *Gravely*
    Calvary.
A very steep hill.
And she did not even feel that she was
    walking.
She did not even feel that her feet were
    carrying her.—
She too had gone up her Calvary.
She too had gone up and up
In the general confusion, lagging a lit-
    tle behind . . .
She wept and wept under a big linen
    veil.
A big blue veil.
A little faded.—
She wept as it will never be granted to
    a woman to weep.
As it will never be asked
Of a woman to weep on this earth.
Never at any time.—

THIRD READER: What was very strange
    was that everyone respected her.

People greatly respect the parents of
    the condemned.
FIRST, SECOND, THIRD READERS:
They even said—Poor woman.

THIRD READER: And at the same time
    they struck at her son.
Because man is like that.—
The world is like that.
Men are what they are and you never
    can change them.
She did not know that, on the con-
    trary, he had come to change
    man.
That he had come to change the world.
She followed and wept.
And at the same time they were beat-
    ing her boy.—
She followed and wept.
Everybody respected her.
Everybody pitied her.

FIRST, SECOND, THIRD READERS: They
    said: Poor woman.

THIRD READER: Because they weren't
    perhaps really bad.
They weren't bad at heart.
They fulfilled the Scriptures.—
They honored, respected and admired
    her grief.
They didn't make her go away, they
    pushed her back only a little
With special attentions
Because she was the mother of the
    condemned.
They thought: It's the family of the
    condemned.
They even said so in a low voice.
They said it among themselves
With a secret admiration.—
She followed and wept, and didn't un-
    derstand very well.

But she understood quite well that the government was against her boy.
And that is a very bad business.—
She understood that all the governments were together against her boy.
The government of the Jews and the government of the Romans.
The government of judges and the government of priests.
The government of soldiers and the government of parsons.
He could never get out of it.

FIRST, SECOND, *and* THIRD READERS:
Certainly not.—

SECOND READER: What was strange was that all derision was heaped on him.
Not on her at all.—
There was only respect for her.
        [*Rapidly build to a climax.*]
For her grief.—
They didn't insult her.
On the contrary.
People even refrained from looking at her too much.
All the more to respect her.
So she too had gone up.
Gone up with everybody else.
Up to the very top of the hill.
Without even being aware of it.
Her legs had carried her and she did not even know it.

She too had made the Way of the Cross.
The fourteen stations of the Way of the Cross.
Were there fourteen stations?
Were there really fourteen stations?—
She didn't know for sure.
She couldn't remember.
Yet she had not missed one.
She was sure of that.
But you can always make a mistake.
In moments like that your head swims. . . .

FIRST, SECOND, *and* THIRD READERS:
Everybody was against him.
Everybody wanted him to die.

FIRST READER: It is strange.
People who are not usually together.
The government and the people.—
That was awful luck.
When you have someone for you and someone against you, sometimes you can get out of it.
You can scramble out of it.

SECOND READER: But he wouldn't.
Certainly he wouldn't.   [*Slowly*]
When you have everyone against you.
But what had he done to everyone?
        [*Clearly*]

THIRD READER: I'll tell you.
        [*Triumphantly*]
He had saved the world.

CHRIST OUR SAVIOUR

DIALOGUES FROM THE GOSPEL OF ST. JOHN

ARRANGED FOR ANTIPHONAL READING BY FREDERICK A. SCHILLING

INTRODUCTION: THE NATURE OF ST. JOHN'S GOSPEL

Among the writings of the New Testament the Gospel of St. John is unsurpassed for its devotional nature. From the second Christian century when Clement of Alexandria called it "the spiritual Gospel," it has been, in worshipful use, the most widely and frequently read of the four Gospels, if not of all the books of the Bible, and has had the strongest appeal to non-Christian readers, especially among the mystically minded people of the Orient.

The reason for this religious popularity is readily found in the Johannine portrait of Jesus. Here Jesus is shown in a stature that transcends the historical. He is the exalted Lord speaking with a living voice and in the universal language of inward spiritual experience. The Palestinian features of the total portrait and its background are but as stage scenery. They are needed for realistic effect. But these details are held to a minimum so that the person of Jesus always stands out distinctly in epic mold, eternal, so that men everywhere can own Him as their divine Master.

In content and style St. John's Gospel has an elevated quality. Its narrative portions are brief and attempt no connected sequence. Throughout runs an element of poetry, like that of hymns and psalms, with rhythmic, well balanced parallelisms or antitheses and liturgical intonations. Even the prose is poetic in its solemn priestly cadences. One cannot read the Gospel without hearing, in the words of Jesus, the Evangelist addressing his churches and leading them in liturgical exercises with responses and confessions of faith. The over-all effect is that of a succession of scenes in a drama. But that is only a loosely fitting description. The drama is not the ordinary drama of a stage play of the life of Jesus, but that of the liturgical act of a worshiping congregation.

Devotional worship and affirmation of faith go together. They stimulate each other. In the atmosphere of meditation and prayer the declaration of love and faith is born. In St. John's Gospel this is perfectly clear, indeed, effectively demonstrated. The teaching elements, and they are prominent, though neither so heavy nor of the formal philosophical or theological kind that many scholars seem to find —for if they were right about it, how could the Gospel ever have been so cherished by common, pious folk?— are varied by dialogue and narrative episodes, clothed in the sublime style of poetry or poetic prose, and relieved by the participation of the body of worshipers. The voices of priest, minister, cantor, chorister and congregation are heard separately or intermingled to produce the richly symphonic Glad Tidings of Jesus Christ according to St. John.

Apostolic personality, prophet and preacher, Bishop of the Church in Ephesus in the perilous years of the closing first century, hymnodist and priest, St. John composed his Gospel so that his people and many others would have a deep and living faith in Jesus as the Christ, the Son of God. But to accomplish this purpose St. John did not write a theological argument or a revision of the earlier narratives and catechisms about Jesus (the Gospels of Mark and Luke and Matthew). Rather, with fresh originality and deep understanding of the human soul he turned to the medium of liturgical forms, words and acts of worship, ripened in the practices of his own churches, as the vehicle of revelation and instruction of the contemporary Christ. To Christ through contemplation and worship is the way of the last of the Gospels. However, it is not the way of the solitary follower, but of the individual strengthened and enlarged as one member of a congregation; and it is in the power and spirit of the united worshiping group and their confession of faith that belief is then transformed into loving, effective, life-giving action, which is the final and complete form of discipleship. Here is then the embodiment of the Exalted Christ. "I do not pray for these only, but also for those who are to believe in me through their word, that they may all be one; even as thou, Father, art in me, and I in thee, that they also may be in us, so that the world may believe that thou hast sent me" (17:20, 21). "By this all men will know that you are my disciples, if you have love for one another" (13:35).

The literary structure of these selected passages makes their appointment to the minister, to the narrator, and to the congregation, very easy. The narrative and explanatory portions naturally fall to the narrator. The questions or replies to Jesus and, certainly, the acceptances and affirmations of faith are the words of the congregation. The role of Jesus is to be taken by the minister.

The directions and rubrics, as well as the brief narrative insertions which are essential to the script of the play but not to its oral presentation, are printed *in italics and are not to be read audibly unless specifically assigned to the narrator.* Thus the entire original text is printed, but it is read without interruptions in the dramatic dialogue.

I. A CANTICLE TO JESUS CHRIST, THE LIVING WORD OF GOD

John 1:1-18

The Prologue to St. John's Gospel gathers up in poetic form the main teaching elements of the entire Gospel: God, Word, Life, Light, Flesh, Glory, Son. Its style and composition clearly mark it as an ancient hymn with which the congregation sang its confession of faith in Christ. While it can be read or chanted in unison, yet its intended effect can best be achieved when it is chanted responsively. The division of the responses is therefore indicated by the placing of the asterisk between the members of the parallelisms, antitheses, or lyric and didactic parts.

The versification of the Prologue follows the arrangement which W. H. Raney, in his "The Relation of the Fourth Gospel to the Christian Cultus," made in the Greek text on the basis of clearly indicated accent rhythms and various kinds of parallelisms. While the rhythms cannot be reproduced to full effect in a translation, yet the parallelisms are obvious in the meaning and structure of the sentences so that the verse arrangement even in translation does preserve much of the literary and psalmic flavor.

This arrangement has made a change in the wording of verses two and three. Instead of the traditional sentence, "And without him was not anything made that was made," we have here the last clause added to the next sentence to produce the reading of that sentence as, "What was made in him was life," instead of simply, "In him was life."

The last verse is the summation which should be said or sung by minister and congregation in unison. It seems appropriate to end this magnificent Christian canticle with the thankful adoration of the liturgical *Gloria Patri*.

[*To be recited responsively, with a definite pause at each asterisk* *.*]

In the beginning was the Word
And the Word was with God*
And the Word was God.

He was in the beginning with God.
All things were made through him*
And without him was not anything
    made.

What was made in him was life*
And the life was the light of men.

The light shines in darkness*
And the darkness has not overcome it.

There was a man sent from God,
Whose name was John.*
He came for testimony,
To bear witness to the Light,
That all should believe through him.

He was not the light,*
But came to bear witness to the light.

The true light that enlightens every
    man was coming into the world;*
He was in the world,
And the world was made through him,
Yet the world knew him not.

He came to his own home,*
And his own people received him not.

But to all who received him,
Who believed in his name,*
He gave power
To become children of God;

Who were born not of blood, nor of
    the will of the flesh*
Nor of the will of man, but of God.

And the Word became flesh
And dwelt among us*
And we have beheld his glory,
Glory as of the only Son of the Father
    full of grace and truth.

John bore witness to him, and cried,*
"This was he of whom I said*
'He who comes after me ranks before
    me*
For he was before me.' "

And from his fulness have we all re-
    ceived,*
Grace upon grace.

For the law was given through Moses,*
Grace and truth came through Jesus
    Christ.

NO ONE HAS EVER SEEN GOD,*
THE ONLY SON, WHO IS IN THE BOSOM
    OF THE FATHER,
HE HAS MADE HIM KNOWN.

———

Glory be to the Father, and to the
Son, and to the Holy Ghost;

As it was in the beginning, is now, and ever shall be, world without end. Amen.

LET US PRAY.

Blessed be thou, O God, who hast given us the light of the knowledge of thy glory in the face of Jesus Christ.†

Glory to thee, O Christ, our ascended and ever present Lord, through whom we have access to the Father.†

Almighty God, who hast poured upon us the new light of thine incarnate Word; Grant that the same light enkindled in our hearts may shine forth in our lives.

O God, whose blessed Son Jesus Christ became man that we might become the sons of God: Grant, we beseech thee, that being made partakers of the divine nature of thy Son, we may be conformed to his likeness; who liveth and reigneth with thee and the Holy Ghost, now and ever. Amen.

II. THE WITNESS OF
THE FORERUNNER

John 1:19-34

The Forerunner points to the Christ, and by so doing is himself distinguished from Him for those of his followers who might (and did, historically) confuse him with the real divine Master. His example is always relevant. Individual Christians, including the minister, and the Church as a

---

† From *The Kingdom, the Power, and the Glory* (New York: Oxford University Press, 1933). Used by permission of the publisher.

total entity, have the role of witnessing like John the Baptist, and pointing to Jesus the Christ as the one of final importance.

The last sentence is the powerful expression of this realization, or, if need be, a reminder, of being witnesses, and of the affirmation of Jesus Christ as the Son of God. Minister and congregation, therefore, make this declaration together.

NARRATOR: *This is the testimony of John, when the Jews sent priests and Levites from Jerusalem to ask him:*

CONGREGATION: "Who are you?"

He confessed, he did not deny, but confessed,

SECOND READER: "I am not the Christ."

And they asked him,

CONGREGATION: "What then? Are you Elija?"

He said,

SECOND READER: "I am not."

CONGREGATION: "Are you the prophet?"

And he answered,

SECOND READER: "No."

They said to him then,

CONGREGATION: "Who are you? Let us have an answer for those who sent us. What do you say about yourself?"

He said,

SECOND READER: "I am the voice of one crying in the wilderness, 'Make straight the way of the

Lord,' as the prophet Isaiah said."

Now they had been sent from the Pharisees. They asked him,

CONGREGATION: "Then why are you baptizing, if you are neither the Christ, nor Elija, nor the prophet?"

John answered them,

SECOND READER: "I baptize with water; but among you stands one whom you do not know, even he who comes after me, the thong of whose sandal I am not worthy to untie."

This took place in Bethany beyond the Jordan, where John was baptizing.

NARRATOR: *The next day he saw Jesus coming toward him, and said,*

SECOND READER: "BEHOLD, THE LAMB OF GOD, WHO TAKES AWAY THE SIN OF THE WORLD! This is he of whom I said, 'After me comes a man, who ranks before me.' I myself did not know him; but for this I came baptizing with water, that he might be revealed to Israel."

And John bore witness,

SECOND READER: "I saw the Spirit descend as a dove from Heaven, and it remained on him. I myself did not know him; but he who sent me to baptize with water said to me,

[Congregation stands.]

MINISTER: 'He on whom you see the Spirit descend and remain, this is he who baptizes with the Holy Spirit.'

And

MINISTER AND CONGREGATION: "I HAVE SEEN AND BORNE WITNESS THAT THIS IS THE SON OF GOD."

GLORY be to God on high, and on earth peace, good will toward men. We praise thee, we bless thee, we worship thee, we give thanks to thee for thy great glory, O Lord God, heavenly King, God the Father Almighty.

O Lord, the only-begotten Son, Jesus Christ; O Lord God, Lamb of God, Son of the Father, that takest away the sins of the world, have mercy upon us. Thou that takest away the sins of the world, receive our prayer. Thou that sittest at the right hand of God the Father, have mercy upon us.

For thou only art holy; thou only art the Lord; thou only, O Christ, with the Holy Ghost, are most high in the glory of God the Father. Amen.

LET US PRAY.

Almighty God, by whose providence thy servant John Baptist was wonderfully born, and sent to prepare the way of thy Son our Saviour by preaching repentance; Make us so to follow his doctrine and holy life, that we may truly repent according to his preaching; and after his example constantly speak the truth, boldly rebuke vice, and patiently suffer for the truth's sake; through the same thy Son Jesus Christ our Lord. Amen.

Almighty God, who didst wonderfully create man in thine own image, and didst yet more wonderfully restore him: Grant, we beseech thee, that as thy Son our Lord Jesus Christ was made in the likeness of men, so we may be made partakers of the divine nature; through the same thy Son, who, with thee and the Holy Ghost, liveth and reigneth one God world without end. Amen.

God, our Shepherd, give to the Church a new vision and a new charity, new wisdom and fresh understanding, the revival of her brightness and the renewal of her unity; that the eternal message of thy Son, undefiled by the traditions of men, may be hailed as the good news of the new age; through him who maketh all things new, Jesus Christ our Lord. Amen.

III. THE MEN WHO FOLLOW

John 1:35-51

The various details of this scene, the different personalities and responses, dramatize the beginnings of early Christian discipleships. At the same time this passage reflects something of the universal experience of becoming followers of Christ. The understanding of Him advances through enlarging and deepening recognitions in their historical contexts toward the highest universal lesson which He sets forth, namely, that He is for all men the eternal link, a two-way channel of communication, between heaven and earth, because He is Son of Man, God-Man. Thus the dialogue arrives at its high point when the congregation, standing, makes Nathanael's confession and receives reverently the words about the greater things yet to be seen.

NARRATOR: *The next day again John was standing with two of his disciples; and he looked at Jesus as he walked, and said:*

SECOND READER: "BEHOLD THE LAMB OF GOD!"

NARRATOR: *The two disciples heard him say this, and they followed Jesus. Jesus turned and saw them following, and said to them:*

MINISTER: "What do you seek?"

And they said to him,

CONGREGATION: "Rabbi (*which means Teacher*), where are you staying?"

He said to them,

MINISTER: "Come and see."

NARRATOR: *They came and saw where he was staying; and they stayed with him that day, for it was about the tenth hour.*
One of the two who heard John speak, and followed him, was Andrew, Simon Peter's brother. He first found his brother Simon, and said to him:

CONGREGATION: "WE HAVE FOUND THE MESSIAH" (*which means Christ*).

NARRATOR: *He brought him to Jesus. Jesus looked at him, and said:*

MINISTER: "So you are Simon the son of John? You shall be called Cephas" (*which means Rock*).

NARRATOR: *The next day Jesus decided to go to Galilee. And he found Philip and said to him:*

MINISTER: "Follow me."

NARRATOR: *Now Philip was from Bethsaida, the city of Andrew and Peter. Philip found Nathanael, and said to him:*

SECOND READER: "WE HAVE FOUND HIM OF WHOM MOSES IN THE LAW AND ALSO THE PROPHETS WROTE, JESUS OF NAZARETH, THE SON OF JOSEPH."

Nathanael said to him,

CONGREGATION: "Can anything good come out of Nazareth?"

Philip said to him,

SECOND LEADER: "Come and see."

NARRATOR: *Jesus saw Nathanael coming to him, and said to him:*

MINISTER: "Behold, an Israelite indeed, in whom is no guile!"

Nathanael said to him,

SECOND LEADER: "How do you know me?"

Jesus answered him,

MINISTER: "Before Philip called you, when you were under the fig tree, I saw you."

Nathanael answered him,

CONGREGATION (*standing*): "Rabbi, YOU ARE THE SON OF GOD! YOU ARE THE KING OF ISRAEL!"

Jesus answered him,

MINISTER: "Because I said to you, 'I saw you under the fig tree,' do you believe? You shall see greater things than these."

And he said to him,

MINISTER: "TRULY, TRULY, I SAY TO YOU, YOU WILL SEE HEAVEN OPENED, AND THE ANGELS OF GOD ASCENDING AND DESCENDING UPON THE SON OF MAN."

LET US PRAY.

Almighty God, who didst give such grace unto thy holy Apostle Saint Andrew, that he readily obeyed the calling of thy Son Jesus Christ, and followed him without delay; Grant unto us all, that we, being called by thy holy Word, may forthwith give up ourselves obediently to fulfil thy holy commandments; through the same Jesus Christ our Lord. Amen.

O Lord Jesus Christ, suffer us not, we beseech thee, to stray from thee, who art the Way, nor to doubt thee, who art the Truth, nor to rest in aught but thee, who art the Life; but by thy Holy Spirit make clear our path, and strong our faith, and sure our everlasting home, who with the Father and the same Spirit livest and reignest ever, one God, world without end. Amen.

O Jesus Christ, the Lord of all good life, who hast called us to build the city of God, do thou enrich and purify our lives and deepen in us our discipleship. Help us daily to know more of thee, and through us, by the power of thy Spirit, show forth thyself to other men. Make us humble, brave, and loving; make us ready for adventure. We do not ask that thou wilt keep us safe, but that thou wilt keep us loyal; who for us didst face death unafraid, and dost live and reign for ever and ever. Amen.†

O Lord, we pray that thou wouldst give to all professing Christians a sense of their responsibility, that they may adorn the doctrine of our Saviour, and by their good example commend the faith to others; and that thou wouldst hasten the time when the gospel shall have been preached to all nations, and the whole world shall be filled with the knowledge of thy love. Amen.†

IV. JESUS, GOD'S TEACHER

John 2:23-3:21

Nicodemus represents the human teacher who is baffled by the ways of God. While these can be felt in their effects, yet in their nature they are intangible like the wind. The one to explain them must come from God and be of God. Jesus is that Teacher, and they who would know and experience the reign of God must have a birth from above as He did.

The person of Jesus in this dialogue merges into that of the author, St. John, and his church. Their testimony is already audible in the "we speak of what we know," and becomes distinct in the praise of God for His love in the giving of His Son for the life of man. They, too, are teachers of God through Christ.

The congregation stands to assert

---

† From *The Kingdom, the Power, and the Glory* (New York: Oxford University Press, 1933). Used by permission of the publisher.

this confident recognition of what Jesus as the Teacher from God means for man.

Services of adult baptisms and confirmations are especially appropriate occasions for the use of this lesson because the rebirth from above, i.e., being born of the Spirit, has from earliest times been realized ritualistically by Christians in the two-fold apostolic experience of baptism and the laying on of hands.

The versification of the latter portion of this reading follows the tracing of the rhythm in the Greek text by W. H. Raney. The power of this hymn is, of course, felt at once. The primary use would naturally be to chant it either responsively (for which purpose asterisks have been inserted to mark the responses) or in unison, or it may be read in chorus.

NARRATOR: *Now when he was in Jerusalem at the Passover feast, many believed in his name when they saw his signs which he did; but Jesus did not trust himself to them, because he knew all men and needed no one to bear witness of man; for he himself knew what was in man.*

Now there was a man of the Pharisees, named Nicodemus, a ruler of the Jews. This man came to Jesus by night and said to him:

CONGREGATION: "Rabbi, WE KNOW THAT YOU ARE A TEACHER COME FROM GOD; for no one can do these signs that you do, unless God is with him."

Jesus answered him,

MINISTER: "TRULY, TRULY, I SAY TO YOU, UNLESS ONE IS BORN ANEW,

HE CANNOT SEE THE KINGDOM OF GOD."

Nicodemus said to him,

CONGREGATION: "How can a man be born when he is old? Can he enter a second time into his mother's womb and be born?"

Jesus answered,

MINISTER: "TRULY, TRULY, I SAY TO YOU, UNLESS ONE IS BORN OF WATER AND THE SPIRIT, HE CANNOT ENTER THE KINGDOM OF GOD. That which is born of the flesh is flesh, and that which is born of the Spirit is spirit. Do not marvel that I said to you, 'You must be born anew.' The wind blows where it wills, and you hear the sound of it, but you do not know whence it comes or whither it goes; so it is with every one who is born of the Spirit."

Nicodemus said to him,

CONGREGATION: "How can this be?"

Jesus answered him,

MINISTER: "Are you a teacher of Israel, and yet you do not understand this? TRULY, TRULY, I SAY TO YOU, WE SPEAK OF WHAT WE KNOW, AND BEAR WITNESS TO WHAT WE HAVE SEEN; but you do not receive our testimony. If I have told you earthly things and you do not believe, how can you believe if I tell you heavenly things? No one has ascended into heaven but he who descended from heaven, the Son of man. And as Moses lifted up the ser-

pent in the wilderness, so must the Son of man be lifted up, that whosoever believes in him may have eternal life."

[Congregation stands.]

MINISTER: (For) GOD SO LOVED THE WORLD,*

CONGREGATION: THAT HE GAVE HIS ONLY SON,*

MINISTER: THAT WHOSOEVER BELIEVES IN HIM SHOULD NOT PERISH*

CONGREGATION: BUT HAVE ETERNAL LIFE.

MINISTER: For God sent the Son into the world,

SECOND READER: Not to condemn the world,*

CONGREGATION: But that the world might be saved through him.

MINISTER: He who believes in him is not condemned;

SECOND READER: He who does not believe is condemned already,*

CONGREGATION: Because he has not believed in the name of the only Son of God.

MINISTER: (And) This is the judgment,*

CONGREGATION: That the light has come into the world,*

MINISTER: And men have loved darkness rather than light,*

CONGREGATION: Because their deeds were evil.

MINISTER: For every one who does evil hates the light,*

SECOND READER: And does not come to the light,

CONGREGATION: Lest his deeds should be exposed.

MINISTER: But he who does what is true comes to the light,*

SECOND READER: That it may be clearly seen that his deeds

CONGREGATION: Have been wrought in God.

LET US PRAY.

Worthy art thou, O God, to receive the honor and the power; for thou didst create all things, and because of thy will they are and were created.

Glory to thee, O Christ, who didst redeem with thy love men of every kindred and tongue and people and nation.

Glory to thee, O Holy Spirit, for thy work in the Church, which will not cease until thou hast made of all mankind one family, to the praise and glory of God.

O living Christ, make us conscious now of thy healing nearness. Touch our eyes that we may see thee; open our ears that we may hear thy voice; enter our hearts that we may know thy love. Overshadow our souls and bodies with thy presence, that we may partake of thy strength, thy love, and thy healing life. Amen.

O Lord Jesus Christ, who art the truth incarnate and the teacher of the faithful; let thy spirit overshadow us in reading thy Word, and conform our thoughts to thy revelation, that learning of thee with honest hearts, we may be rooted and built up in thee; who livest and reignest with the Holy Ghost, one God, world without end. Amen.

O Thou who art the Light of the minds that know thee, the Life of the souls that love thee, and the Strength of the wills that serve thee, help us to know thee that we may truly love thee, so to love thee that we may fully serve thee, whom to serve is perfect freedom; through Jesus Christ our Lord. Amen.

O God, our great Companion, lead us ever more deeply into the knowledge of thy life and ours, and make us faithful interpreters of life to our fellows; through Jesus Christ our Lord. Amen.

V. JESUS THE SAVIOUR
OF THE WORLD

John 4:1-42

In this vivid scene outside of the Samaritan village we see Jesus and His Gospel actively engaged in missionary effort beyond the borders of the homeland. History and geography place no limitations upon either the actions of God or man's experience of Him. Only one condition obtains, and that is the spirit of truth. Jesus is Saviour for all men everywhere. He is the never-failing spring of life. Men need but to be thirsty and drink.

The words, "I who speak to you am he," render the original, "I Am is he who is speaking to you," and reveal the Exalted Lord not only as Messiah, but verily as God, the "I Am" of the Old Testament and the ever-living God of all mankind.

The Christian's perpetual mission is reflected in Jesus' own action; and in the responses of the Samaritan woman and her village folk are expressed the awakened conscience and thought of the convert.

The conclusion offers to the entire body of worshipers the exercise of an effective declaration of conviction based on immediate personal experience.

NARRATOR: *Now when* THE LORD *knew that the Pharisees had heard that Jesus was making and baptizing more disciples than John (although Jesus himself did not baptize, but only his disciples), he left Judea and departed again to Galilee. He had to pass through Samaria. So he came to a city of Samaria, called Sychar, near the field that Jacob gave to his son Joseph. Jacob's well was there, and so Jesus, wearied as he was with his journey, sat down beside the well. It was about the sixth hour.*
There came a woman of Samaria to draw water. Jesus said to her:

MINISTER: "Give me a drink."

For his disciples had gone away into the city to buy food. The Samaritan woman said to him,

CONGREGATION: "How is it that you, a Jew, ask a drink of me, a woman of Samaria?"

Jesus answered her,

MINISTER: "If you knew the gift of God, and who it is that is saying to you, 'Give me a drink,' you would have asked him, and he would have given you living water."

The woman said to him,

CONGREGATION: "Sir, you have nothing to draw with, and the well is deep; where do you get that living water? Are you greater than our father Jacob, who gave us the well, and drank from it himself, and his sons, and his cattle?"

Jesus said to her,

MINISTER: "Everyone who drinks of this water will thirst again, but WHOEVER DRINKS OF THE WATER THAT I SHALL GIVE HIM WILL NEVER THIRST; the water that I shall give him will become in him a spring of water welling up to eternal life."

The woman said to him,

CONGREGATION: "Sir, give me this water, that I may not thirst, nor come here to draw."

Jesus said to her,

MINISTER: "Go, call your husband, and come here."

The woman answered him,

CONGREGATION: "I have no husband."

Jesus said to her,

MINISTER: "You are right in saying, 'I have no husband'; for you have had five husbands, and he whom you now have is not your husband; this you said truly."

The woman said to him,

CONGREGATION (*standing*): "SIR, I PERCEIVE THAT YOU ARE A PROPHET. Our fathers worshiped on this mountain; and you say that in Jerusalem is the place where men ought to worship."

Jesus said to her,

MINISTER: "Woman, believe me, the hour is coming when neither on this mountain nor in Jerusalem will you worship the Father. You worship what you do not know; we worship what we know, for salvation is from the Jews.

MINISTER AND CONGREGATION: "The hour is coming, and now is, when the true worshipers will worship the Father in spirit and truth, for such the Father seeks to worship him. God is spirit, and those who worship him must worship in spirit and truth."

The woman said to him,

CONGREGATION: "I know that Messiah is coming (he who is called Christ); when he comes, he will show us all things."

Jesus said to her,

MINISTER: "I who speak to you am he."

[*Congregation is seated. Pause.*]

NARRATOR: *Just then his disciples came. They marveled that he was talking with a woman, but none said, "What do you wish?" or "Why are you talking with her?" So the woman left her water jar, and went away into* the city, and said to the people, "Come, see a man who told me all that I ever did. Can this be the Christ?" They went out of the city and were coming to him. Meanwhile the disciples besought him, saying "Rabbi, eat."

But he said to them,

MINISTER: "I have food to eat of which you do not know."

NARRATOR: *So the disciples said to one another, "Has anyone brought him food?"*

Jesus said to them,

MINISTER: "MY FOOD IS TO DO THE WILL OF HIM WHO SENT ME, AND TO ACCOMPLISH HIS WORK. Do you not say, 'There are yet four months, then comes the harvest?' I tell you, lift up your eyes, and see how the fields are already white for harvest. He who reaps receives wages, and gathers fruit for eternal life, so that sower and reaper may rejoice together. For here the saying holds true, 'One sows and another reaps.' I sent you to reap that for which you did not labor; others have labored, and you have entered into their labor."

NARRATOR: *Many Samaritans from that city believed in him because of the woman's testimony, "He told me all that I ever did." So when the Samaritans came to him, they asked him to stay with them; and he stayed there two days. And many more believed because of his word. They said to the woman:*

CONGREGATION (*standing*): "It is no longer because of your words that we believe, for we have heard for ourselves, and WE KNOW THAT THIS IS INDEED THE SAVIOUR OF THE WORLD."

LET US PRAY.

Lord Jesus, if we thirst not, give us thirst; if we thirst, give us to drink. Withhold not from us Thyself and Thy Most Holy Spirit, that we thirst no more, neither go elsewhere to draw.

Grant, O Lord, that all who worship within this place may present their bodies a living sacrifice, holy, acceptable unto thee; and that they may themselves be temples of the Holy Ghost, wherein thou wilt dwell for evermore. Amen.

O God, who in the exaltation of thy Son Jesus Christ dost sanctify thy universal Church; shed abroad in every race and nation the gift of his Spirit; that the work wrought by his power at the first preaching of the gospel may be extended throughout the whole world; through the same our Lord Jesus Christ, who liveth and reigneth with thee in the unity of the same Spirit now and ever. Amen.†

O Heavenly Father, Lord of the Harvest, have respect, we beseech thee, to our prayers, and send forth laborers into thy harvest. Fit and prepare them by thy grace for the work of their ministry, and grant that both by their lives and labors they may show forth thy glory and set forward

the salvation of all men, through Jesus Christ our Lord. Amen.

O God, who hast made of one blood all nations of men for to dwell on the face of the whole earth, and didst send thy blessed Son to preach peace to them that are far off and to them that are nigh; Grant that all men everywhere may seek after thee and find thee. Bring the nations into thy fold, pour out thy Spirit upon all flesh, and hasten thy kingdom; through the same thy son Jesus Christ our Lord. Amen.

VI. JESUS THE BREAD OF LIFE

John 6 (Verses 15-21, 64b, 65, 70, 71 are omitted.)

The account of the miraculous meal of the multitude is here used as an allegory or parable with interpretation added in the form of Jesus' discourse on the following day. His words, His character, His Life are nourishment to our souls. He is the spiritual bread that is always available and sufficient, and gives life eternal.

It seems quite certain that St. John contributed this lesson especially for use at the service of "the Breaking of Bread" or "Lord's Supper" which was everywhere observed in general accordance with the tradition established by the early apostles. Thus St. John balances the rite of Christ's sacrificial death with the spiritual emphasis upon the Risen Lord as the Bread of Life.

This reading may be used on any occasion. In the indicated responses the congregation has an important part in the liturgy. They stand to receive

---

† From *The Kingdom, the Power, and the Glory* (New York: Oxford University Press, 1933). Used by permission of the publisher.

the sublime Johannine affirmation of the Life which the believer has in his communion with Christ (vs. 63), and to end the service by declaring their faith in Christ with the words of Simon Peter, "You have the words of eternal life." This moving act of consecration may be sealed by having the congregation say the first of the suggested prayers in unison with the minister.

Regarding the indicated omissions from the text of this chapter it need only be said that they have been made in order to preserve the narrative and line of thought in unbroken sequence for the purpose of this liturgical exercise. Nothing of material relevance has been lost.

NARRATOR: *After this Jesus went to the other side of the sea of Galilee, which is the sea of Tiberias. And a multitude followed him, because they saw the signs which he did on those who were diseased. Jesus went up into the hills, and there sat down with his disciples. Now the Passover, the feast of the Jews, was at hand. Lifting up his eyes, then, and seeing that a multitude was coming to him, Jesus said to Philip:*

MINISTER: "How are we to buy bread, so that these people may eat?"

NARRATOR: *This he said to test him, for he himself knew what he would do. Philip answered him, "Two hundred denarii would not buy enough bread for each of them to get a little." One of his disciples, Andrew, Simon Peter's brother, said to him, "There is a lad here who has five barley loaves and two fish; but what are they among so many?" Jesus said:*

MINISTER: "Make the people sit down."

NARRATOR: *Now there was much grass in the place; so the men sat down, in number about five thousand. Jesus then took the loaves, and when he had given thanks, he distributed them to those who were seated; so also the fish, as much as they wanted. And when they had eaten their fill, he told his disciples:*

MINISTER: "Gather up the fragments left over, that nothing may be lost."

NARRATOR: *So they gathered them up and filled twelve baskets with fragments from the five barley loaves, left by those who had eaten. When the people saw the sign which he had done, they said:*

CONGREGATION (*standing*): "THIS IS INDEED THE PROPHET WHO IS TO COME INTO THE WORLD!"

[*Congregation is seated. Pause.*]

NARRATOR: *On the next day the people who remained on the other side of the sea saw that there had been only one boat there, and that Jesus had not entered the boat with his disciples, but that his disciples had gone away alone. However, boats from Tiberias came near the place where they ate the bread after the Lord had given thanks. So when the people saw that Jesus was not there, nor his disciples, they themselves got into the boats and went to Capernaum, seeking Jesus. When they found him on the other side of the sea, they said to him:*

CONGREGATION: "Rabbi, when did you come here?"

Jesus answered them,

MINISTER: "TRULY, TRULY, I SAY TO YOU, YOU SEEK ME, NOT BECAUSE YOU SAW SIGNS, BUT BECAUSE YOU ATE YOUR FILL OF THE LOAVES. DO NOT LABOR FOR THE FOOD WHICH PERISHES, BUT FOR THE FOOD WHICH ENDURES TO ETERNAL LIFE, WHICH THE SON OF MAN WILL GIVE TO YOU; FOR ON HIM HAS GOD THE FATHER SET HIS SEAL."

Then they said to him,

CONGREGATION: "What must we do, to be doing the work of God?"

Jesus answered them,

MINISTER: "This is the work of God, that you believe in him whom he has sent."

So they said to him,

CONGREGATION: "Then what sign do you do, that we may see, and believe you? What work do you perform? Our fathers ate the manna in the wilderness; as it is written, 'He gave them bread from heaven to eat.' "

Jesus then said to them,

MINISTER: "TRULY, TRULY, I SAY TO YOU, IT WAS NOT MOSES WHO GAVE YOU THE BREAD FROM HEAVEN; MY FATHER GIVES YOU THE TRUE BREAD FROM HEAVEN. FOR THE BREAD OF GOD IS THAT WHICH COMES DOWN FROM HEAVEN, AND GIVES LIFE TO THE WORLD."

They said to him,

CONGREGATION (*standing*): "LORD, GIVE US THIS BREAD ALWAYS."

Jesus said to them,

MINISTER: "I am the bread of life; he who comes to me shall not hunger, and he who believes in me shall never thirst. But I said to you that you have seen me and yet do not believe. All that the Father gives me will come to me; and him who comes to me I will not cast out. For I have come down from heaven, not to do my own will, but the will of him who sent me; and this is the will of him who sent me, that I should lose nothing of all that he has given me, but raise it up at the last day. For this is the will of my Father, that every one who sees the Son and believes in him should have eternal life; and I will raise him up at the last day."

[*Congregation is seated.*]

NARRATOR: *The Jews then murmured at him, because he said, "I am the bread which came down from heaven." They said, "Is not this Jesus, the son of Joseph, whose father and mother we know? How does he now say, 'I have come down from heaven'?"*

Jesus answered them,

MINISTER: "Do not murmur among yourselves. No one can come to me unless the Father who sent me draws him; and I will raise him up at the last day. It is written in the prophets, 'And they shall be taught by God.' Every one who has heard and learned from the Father comes to me. Not that anyone has seen the Father except him who is from God; he has seen the Father. Truly, truly, I say to you, he who believes has eternal life. I am the bread of life. Your fathers ate the manna in the wilderness, and they died. This is the bread which comes down from heaven; if any one eats of this bread, he will live forever; and the bread which I shall give for the life of the world is my flesh."

NARRATOR: *The Jews then disputed among themselves, saying, "How can this man give us his flesh to eat?"*

So Jesus said to them,

MINISTER: "TRULY, TRULY, I SAY TO YOU, UNLESS YOU EAT THE FLESH OF THE SON OF MAN AND DRINK HIS BLOOD, YOU HAVE NO LIFE IN YOU; HE WHO EATS MY FLESH AND DRINKS MY BLOOD HAS ETERNAL LIFE, AND I WILL RAISE HIM UP AT THE LAST DAY. For my flesh is food indeed, and my blood is drink indeed. He who eats my flesh and drinks my blood abides in me, and I in him. As the living Father sent me, and I live because of the Father, so he who eats me will live because of me. This is the bread which came down from heaven, not such as the fathers ate and died; he who eats this bread will live forever."

This he said in the synagogue, as he taught in Capernaum. Many of his

disciples, when they heard it, said,

CONGREGATION (*standing*): "This is a hard saying; who can listen to it?"

But Jesus, knowing in himself that his disciples murmured at it, said to them,

MINISTER: "Do you take offense at this? Then what if you were to see the Son of man ascending where he was before? IT IS THE SPIRIT THAT GIVES LIFE, THE FLESH IS OF NO AVAIL; THE WORDS THAT I HAVE SPOKEN TO YOU ARE SPIRIT AND LIFE. But there are some of you that do not believe."

[Pause.]

After this many of his disciples drew back and no longer went about with him. Jesus said to the twelve,

MINISTER: "Will you also go away?"

Simon Peter answered him,

CONGREGATION: "LORD, TO WHOM SHALL WE GO? YOU HAVE THE WORDS OF ETERNAL LIFE: AND WE HAVE BELIEVED, AND WE HAVE COME TO KNOW, THAT YOU ARE THE HOLY ONE OF GOD."

LET US PRAY.

Lord Jesus, evermore give us this Bread, give us Thyself. Thou Who in love givest Thyself to us in the Blessed Sacrament of Thy Body and Blood, grant us grace in love to receive Thee, in love to retain Thee, in love to be joined to Thee eternally.

O Lord Christ, who didst say to thine apostles when they would send away the hungry multitude, They need not depart, give ye them to eat; enable us so to use thy Father's gifts as to relieve the necessities of our brethren, and chiefly help us in our daily work so to reflect the glory of thy spirit that they may come to thee, the Bread of Life, and see their soul's desire and be satisfied; who livest and reignest with the Father and the Holy Spirit, one God for ever and ever. Amen.†

Almighty God, who hast given to thy people the true Bread who cometh down from heaven, even thy Son Jesus Christ; grant that our souls may be so fed by him who giveth health unto the world, that we may abide in him and he in us, and thy Church be filled with the power of his deathless life; through the same Jesus Christ our Lord. Amen.†

Blessed Lord, who hast caused all holy Scriptures to be written for our learning; Grant that we may in such wise hear them, read, mark, learn, and inwardly digest them, that by patience and comfort of thy holy Word, we may embrace, and ever hold fast, the blessed hope of everlasting life, which thou hast given us in our Saviour Jesus Christ. Amen.

O God, whose blessed Son did manifest himself to his disciples in the breaking of bread; Open, we pray thee,

---

† From *The Kingdom, the Power, and the Glory* (New York: Oxford University Press), 1933). Used by permission of the publisher.

the eyes of our faith, that we may behold thee in all thy works; through the same thy Son Jesus Christ our Lord. Amen.

VII. JESUS THE MESSIANIC PROPHET

John 7:10-46

Jesus is hailed as the messianic Prophet because He is the one than whom no man can do more signs. This description of Christ is meaningful in the dramatic setting of the critical event in Jerusalem. But this scene is typical of many situations elsewhere since then. There are strong controversial undertones. Judgment impends against people of prejudice, and there is the dark hint of turning away from them to the simple but teachable wherever and whoever they may be. Lowly and alien people—in the story they are the "some of the people," the "officers," Greeks—have neither educated minds to comprehend nor trained language to express the full truth of Christ. But they have the instinct that recognizes His superiority, and awareness of the divine in Him. Also to such Jesus is the Prophet sent with heaven's anointing.

The thought of this lesson moves out of the context of formal and traditional language to the wider and simpler affirmation, "No man ever spoke like this man."

It is helpful from time to time to lay aside the terms and descriptions which have become conventional, the technical words fraught by their history with the spirit of argument and controversy, and to think and speak the elemental, unsophisticated language of humble admiration and faith. What fresh and delightful meanings are found!

NARRATOR: *After his brothers had gone up to the feast, then he also went up, not publicly but in private. The Jews were looking for him at the feast, and saying, "Where is he?" And there was much muttering about him among the people. While some said, "He is a good man," others said, "No, he is leading the people astray." Yet for fear of the Jews no one spoke openly of him.*
About the middle of the feast Jesus went up into the temple and taught. The Jews marveled at it, saying:

CONGREGATION: "How is it that this man has learning, when he has never studied?"

So Jesus answered them,

MINISTER: "My teaching is not mine, but his who sent me; if any man's will is to do his will, he shall know whether the teaching is from God or whether I am speaking on my own authority. He who speaks on his own authority seeks his own glory; but he who seeks the glory of him who sent him is true, and in him there is no falsehood. Did not Moses give you the law? Yet none of you keeps the law. Why do you seek to kill me?"

The people answered,

CONGREGATION: "You have a demon! Who is seeking to kill you?"

Jesus answered them,

MINISTER: "I did one deed, and you all marvel at it. Moses gave you circumcision (not that it is from Moses, but from the fathers), and you circumcise a man upon the sabbath. If on the sabbath a man receives circumcision, so that the law of Moses may not be broken, are you angry with me because on the sabbath I made a man's whole body well? Do not judge by appearances, but judge with right judgment."

Some of the people of Jerusalem therefore said,

CONGREGATION: "Is not this the man whom they seek to kill? And here he is, speaking openly, and they say nothing to him! Can it be that the authorities really know that this is the Christ? Yet we know where this man comes from; and when the Christ appears, no one will know where he comes from."

So Jesus proclaimed, as he taught in the temple,

MINISTER: "You know me, and you know where I come from? But I have not come of my own accord; he who sent me is true, and him you do not know. I know him, for I come from him, and he sent me."

NARRATOR: *So they sought to arrest him; but no one laid hands on him, because his hour had not yet come. Yet many of the people believed in him; they said:*

CONGREGATION: "WHEN THE CHRIST APPEARS, WILL HE DO MORE SIGNS THAN THIS MAN HAS DONE?"

NARRATOR: *The Pharisees heard the crowd thus muttering about him, and the chief priests and Pharisees sent officers to arrest him.*

Jesus then said,

MINISTER: "I shall be with you a little longer, and then I go to him who sent me; you will seek me and you will not find me; where I am you cannot come."

The Jews said to one another,

CONGREGATION: "Where does this man intend to go that we shall not find him? What does he mean by saying, 'You will seek me and you will not find me, and 'Where I am you cannot come'?"

On the last day of the feast, the great day, Jesus stood up and proclaimed,

[*Congregation stands.*]

MINISTER: "If any one thirst, let him come to me and drink. He who believes in me, as the scripture has said, 'Out of his heart shall flow rivers of living water'."

Now this he said about the Spirit, those who believed in him were to receive; for as yet the Spirit had not been given, because Jesus was not yet glorified.

When they heard these words, some of the people said,

CONGREGATION: "THIS IS REALLY THE PROPHET."

Others said,

CONGREGATION: "THIS IS THE CHRIST."

[*Congregation is seated.*]

NARRATOR: *But some said, "Is the Christ to come from Galilee? Has not the scripture said that the Christ is descended from David, and comes from Bethlehem, the village where David was?"*

So there was a division among the people over him. Some of them wanted to arrest him, but no one laid hands on him.

The officers then went back to the chief priests and the Pharisees, who said to them:

SECOND READER: "Why did you not bring him?"

The officers answered,

CONGREGATION: "NO MAN EVER SPOKE LIKE THIS MAN!"

LET US PRAY.

Grant, O Lord, we pray thee, that as we seek for truth we may find that the search leads us to thyself. Give us courage to seek honestly, and reverence to seek humbly; and when our minds are perplexed and we cannot find thee, give us patience to go on with our daily duties; through Jesus Christ our Lord. Amen.

O Eternal God, who hast set within us a spirit which answers to Thine own, give us the faith to follow that image of Jesus which can keep Thy spirit so plainly before us. To our questioning hearts he is ever the answer. Teach us to be led by him in pursuit of Thee until we find, and let the whole world feel and see, that things which were cast down are being raised up, and things which had grown old are being made new; through Him whose good cheer can overcome the world, the same Jesus Christ. Amen.†

O Lord Jesus Christ, Who art the Way, the Truth and the Life, we pray Thee suffer us not to stray from Thee, Who art the Way, nor to distrust Thee, Who art the Truth, nor to rest in any other thing than Thee, Who art the Life. Teach us by Thy Holy Spirit what to believe, what to do, and wherein to take our rest. For Thine own name's sake we ask it. Amen.

O God, whose revelation never faileth and who showeth a new aspect of Thy eternal truth to each generation, grant unto us to see the truth as Thou dost set it before us in this our day and to strive for its realization among our fellows; through Jesus Christ our Lord. Amen.

VII. JESUS THE LIGHT OF MANKIND

John 9:1-38

The story of how Jesus gave sight to the man who had been born blind and his resulting experience at the hands of various people is a lesson of deep moral significance and universal experience.

---

† Donald B. Aldrich, *The Golden Book of Prayer* (New York: Dodd Mead & Co., 1941). Used by permission of the publisher.

In natural birth every man is blind to deeper spiritual realities, to the vision of God; but by the hand of Jesus Christ his eyes are opened to see. Doubts are cast upon the validity of the healing and the authenticity of its agent. But scoffing, argument or even the inability to explain cannot refute the fact of the experience. Firmly stands the repeated testimony: "He opened my eyes . . . If this man were not from God, he could do nothing," and finally the humbly grateful declaration of devotion, "Lord, I believe." This is the simple faith that needs no argument either in defense or in explanation. That there is sight where there had been none is proof enough and beyond contradiction; it needs but to be exhibited.

NARRATOR: *As he passed by, he saw a man blind from his birth. And his disciples asked him:*

CONGREGATION: "Rabbi, who sinned, this man or his parents, that he was born blind?"

Jesus answered,

MINISTER: "It was not that this man sinned, or his parents, but that the works of God might be made manifest in him. We must work the works of him who sent me, while it is day; night comes when no one can work. As long as I am in the world, I am the light of the world."

NARRATOR: *As he said this, he spat on the ground and made clay of the spittle and anointed the man's eyes with the clay, saying to him:*

MINISTER: "Go, wash in the pool of Siloam" (*which means Sent*).

NARRATOR: *So he went and washed and came back seeing. The neighbors and those who had seen him before as a beggar, said, "Is not this the man who used to sit and beg?" Some said, "It is he"; others said, "No, but he is like him." He said:*

CONGREGATION: "I am the man."

They said to him,

NARRATOR: *"Then how were your eyes opened?"*

He answered,

CONGREGATION: "The man called Jesus made clay and anointed my eyes and said to me, 'Go to Siloam and wash'; so I went and washed and received my sight."

They said to him,

NARRATOR: *"Where is he?"*

He said,

CONGREGATION: "I do not know."

NARRATOR: *They brought to the Pharisees the man who had formerly been blind. Now it was a sabbath day when Jesus made the clay and opened his eyes. The Pharisees again asked him how he had received his sight. And he said to them:*

CONGREGATION (*standing*): "He put clay on my eyes, and I washed, and I see."

NARRATOR: *Some of the Pharisees said, "This man is not from God, for he does not keep the sabbath." But others* said, "How can a man who is a sinner do such signs?" There was a division among them. So they again said to the blind man, "What do you say about him, since he has opened your eyes?"

He said,

CONGREGATION: "HE IS A PROPHET."

[Congregation is seated. Pause.]

NARRATOR: *The Jews did not believe that he had been blind and had received his sight, until they called the parents of the man who had received his sight, and asked them, "Is this your son, who you say was born blind? How then does he now see?" His parents answered, "We know that this is our son, and that he was born blind; but how he now sees we do not know, nor do we know who opened his eyes. Ask him; he is of age, he will speak for himself." His parents said this because they feared the Jews, for the Jews had already agreed that if any should confess him to be Christ, he was to be put out of the synagogue. Therefore his parents said, "He is of age, ask him." So for the second time they called the man who had been blind, and said to him, "Give God the praise; we know that this man is a sinner."*

He answered,

CONGREGATION: "Whether he is a sinner, I do not know; one thing I know, that though I was blind, now I see."

They said to him,

NARRATOR: *"What did he do to you? How did he open your eyes?"*

He answered them,

CONGREGATION: "I have told you already, and you would not listen. Why do you want to hear it again? Do you too want to become his disciples?"

And they reviled him, saying,

NARRATOR: *"You are his disciple, but we are disciples of Moses. We know that God has spoken to Moses, but as for this man, we do not know where he comes from."*

The man answered,

CONGREGATION (*standing*): "WHY, THIS IS A MARVEL! YOU DO NOT KNOW WHERE HE COMES FROM, AND YET HE OPENED MY EYES. WE KNOW THAT GOD DOES NOT LISTEN TO SINNERS, BUT IF ANY ONE IS A WORSHIPER OF GOD AND DOES HIS WILL, GOD LISTENS TO HIM. NEVER SINCE THE WORLD BEGAN HAS IT BEEN HEARD THAT ANY ONE OPENED THE EYES OF A MAN BORN BLIND. IF THIS MAN WERE NOT FROM GOD, HE COULD DO NOTHING."

They answered him,

NARRATOR: *"You were born in utter sin, and would you teach us?" And they cast him out. Jesus heard that they had cast him out, and having found him he said,*

MINISTER: "Do you believe in the Son of man?"

He answered,

CONGREGATION: "And who is he, sir, that I may believe in him?"

Jesus said to him,

MINISTER: "You have seen him, and it is he who speaks to you."

He said,

CONGREGATION: "LORD, I BELIEVE,"

and he worshiped him.

LET US PRAY.

Lord Jesus, suffer us not to love darkness rather than light; but help us so to do good works and come into the light, that our deeds may be manifest that they are wrought in God.

O Thou who art the Sun of Righteousness, evermore arising and never going down, flooding the world with life and gladness, shed upon us, we pray thee, thy glorious beams to scatter the night of sin and the mists of doubt and ignorance, that we may walk purely as in the day, and joyfully in thee, the one true Light, who livest and reignest with the Father and the Holy Spirit, one God, for ever and ever. Amen.

Almighty God, who at the baptism of thy blessed Son Jesus Christ in the river Jordan didst manifest his glorious Godhead: Grant, we beseech thee, that the brightness of his presence may shine in our hearts, and his glory be set forth in our lives; through the same Jesus Christ our Lord. Amen.

O Almighty God, who willest to be glorified in thy Saints, and dost raise up thy servants to shine as lights in the world: Shine, we pray thee, in our hearts, that we also, in our generation, may show forth thy praises, who hast called us out of darkness into thy marvellous light; through Jesus Christ our Lord. Amen.

IX. JESUS THE LIFE ETERNAL

John 11:1-44

The touchingly beautiful story of the death of Lazarus, the grief of the sisters, their appeal to Jesus, and His restoring Lazarus to life was written to show that Jesus Christ is for those who believe in Him the assurance of eternal life. The believer will experience resurrection because his Lord did, and just as He did. For him the questions of "why death?" and "when the resurrection?" have lost their relevance.

Obviously this reading reaches its high point when the congregation stands to hear the words, "I am the resurrection and the life," and responds, "Yes, Lord, I believe." This is one of the most important expressions of Christian faith.

It is to be noted that the phrase, "shall never die," should be rendered according to the literal Greek, "shall not die into eternity," meaning, "death will not last." This is what the case of Lazarus teaches.

It is impossible to read this lesson without sensing the subtle implication of a secondary, spiritual reference to those who are dead in sin. For them Christ brings life; even for those who are far gone in sin. This restored life is the promise of resurrection. Meanwhile, as the revival from moral death takes place, the Christian family has a responsibility toward them: "Unbind him, and let him go!"

NARRATOR: *Now a certain man was ill, Lazarus of Bethany, the village of Mary and her sister Martha. It was Mary who anointed the Lord with ointment and wiped his feet with her hair, whose brother Lazarus was ill. So the sisters sent to him, saying:*

CONGREGATION: "Lord, he whom you love is ill."

But when Jesus heard it, he said,

MINISTER: "This illness is not unto death; it is for the glory of God, so that the Son of God may be glorified by means of it."

NARRATOR: *Now Jesus loved Martha and her sister and Lazarus. So when he heard that he was ill, he stayed two days longer in the place where he was. Then after this he said to his disciples:*

MINISTER: "Let us go into Judea again."

The disciples said to him,

CONGREGATION: "Rabbi, the Jews were but now seeking to stone you, and are you going there again?"

Jesus answered,

MINISTER: "Are there not twelve hours in the day? If any one walks in the day, he does not stumble, because he sees the light of this world. But if any one walks in the night, he stumbles, because the light is not in him."

Thus he spoke, and then he said to them,

MINISTER: "Our friend Lazarus has fallen asleep, but I go to awake him out of sleep."

The disciples said to him,

CONGREGATION: "Lord, if he has fallen asleep, he will recover."

Now Jesus had spoken of his death, but they thought that he meant taking rest in sleep. Then Jesus told them plainly,

MINISTER: "Lazarus is dead; and for your sake I am glad that I was not there, so that you may believe. But let us go to him."

Thomas called the Twin, said to his fellow disciples,

SECOND READER: "Let us also go, that we may die with him."

NARRATOR: *Now when Jesus came, he found that Lazarus had already been in the tomb four days. Bethany was near Jerusalem, about two miles off, and many of the Jews had come to Martha and Mary to console them concerning their brother. When Martha heard that Jesus was coming, she went and met him, while Mary sat in the house.*

Martha said to Jesus,

CONGREGATION: "Lord, if you had been here, my brother would not have died. And even now I know that whatever you ask from God, God will give you."

Jesus said to her,

MINISTER: "Your brother will rise again."

Martha said to him,

CONGREGATION: "I know that he will rise again in the resurrection at the last day."

Jesus said to her,

[Congregation stands.]

MINISTER: "I AM THE RESURRECTION AND THE LIFE; HE WHO BELIEVES IN ME, THOUGH HE DIE, YET SHALL HE LIVE, AND WHOEVER LIVES AND BELIEVES IN ME SHALL NEVER DIE. DO YOU BELIEVE THIS?"

She said to him,

CONGREGATION: "YES, LORD; I BELIEVE THAT YOU ARE THE CHRIST, THE SON OF GOD, HE WHO IS COMING INTO THE WORLD."

[Congregation is seated.]

NARRATOR: *When she had said this, she went and called her sister Mary, saying quietly:*

CONGREGATION: "The teacher is here and is calling for you."

NARRATOR: *And when she heard it, she rose quickly and went to him. Now Jesus had not yet come to the village, but was still in the place where Martha had met him. When the Jews who were with her in the house, consoling her, saw Mary rise quickly and go out, they followed her, supposing that she was going to the tomb to weep there. Then Mary, when she came where Jesus was and saw him, fell at his feet, saying to him:*

CONGREGATION: "Lord, if you had been here, my brother would not have died."

NARRATOR: *When Jesus saw her weeping, and the Jews who came with her also weeping, he was deeply moved in spirit and troubled. And he said:*

MINISTER: "Where have you laid him?"

They said to him,

CONGREGATION: "Lord, come and see."

NARRATOR: *Jesus wept.*

So the Jews said,

SECOND READER: "See how he loved him!"

But some of them said,

CONGREGATION: "Could not he who opened the eyes of the blind man have kept this man from dying?"

NARRATOR: *Then Jesus, deeply moved again, came to the tomb; it was a cave, and a stone lay upon it.*

Jesus said,

MINISTER: "Take away the stone."

Martha, the sister of the dead man, said to him,

CONGREGATION: "Lord, by this time there will be an odor, for he has been dead four days."

Jesus said to her,

MINISTER: "Did I not tell you that if you would believe you would see the glory of God?"

NARRATOR: *So they took away the stone.*

And Jesus lifted up his eyes and said,

[Congregation stands.]

MINISTER: "Father, I thank thee that thou hast heard me. I knew that thou hearest me always, but I have said this on account of the people standing by, that they may believe that thou didst send me."

When he had said this, he cried with a loud voice,

MINISTER: "Lazarus, come out."

NARRATOR: *The dead man came out, his hands and feet bound with bandages, and his face wrapped with a cloth. Jesus said to them,*

MINISTER: "Unbind him, and let him go."

LET US PRAY.

Lord Jesus, in whose hand is the soul of every living thing and the breath of mankind, to the lifeless impart life, to the living increase life: for Thou Thyself art the Life, and apart from Thee we have no life.

Almighty God, who through thine only-begotten Son Jesus Christ hast overcome death, and opened unto us the gate of everlasting life; We humbly beseech thee that, as by thy special grace preventing us thou dost put into our minds good desires, so by thy continual help we may bring the same to good effect; through the same Jesus Christ our Lord, who liveth and reigneth with thee and the Holy Ghost ever, one God, world without end. Amen.

O God, who for our redemption didst give thine only-begotten Son to the death of the Cross, and by his glorious resurrection hast delivered us from the power of our enemy; Grant us so to die daily from sin, that we may evermore live with him in the joy of his resurrection; through the same thy Son Christ our Lord. Amen.

O Thou God of our immortal souls, suffer us not through sin and neglect to live apart from Thee. Enlighten us with the knowledge of Thy being, strengthen us with Thy presence, enlarge and refine our spirits with the thought of our eternal life, that we may here and now prepare ourselves for greater love and service in the greater life to be.

So that at last when the time of our going cometh, we may be no strangers to the thought and may give ourselves, our souls and bodies, into Thy tender, unwasteful care and keeping for such use and service as Thy wisdom may find best. All which we ask for His sake Who died for us, Who rose again for us, Jesus Christ, our Lord. Amen.

O Lord, may there be for me a life beyond this life, and in that life may there be work to do and tasks to be accomplished. Amen.

X. JESUS THE MINISTER
OF LOVE

John 13

In the surprising act of performing the function of a slave or servant, Jesus expressed the whole meaning of His life and ministry: a giving of Himself in self-forgetful, loving service. That is His ever-new lesson to all who would belong to His cause. This reading becomes, therefore, a solemn act of consecration to a life which finds its fulfillment in making the journey of life easier for others.

There is no time when the use of this reading is not appropriate and meaningful. However, a special use is indicated by the fact that it stands in St. John's Gospel in place of the account of the Lord's Supper. The Supper forms the background and frame of reference for Chapter Six and is there suggested as an established ritual of the Church. In this lesson there is also an allusion to baptism in the reference to him "who has bathed."

St. John writes up this act of Jesus to add two meanings to the Lord's Supper: 1) that it is a taking or renewing the obligation of a life of service in imitation of the Master; 2) that the Lord's Supper is itself a repeated washing of the disciples' feet which are always, in their very life of service, soiled with the grime of this world.

This chapter is divided into these sections: 1-20, The Foot Washing; 21-30, The Betrayer; 31-35, The New Commandment of Love. The Warning to Peter, 36-38, is omitted here.

NARRATOR: *Now before the feast of the Passover, when Jesus knew that his hour had come to depart out of this world to the Father, having loved his own who were in the world, he loved them to the end. And during supper, when the devil had already put it into the heart of Judas Iscariot, Simon's son, to betray him, Jesus, knowing that the Father had given all things into his hands, and that he had come from God and was going to God, rose from supper, laid aside his garments, and girded himself with a towel. Then he poured water into a basin, and began to wash the disciples' feet, and to wipe them with the towel with which he was girded. He came to Simon Peter; and Peter said to him:*

CONGREGATION: "Lord, do you wash my feet?"

Jesus answered him,

MINISTER: "What I am doing you do not know now, but afterward you will understand."

Peter said to him,

CONGREGATION: "You shall never wash my feet."

Jesus answered him,

MINISTER: "IF I DO NOT WASH YOU, YOU HAVE NO PART IN ME."

Simon Peter said to him,

CONGREGATION: "Lord, not my feet only but also my hands and my head!"

Jesus said to him,

MINISTER: "He who has bathed does not need to wash, except for his feet, but he is clean all over; and you are clean, but not all of you."

NARRATOR: *For he knew who was to betray him; that was why he said, "You are not all clean."*
When he had washed their feet, and taken up his garments, and resumed his place, he said to them:

[Congregation stands.]

MINISTER: "Do you know what I have done to you? You call me Teacher and Lord; and you are right, for so I am. If I then, your LORD and TEACHER, have washed your feet, you also ought to wash one another's feet. FOR I HAVE GIVEN YOU AN EXAMPLE, THAT YOU ALSO SHOULD DO AS I HAVE DONE TO YOU. Truly, I say to you, a servant is not greater than his master; nor is he who is sent greater than he who sent him. If you know these things, blessed are you if you do them. I am not speaking of you all; I know whom I have chosen; it is that the scripture may be fulfilled, 'He who ate my bread has lifted his heel against me.' I tell you this now, before it takes place, that when it does take place, you may believe that I am he. Truly, truly, I say to you, he who receives any one whom I send receives me; and he who receives me receives him who sent me."

[Congregation is seated.]

When Jesus had thus spoken, he was troubled in spirit, and testified,

MINISTER: "Truly, truly, I say to you, one of you will betray me."

NARRATOR: *The disciples looked at one another, uncertain of whom he spoke. One of his disciples, whom Jesus loved, was lying close to the breast of Jesus; so Simon Peter beckoned to him and said, "Tell us who it is of whom he speaks." So lying thus, close to the breast of Jesus, he said to him, "Lord, who is it?" Jesus answered:*

MINISTER: "It is he to whom I shall

give this morsel when I have dipped it."

NARRATOR: *So when he had dipped the morsel, he gave it to Judas, the son of Simon Iscariot. Then after the morsel, Satan entered into him. Jesus said to him:*

MINISTER: "What you are going to do, do quickly."

NARRATOR: *Now no one at the table knew why he said this to him. Some thought that, because Judas had the money box, Jesus was telling him, "Buy what we need for the feast"; or, that he should give something to the poor. So, after receiving the morsel, he immediately went out; and it was night.*

[*Pause.*]

When he had gone out, Jesus said,

MINISTER: "Now is the Son of man glorified, and in him God is glorified; if God is glorified in him, God will also glorify him in himself, and glorify him at once.

[*Pause.*]

MINISTER: "Little children, yet a little while I am with you. You will seek me; and as I said to the Jews so now I say to you, 'Where I am going you cannot come.' A NEW COMMANDMENT I GIVE TO YOU, THAT YOU LOVE ONE ANOTHER; EVEN AS I HAVE LOVED YOU, THAT YOU ALSO LOVE ONE ANOTHER. By this all men will know that you are my disciples, if you have love for one another."

LET US PRAY.

Almighty and most merciful Father, who hast given us a new commandment that we should love one another; give us also grace that we may fulfill it. Make us gentle, courteous, and forbearing. Direct our lives so that we may look each to the good of the other in word and deed. And hallow all our friendships by the blessing of thy Spirit; for his sake who loved us and gave himself for us, Jesus Christ our Lord. Amen.

O Lord, our heavenly Father, whose blessed Son came not to be ministered unto, but to minister; we beseech thee to bless all who, following in his steps, give themselves to the service of their fellow men. Endue them with wisdom, patience, and courage to strengthen the weak and raise up those who fall that, being inspired by thy love, they may worthily minister in thy Name to the suffering, the friendless, and the needy; for the sake of him who laid down his life for us, the same thy son, our Saviour Jesus Christ. Amen.

Blessed Lord, who for our sakes wast content to bear sorrow and want and death, grant unto us such a measure of thy Spirit that we may follow thee in all thy courage and self-denial, and help us by thy great love to succor the afflicted, to relieve the needy and destitute, to share the burden of the heavy laden, and to see thee in all who are poor and desolate; who livest and reignest with the Father and the Holy Spirit, one God, world without end. Amen.†

† From *The Kingdom, the Power, and the Glory* (New York: Oxford University Press, 1933). Used by permission of the publisher.

Almighty God, who hast given us to receive the body and blood of thy son our Saviour Jesus Christ, that by means thereof we may receive the washing away of our besetting sins and be united more and more closely unto thee, grant that we may be servants of cleansing and refreshment unto all men, and so to promote unity and fellowship among them; through the same Jesus Christ our Lord, who liveth and reigneth with thee and the Holy Spirit, one God, world without end. Amen.

XI. JESUS, LORD AND GOD

John 20:19-31

The sequence of confessional exercises in St. John's Gospel reaches its climax in this brief but tremendously dramatic act. It is the supreme confession of faith in Christ, inspired by the evidence of His resurrection, and, written as it is at the end of the century, is filled with the power of conviction established by the vision of Christ's exaltation and the continuing experience of His very real presence.

Thomas is made to represent the second generation of Christians, those who were not present at the first resurrection appearances, but still had something of the sight and the touch of its marvel. The words of the Lord, "Blessed are those who have not seen and yet believe," go beyond the primary apostles and Thomas to all later generations, even to us, who have in our experiences of the spiritual manifestations of the Present Christ an equally valid foundation of faith. The past and present are nowhere in the Gospel so effectively merged as in this reading and confession: "My Lord and My God"—always.

NARRATOR: *On the evening of that day, the first day of the week, the doors being shut where the disciples were, for fear of the Jews, Jesus came and stood among them and said to them:*

MINISTER: "Peace be with you."

NARRATOR: *When he had said this, he showed them his hands and his side. Then the disciples were glad when they saw the Lord:*

Jesus said to them again,

MINISTER: "Peace be with you. As the Father has sent me, even so I send you."

And when he had said this, he breathed on them, and said to them,

MINISTER: "Receive the Holy Spirit. If you forgive the sins of any, they are forgiven; if you retain the sins of any, they are retained."

NARRATOR: *Now Thomas, one of the twelve, called the Twin, was not with them when Jesus came. So the other disciples told him:*

SECOND READER: "We have seen the Lord."

But he said to them,

CONGREGATION: "Unless I see in his hands the print of the nails, and place my finger in the mark of the nails, and place my hand in his side, I will not believe."

[Congregation stands.]

NARRATOR: *Eight days later, his disciples were again in the house, and Thomas was with them. The doors were shut, but Jesus came and stood among them, and said:*

MINISTER: "Peace be with you."

Then he said to Thomas,

MINISTER: "Put your finger here, and see my hands; and put out your hand, and place it in my side; do not be faithless, but believing."

Thomas answered him,

CONGREGATION: "MY LORD AND MY GOD!"

Jesus said to him,

MINISTER: "Have you believed because you have seen me? Blessed are those who have not seen and yet believe."

[Congregation is seated.]

NARRATOR: *Now Jesus did many other signs in the presence of the disciples, which are not written in this book; but these are written that you may believe that Jesus is the Christ, the Son of God, and that believing you may have life in his name.*

LET US PRAY.

Almighty and everlasting God, who for the greater confirmation of the faith, didst suffer thy holy Apostle Thomas to be doubtful in thy Son's resurrection; Grant us so perfectly, and without all doubt, to believe in thy Son Jesus Christ, that our faith in thy sight may never be reproved. Hear us, O Lord, through the same Jesus Christ, to whom, with thee and the Holy Ghost, be all honor and glory, now and for evermore. Amen.

O Saviour of men, Who sufferest not Thy beloved Disciple to exclude us, even us, from any height or depth of beatitude, give us grace to be of those blessed who not seeing believe.

O God, that there are things I cannot understand is but the evidence of their infinity and that there are times of doubt reveals but mine own fault.

I would not assume that what I am unable to grasp cannot be nor yet that the whole of which I am a part is beyond my reach. Rather do I know that Thou hast not given me the longing to understand simply to torment it with impossibility but rather to satisfy it with increasing knowledge when it seeks worthily.

May not be mine the part of the coward who fears the truth nor of the laggard unwilling to pay the price of it in labour and sincerity.

If my steps on the path are slow, may they be nonetheless sure, and while I strive on toward the goal where faith will be seeing and belief will be knowing, may I receive strength and inspiration from those on whose vigils has long since broken the eternal day of their faith's justification. Through Jesus Christ, our Lord. Amen.

O God, from whom all holy desires, all good counsels, and all just works do proceed: Give unto thy servants that peace which the world cannot give; that our hearts may be set to obey thy commandments, and also that by thee we being defended from the fear of our enemies may pass our time in rest and quietness; through the merits of Jesus Christ our Saviour. Amen.

The Peace of God, which passeth all understanding, keep our hearts and minds in the knowledge and love of God, and of his son Jesus Christ our Lord: and the Blessing of God Almighty, the Father, the Son, and the Holy Ghost, be amongst us, and remain with us always. Amen.

XII. A LITURGY
OF PREPARATION

John 6:1-14, 22-64a; 13:33-38, 1-32; and 6:67a-69

This reading is an arrangement of readings VI and X into a unified order of service for use at any desired time, or as a liturgy or service of preparation.

Apart from such a special occasion, this reading is a deeply spiritual ending to this series of liturgical exercises. Having heard again His living voice, we cannot but say that there is no other Lord for us. "You have the words of eternal life." The prayers which follow are finally gathered up in the majestic tones of the second portion of the Te Deum, to be said or sung by all standing.

NARRATOR: *After this Jesus went to the other side of the sea of Galilee, which is the sea of Tiberias. And a multitude followed him, because they saw the signs which he did on those who were diseased. Jesus went up into the hills, and there sat down with his disciples. Now the Passover, the feast of the Jews, was at hand. Lifting up his eyes, then, and seeing that a multitude was coming to him, Jesus said to Philip:*

MINISTER: "How are we to buy bread, so that these people may eat?"

NARRATOR: *This he said to test him, for he himself knew what he would do. Philip answered him, "Two hundred denarii would not buy enough bread for each of them to get a little." One of his disciples, Andrew, Simon Peter's brother, said to him, "There is a lad here who has five barley loaves and two fish; but what are they among so many?"*

Jesus said,

MINISTER: "Make the people sit down."

NARRATOR: *Now there was much grass in the place; so the men sat down, in number about five thousand. Jesus then took the loaves, and when he had given thanks, he distributed them to those who were seated; so also the fish, as much as they wanted. And when they had eaten their fill, he told his disciples:*

MINISTER: "Gather up the fragments left over, that nothing may be lost."

NARRATOR: *So they gathered them up and filled twelve baskets with fragments from the five barley loaves, left by those who had eaten. When the people saw the sign which he had done, they said:*

CONGREGATION (*standing*): "THIS IS INDEED THE PROPHET WHO IS TO COME INTO THE WORLD!"

[Congregation is seated. Pause.]

NARRATOR: *On the next day the people who remained on the other side of the sea saw that there had been only one boat there, and that Jesus had not entered the boat with his disciples, but that his disciples had gone away alone. However, boats from Tiberias came near the place where they ate the bread after the Lord had given thanks. So when the people saw that Jesus was not there, nor his disciples, they themselves got into the boats and went to Capernaum, seeking Jesus.*

When they found him on the other side of the sea, they said to him:

CONGREGATION: "Rabbi, when did you come here?"

Jesus answered them,

MINISTER: "Truly, truly, I say to you, you seek me, not because you saw signs, but because you ate your fill of the loaves. Do not labor for the food which perishes, but for the food which endures to eternal life, which the Son of man will give to you; for on him has God the Father set his seal."

CONGREGATION: "What must we do, to be doing the work of God?"

Jesus answered them,

MINISTER: "This is the work of God, that you believe in him whom he has sent."

So they said to him,

CONGREGATION: "Then what sign do you do, that we may see, and believe you? What work do you perform? Our fathers ate the manna in the wilderness; as it is written, 'He gave them bread from heaven to eat.' "

Jesus then said to them,

MINISTER: "Truly, truly, I say to you, it was not Moses who gave you the bread from heaven; my Father gives you the true bread from heaven. For the bread of God is that which comes down from heaven, and gives life to the world."

They said to him,

CONGREGATION (*standing*): "LORD, GIVE US THIS BREAD ALWAYS."

Jesus said to them,

MINISTER: "I am the bread of life; he who comes to me shall not hunger, and he who believes in me shall never thirst. But I said to you that you have seen me and yet do not believe.

All that the Father gives me will come to me; and him who comes to me I will not cast out. For I have come down from heaven, not to do my own will, but the will of him who sent me; and this is the will of him who sent me, that I should lose nothing of all that he has given me, but raise it up at the last day. For this is the will of my Father, that everyone who sees the Son and believes in him should have eternal life; and I will raise him up at the last day."

[Congregation is seated.]

NARRATOR: *The Jews then murmured at him, because he said, "I am the*

*bread which came down from heaven."
They said, "Is not this Jesus, the son
of Joseph, whose father and mother we
know? How does he now say, 'I have
come down from heaven'?"*

Jesus answered them,

MINISTER: "Do not murmur among
yourselves. No one can come to
me unless the Father who sent me
draws him; and I will raise him
up at the last day. It is written in
the prophets, 'And they shall all
be taught by God.' Every one
who has heard and learned from
the Father comes to me. Not that
any one has seen the Father except him who is from God; he has
seen the Father. Truly, truly, I
say to you, he who believes has
eternal life. I am the bread of life.
Your fathers ate the manna in the
wilderness, and they died. This is
the bread from heaven; if any one
eats of this bread, he will live for
ever; and the bread which I shall
give for the life of the world is my
flesh."

NARRATOR: *The Jews then disputed
among themselves, saying, "How can
this man give us his flesh to eat?"*

So Jesus said to them,

MINISTER: "Truly, truly, I say to you,
unless you eat the flesh of the Son
of man and drink his blood, you
have no life in you; he who eats
my flesh and drinks my blood has
eternal life, and I will raise him
up at the last day. For my flesh
is food indeed, and my blood is
drink indeed. He who eats my
flesh and drinks my blood abides
in me, and I in him. As the living

Father sent me, and I live because
of the Father, so he who eats me
will live because of me. This is
the bread which came down from
heaven, not such as the fathers ate
and died; he who eats this bread
will live forever."

*This he said in the syna-
gogue, as he taught in
Capernaum.*

[*Pause.*]

*Many of his disciples,
when they heard it, said,*

CONGREGATION (*standing*): "This is a
hard saying: who can listen to
it?"

*But Jesus, knowing in
himself that his disciples
murmured at it, said to
them,*

MINISTER: "Do you take offense at
this? Then what if you were to
see the Son of man ascending
where he was before? IT IS THE
SPIRIT THAT GIVES LIFE, THE
FLESH IS OF NO AVAIL: THE
WORDS THAT I HAVE SPOKEN TO
YOU ARE SPIRIT AND LIFE. . . .
But there are some of you that do
not believe."

[*Congregation is seated. Pause.*]

*After this many of his dis-
ciples drew back and no
longer went about with
him.*

MINISTER: "Little children, yet a little
while I am with you. You will
seek me; and as I said to the
Jews so now I say to you, 'Where
I am going you cannot come.'

A NEW COMMANDMENT I GIVE TO YOU, THAT YOU LOVE ONE AN-OTHER; EVEN AS I HAVE LOVED YOU, THAT YOU ALSO LOVE ONE ANOTHER. By this all men will know that you are my disciples, if you have love for one another."

Simon Peter said to him,

CONGREGATION: "Lord, where are you going?"

Jesus answered,

MINISTER: "Where I am going you cannot follow me now; but you shall follow afterward."

Peter said to him,

CONGREGATION: "Lord, why cannot I follow you now? I will lay down my life for you."

MINISTER: "Will you lay down your life for me? Truly, truly, I say to you, the cock will not crow, till you have denied me three times."

[Pause.]

NARRATOR: *Now before the feast of the Passover, when Jesus knew that his hour had come to depart out of this world to the Father, having loved his own who were in the world, he loved them to the end. And during supper, when the devil had already put it into the heart of Judas Iscariot, Simon's son, to betray him, Jesus, knowing that the Father had given all things into his hands, and that he had come from God and was going to God, rose from supper, laid aside his garments, and girded himself with a towel. Then he poured water into a basin, and began to wash the disciples' feet, and to wipe*

them with the towel with which he was girded. He came to Simon Peter; and Peter said to him:

CONGREGATION: "Lord, do you wash my feet?"

Jesus answered him,

MINISTER: "What I am doing you do not know now, but afterward you will understand."

Peter said to him,

CONGREGATION: "You shall never wash my feet."

Jesus answered him,

MINISTER: "IF I DO NOT WASH YOU, YOU HAVE NO PART IN ME."

Simon Peter said to him,

CONGREGATION: "Lord, not my feet only but also my hands and my head!"

Jesus said to him,

MINISTER: "He who has bathed does not need to wash, except for his feet, but he is clean all over; and you are clean, but not all of you."

NARRATOR: *For he knew who was to betray him; that was why he said, "You are not all clean."*
When he had washed their feet, and taken up his garments, and resumed his place, he said to them:

[Congregation stands.]

MINISTER: "Do you know what I have done to you? You call me Teacher and Lord; and you are right, for so I am. If I then, your LORD AND TEACHER, have washed your feet, you also ought to wash one another's feet. FOR I HAVE GIVEN YOU AN EXAMPLE, THAT YOU ALSO SHOULD DO AS I HAVE DONE TO YOU. Truly, truly, I say to you, a servant is not greater than his master; nor is he who is sent greater than he who sent him. If you know these things, blessed are you if you do them. I am not speaking of you all; I know whom I have chosen; it is that the scripture may be fulfilled, 'He who ate my bread has lifted his heel against me.' I tell you this now, before it takes place, that when it does take place you may believe that I am he. Truly, truly, I say to you, he who receives any one whom I send receives me; and he who receives me receives him who sent me."

[*Congregation is seated.*]

When Jesus had thus spoken, he was troubled in spirit, and testified,

MINISTER: "Truly, truly, I say to you, one of you will betray me."

NARRATOR: *The disciples looked at one another, uncertain of whom he spoke. One of his disciples, whom Jesus loved, was lying close to the breast of Jesus; so Simon Peter beckoned to him and said, "Tell us who it is of whom he speaks." So lying thus, close to the breast of Jesus, he said to him, "Lord, who is it?" Jesus answered:*

MINISTER: "It is he to whom I shall give this morsel when I have dipped it."

NARRATOR: *So when he had dipped the morsel, he gave it to Judas, the son of Simon Iscariot. Then after the morsel, Satan entered into him. Jesus said to him:*

MINISTER: "What you are going to do, do quickly."

NARRATOR: *Now no one at the table knew why he said this to him. Some thought that, because Judas had the money box, Jesus was telling him, "Buy what we need for the feast"; or, that he should give something to the poor. So after receiving the morsel, he immediately went out; and it was night.*

[*Pause.*]

When he had gone out, Jesus said,

[*Congregation stands.*]

MINISTER: "Now is the Son of man glorified, and in him God is glorified; if God is glorified in him, God will also glorify him in himself, and glorify him at once."

[*Pause.*]

Jesus said to the twelve,

MINISTER: "Will you also go away?"

Simon Peter answered him,

CONGREGATION: "LORD, TO WHOM SHALL WE GO? YOU HAVE THE WORDS OF ETERNAL LIFE: AND WE HAVE BELIEVED, AND WE HAVE COME TO KNOW, THAT YOU ARE THE HOLY ONE OF GOD."

LET US PRAY.

Grant us, O Lord, the help of thy grace, that at this holy sacrament we may bring all our thoughts and desires into subjection to thy blessed will, and may offer our souls and bodies as a living sacrifice unto thee, in union with the perfect sacrifice of thy Son, our Saviour Jesus Christ. Amen.†

O Christ, the true Vine and the source of life, ever giving thyself that the world may live, who also hast taught us that those who follow thee must will to lose their lives for thy sake; grant us so to receive within our souls the power of thine eternal sacrifice that in sharing thy cup we may share thy glory and at the last be made perfect in thy love; to the honor of thy holy name. Amen.†

Grant, we beseech thee, O Christ, that as we all share in one life, being members of thy body, so we may all use thy gifts for the perfecting of the saints, unto the work of ministering, unto the building up of thy body, till we attain unto the unity of the faith, and of the knowledge of thee, unto a full-grown man, unto the measure of

---

† From *The Kingdom, the Power, and the Glory* (New York: Oxford University Press, 1933). Used by permission of the publisher.

the stature of thy fullness, to whom be all praise and glory now and forever more. Amen.†

Teach us, good Lord, to serve thee as thou deservest; to give and not to count the cost; to fight and not to heed the wounds; to toil and not to seek for rest; to labor and not to ask for any reward, save that of knowing that we do thy will, through Jesus Christ our Lord. Amen.

Thou art the King of Glory, O Christ.

Thou art the everlasting Son of the Father.

When thou tookest upon thee to deliver man, thou didst humble thyself to be born of a Virgin.

When thou hadst overcome the sharpness of death, thou didst open the Kingdom of Heaven to all believers.

Thou sittest at the right hand of God, in the glory of the Father.

We believe that thou shalt come to be our Judge.

We therefore pray thee, help thy servants, whom thou hast redeemed with thy precious blood.

Make them to be numbered with thy Saints, in glory everlasting. Amen.

Suggestions for the Director of a Speaking Choir

Suggestions for the Director of a Speaking Choir

The selection of a suitable leader or director is critically important for the presentation of these readings. Ideally, he or she should have had some previous experience either as a participant or as a leader of a speech choir. If no such person is available, someone who has had experience in dramatics can do a very creditable job. The director should be able to read poetry meaningfully and expressively himself; he should be ear-minded and sensitive to sound effects and rhythms. And, of course, the director must be able to make suggestions, criticize, drill, and encourage members of the group without arousing antagonism. He must also be able to arouse a fine sense of devotion and group spirit in accomplishing an important artistic and religious task.

Tryouts. Just as in the selection of characters for a play, tryouts are essential for a good speaking choir. The director must know in advance about the pitch and character and carrying power of each voice. Equally important, he needs to know how effectively each person can read aloud since this is almost a lost art. It is amazing how many adults are stumbling and clumsy readers.

The suggestions in the section on "Tryouts" in Book I are also applicable to the selection of members for a speech choir. It may, however, be necessary to invite people specially to come to the tryouts and not rely on volunteers alone.

Preliminary study. If, in the first rehearsal, people are asked to read parts without preliminary preparation, they are very likely to establish habit patterns that are very hard to correct later. It is advisable, therefore, for the group to read the selection over together and often to rephrase and *state in their own words* what the author is saying poetically. Correct emphasis and rhythm in subsequent group rehearsals is much easier to achieve in this way. Meaning is always important in poetry, but this is especially true in the case of religious verse.

Special precautions. A speaking choir does not differ from other dramatic groups in requiring that voices be sufficiently loud to carry and that enunciation be sharp and clear. Indeed, clarity and adequate voice carrying power (even to the very back of the church) are even more important here than in the drama, for there are no actions here to help carry the meaning.

An element unique to the speech choir is the necessity of precision in *synchronization* when several people are reciting aloud together. Without perfect synchronization the listener gets only a meaningless and frustrating jumble of sound. Only patient and disciplined practice can achieve such synchronization. The use of a tape recorder in the back of the church during rehearsal can greatly assist a group in achieving clarity, volume, and synchronization.

Music. Musical themes to accompany these selections can readily be adapted from the music provided.

168-1156-C-7.5